Truth in Dating

FINDING LOVE BY GETTING REAL

Susan M. Campbell, Ph.D.

Foreword by Gay Hendricks

H J Kramer

New World Library

An H J Kramer Book
published in a joint venture with
New World Library

Editorial office:
P.O. Box 1082
Tiburon, California 94920

Administrative office:
14 Pamaron Way
Novato, California 94949

Front cover design by Mary Ann Casler
Text design and typography by Tona Pearce Myers

Library of Congress Cataloging-in-Publication Data
Campbell, Susan M.
  Truth in dating : finding love by getting real / Susan M. Campbell.
     p.   cm.
  ISBN 1-932073-06-X (Pbk. : alk. paper)
  1. Dating (Social customs)—United States. 2. Man-woman
relationships—United States. I. Title.
HQ801.C2738 2004
646.7'7—dc22   2003018061

First Printing, January 2004
ISBN 1-932073-06-X
Printed in Canada on partially recycled, acid-free paper
Distributed to the trade by Publishers Group West

10 9 8 7 6 5 4 3 2 1

To Randy Mack, my Truth in Dating practice partner,
who has helped me prove that these ideas really work

Honesty is the only hope
for relationships.

Contents

Part I: Why Truth in Dating?

Part II: Dating 101

Part III: Advanced Dating

Part IV: Ending It

Foreword

By Gay Hendricks

Whether you are single or in an intimate relationship, this book is an important resource for you. In page after page of clear insight, Susan Campbell provides a much-needed map to a territory still largely unexplored: authenticity in our romantic relationships.

Like many of you, I was given no training in high school or college about how to communicate with the interior of myself, or how to communicate with any degree of authenticity with other people around me. In research done with several thousand couples for our book *Lasting Love*, my wife, Kathlyn, and I found that 98 percent of them had, like us, never received even ten minutes of instruction about how to communicate or solve problems in a close relationship. If the same level of training were given in driver education, the roadways would be as clogged with wrecked cars as our courts are with divorce petitions.

It's time for change, and now Susan Campbell has given the millions of people who start new relationships every year a powerful way to make those changes. This book offers a great deal more than just the notion that honesty is a good idea. It offers communication skills and awareness practices that make it much easier and safer to navigate the sometimes tricky passages of honesty in relationships.

If you will take to heart the lessons in *Truth in Dating*, you can solve what I consider to be the single biggest problem that keeps people from experiencing lasting love. Susan puts it this way:

> Most people look for love in all the wrong places. They seek a person who is attractive, who is worthy of their love, and who loves them in return — all positive things. But they do not know how to be in a state of love themselves. So, even if they are lucky enough to find somebody to love, their attention is not really free to love this person because most of their attention is on avoiding some feared consequence (like being criticized, hurt, abandoned, not seen, et cetera). When your attention is dominated by fear, love gets squeezed out of the picture.

Truth in Dating not only busts up the dangerous mythology most of us inherited, it also gives us the power tools to create something radically new.

Practicing the ten truth skills in the book will help you to stay in the present, open to the reality of right now, rather than trying to control the outcome of the moment by presenting a false image of yourself. If relationships can begin in authenticity, their chances of success are remarkably enhanced. In this spirit of learning from every moment, it truly doesn't matter whether the date lasts an hour or leads to a romance that lasts a lifetime. What matters is that you use the process to become more transparent to your own essential depths and create an open space for your companion to make the same benign leap into discovery.

Truth in Dating is an essential guidebook for the journey.

Acknowledgments

I would like to express my love and gratitude to my mother and father, who encouraged me back in high school to practice Truth in Dating with my boyfriends, and who gave me plenty of feedback when they suspected I was being too much of a people-pleaser.

I am deeply grateful to my friend and practice partner, Randy Mack. His careful reading and critiquing of various versions of the manuscript have been invaluable.

I owe so much to my early teachers: Fritz Perls, Marilyn Rosanes-Beret, Erv Polster, Miriam Polster, Robert Resnick, Jim Simkin, Bernie Gunther, Charlotte Selver, and Virginia Satir, and to my more recent teachers: Brad Blanton, Paul Lowe, and Dhiravamsa. The challenging support I have received from these gifted mentors has enabled me to offer a similar type of mentoring to others.

Much appreciation also goes to the wonderful people at H J Kramer/New World Library, who have helped me get the book ready for publication: Linda Kramer, Hal Kramer, Georgia Hughes, and Kevin Bentley.

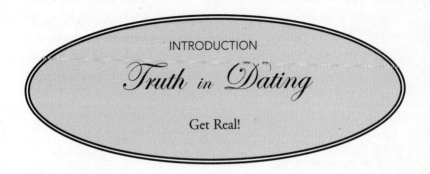

INTRODUCTION

Truth in Dating

Get Real!

After spending most of my adult life as a married woman, ten years ago (at age fifty), I joined the ranks of the approximately eighty million singles in the U.S. I am the type of person who always seems to be doing research on topics that I struggle with personally, so it's no surprise that I turned my attention to the subject of dating. I started asking questions. Is there a way to navigate the singles scene that will maximize your chances for finding true love? Why have so many singles given up on dating? Why do even very psychologically sophisticated people have difficulty beginning a new relationship? How can single people learn to enjoy the process of meeting new people without being so focused on the outcome that they feel like failures when things don't work out? Are there ways to find meaning in the difficulties so you don't wind up feeling hopeless? These are some of the questions that motivated a yearlong research study I conducted to explore how single men and women are dealing with the challenge of meeting their intimacy needs as they search for a life partner or a network of kindred spirits. My research project sought to identify other conscious, aware singles and compare my experiences with theirs. I interviewed 75 singles and surveyed 150 others in an attempt to discover what singles in this country are discovering about how to find lasting love. And over the past thirty-five years, as a dating coach and seminar leader, I have listened to the stories of thousands of other single people.

I'd Rather Be Single Than Settle

One of the most striking of my findings is the fact that many single people over the age of thirty-five have come to the decision that they would rather be single than "settle"; in other words they are not willing to compromise their integrity or their desires in order to have or keep a relationship. As one forty-something man said to me, "I used to think I had to settle for a relationship where I couldn't be myself. I'm not willing to do that anymore. And now that I'm giving myself permission to be honest about what I want and who I am, I'm discovering that there are quite a few women out there who can accept me as I am." It makes sense that if you want to find a relationship where you can be yourself, you need to conduct your dating activities with this goal in mind. You also need to recognize the sad fact that most people do not feel safe about being totally honest. They fear being hurt, causing hurt, being rejected, being judged as not good enough, or being told, "I'm not interested in seeing you again." There's a lot of fear in the dating world. Many people told me that they see dating as "dangerous." And many others more subtly revealed their unconscious fears through the defensive or self-protective way they answered my questions. So before even thinking about being more truthful in your dating relationships, it's important that you recognize how much fear exists in today's dating scene.

> I used to think I had to settle for a relationship where I couldn't be myself. I'm not willing to do that anymore.

Yet there is a way to make being honest feel safer and that's what this book is about. Truth in Dating is an approach to finding love that involves learning and practicing ten "truth skills." These skills are designed to help you speak your truth more skillfully and compassionately while at the same time helping you lighten up on your need for other people's approval. It's a way to change the rules of the dating game — toward more honesty and spontaneity, and less worry about the outcome. As you become more fluent with these skills, you will discover an increasing sense of self-trust and trust in life — so that you no longer need to control the outcome in order to feel okay.

Intimacy as a Spiritual Voyage

Since my best-selling book *The Couple's Journey* came out in 1980, I have been teaching partners how to use the hurts and struggles in their long-term relationships to deepen their contact with their spiritual essence. Now, as a single person, I find that many of these same practices can be used in a dating relationship.

Many people are beginning to realize that honesty is the only hope for relationships. As a result they have shifted their intent in dating — letting go of the intent to impress and taking on the intent to be honest. When you make honesty your conscious intent, then you will notice when you are not being truthful, and you can ask yourself, "What belief am I unconsciously harboring about myself or about people that tells me it's not safe to be honest in this situation? What am I afraid of?" Of course, the singles I talked with were not 100 percent honest all the time; but they seemed to feel that just the intent to be created richer, more rewarding dating experiences and a deepening sense of themselves. The other good news is that you can start using honesty as a way to practice being more aware and present even on a first date. You don't have to wait until you find your soul mate to enjoy the learning and growth usually associated with long-term commitments.

How I Found Myself on This Path

Since I was a teenager, I have been interested in how relationships can be paths to healing and self-realization. I was blessed to have the kind of parents who talked openly about their relationship struggles in a way that modeled to me what I now call "grown-up love." Grown-up love allows you to love another person even if you're angry with him or her. It's the kind of love where you don't blame your partner when you are feeling upset — even if it was your partner's actions that triggered your pain. Grown-up love understands that no one is going to meet all your emotional needs. But this is no reason to hide the fact that you have such needs. In grown-up love, two people accept each other, and themselves, as they are. Seeing this model for what a relationship could be, and believing that few adults have the inner strength to pull it off, I became interested in how my parents managed to be so mature in their behavior and expectations toward each other (especially in light of the fact that their own parents were quite dysfunctional).

My parents did not always practice grown-up love. They grew into it. I remember as a little girl watching my dad get angry at my mom for forgetting to take care of something and my mom crying and telling him she was hurt. It took my dad a little while, perhaps a couple of years, before he realized that her expressions of hurt feelings were not an indictment of him.

One thing that really helped my parents was that they were always reading self-improvement books. In my family, we didn't watch much television. We read together in the evenings. This was in an era when you had to really search to find inspiring self-help literature. I remember seeing around our home books by Krishnamurti, Lao-tzu, and Carl Jung. *Summerhill* by A. S. Neill was a family favorite, as was a lesser-known title by Hugh Missildine, *Your Inner Child of the Past*. Books like these helped my parents develop a healthy philosophy of married life. Whenever they read a book that inspired them, they would talk about it with me and my brothers and urge us to read it too.

Having parents like mine was a decided advantage in many ways. I have often praised them for giving me a jump start on life. So it seems to be my destiny to be somewhat ahead of the times in terms of my independence from the prevailing social norms. In college, when most of my girlfriends were seeking to marry a doctor, I wanted to be a doctor. And when most of the eligible men I was meeting wanted to impress me with their brilliance or their achievements, I was more interested in learning about their shadow sides, the things they usually didn't feel comfortable sharing with a girlfriend.

> One of the beneficial by-products of my personal Truth in Dating practice has been a consistent spaciousness of attention, or presence, in the face of disturbing information.

As I sit down to write a book about Truth in Dating, I wonder: Is this idea too far ahead of our present culture? The people I interviewed felt an affinity for using honesty to become more conscious, but is anyone strong enough to actually do it? Will my well-intentioned interviewees revert back to sugarcoating and avoiding conflict when they become emotionally involved? And I must admit that even I, who have been using dating as an awareness practice for ten years, sometimes think, "I can't keep doing this. The truth hurts too much." It hurts to hear that my boyfriend is turned off by how I talk or laugh or that he is fantasizing about another woman when he is making love with me. I get my feelings hurt, or my ego bruised, just like everyone else, so I'm pretty aware of how a blow to our ego or pride can trigger an unconscious reaction and make us want to fight or flee. But I also know that it is my mission to tell the world the other side of this story — the story of how good I feel about myself when I am able to speak and hear what's real and honest. I respect and trust myself so much more now than I did before I began this practice. One of the beneficial by-products of my personal Truth in Dating practice has been a consistent spaciousness of attention, or presence, in the face of disturbing information. I can listen to bad

news from someone I'm dating without freaking out or jumping to conclusions like, "I'm outta here!" I have learned, through practice, to allow
my buttons to be pushed and to feel my feelings without resorting to
such typical defense mechanisms as
blaming, punishing, with-
drawing, or running away.
As I have become more
open toward others and
trusting toward myself,
I have come to like myself
better. My inner life — my
relationship with myself and with all
creation — is richer. So I find I am less dependent upon a man-
woman relationship for my sense of well-being.

> If I react with hurt feelings when my date tells me he doesn't want to go out with me again, there's something in me that's calling out for healing — an old outdated belief, or a childhood-based fear that there's something wrong with me.

Truth in Dating? Get Real!

Many people laugh when they first hear the phrase "Truth in Dating."
"Yeah, sure," they chuckle, "Like I'm really going to tell a woman I'm
seeing that I am attracted to her best friend," or "You think I'm going to
tell a man that I'm turned off by how he smells?!"

Popular wisdom has it that the truth hurts, so if you can't say something nice don't say anything at all. Yes, the truth does hurt sometimes.
But when I am hurt, it's because there's buried pain already inside me
that needs to be felt, acknowledged, and healed. If I react with fear or
hurt feelings when my date tells me he doesn't want to go out with me
again, there's something in me that's calling out for attention and for
healing — an old outdated belief, or a childhood-based fear that there's
something wrong with me. Sure, I can blame him or label him as inca-
pable of intimacy. I can say good riddance and keep searching for someone who will not push any of my buttons. If I'm able to find such a
person, my reward is that I don't have to face myself honestly, and I get
to keep my addictions and my neuroses intact. But if I decide to face my
fears and uncover my outdated beliefs about myself, I become more real,

more of who I really am. And I become more confident that I can handle people's reactions to my honesty.

Many people are still seeking someone who will feed their addictions for security and control. And many believe that in order to have a loving relationship that endures, they have to lie a little or a lot to make the other person feel secure.

Truth in Dating challenges this assumption. The fact is, no one can make another person feel anything — secure or insecure. If you feel pain, I didn't make you feel it. It was there already. As your friend, it is my commitment to give you my honest feedback or response. That's the greatest gift I can give to another person — my honesty. It's more valuable than a promise to love you forever because it respects you enough to treat you like a grown-up. A mutual agreement to be honest calls both partners out to a higher standard of relating. It is my conviction that we all need to do this for one another. As your friend and fellow sojourner, it is my responsibility to provide you with accurate data concerning my feelings, my wants, and my thoughts about you, for that is how you learn — through honest feedback.

Through my research conversations, I found that while few people practice Truth in Dating all the time, there are a great many singles of all ages who sincerely desire to be more honest. They know it's not easy. Some have tried being honest, perhaps without developing the requisite truth skills, and found their relationships couldn't take it. But most of the individuals I polled or interviewed* said they would give this kind of honesty another chance if they could find someone willing to try it with them.

Honesty Requires Skill

The reason most people haven't fared so well when they have ventured forth into honest relating is that they lack the skill and confidence to pull

---

* My interviews and questionnaires asked such questions as: In what areas do you find it most difficult to be honest with someone you're just getting to know? Tell me about a time when you told the truth in a dating situation and it turned out badly. Tell me about a time when you told the truth, and it turned out well.

it off. They need to develop better truth skills. Your ability to accurately hear what the other person actually said, instead of embellishing what you hear with fear-based interpretations, is a truth skill; the ability to ask for and listen to feedback without deflecting it or defending yourself is another. These truth skills will be described in chapter 3. When you know and use these skills, honesty becomes easier — less hurtful, less scary, and even exciting.

In the pages that follow, you will have the opportunity to try on Truth in Dating to see if it fits you. In part I, "Why Truth in Dating?" you'll learn about the benefits and the pitfalls of this approach. You'll take a quiz to help you assess your values and habits with respect to honest relating. And you will be introduced to the ten truth skills. In part II, "Dating 101," you will see how the ten truth skills can be applied in many of the typical dating situations that most singles find themselves dealing with — situations like deciding when to have sex, or telling someone you're not attracted to them. Part III, "Advanced Dating," is devoted to more high-risk dating practices — ways to move your relationship along faster so you can see each other's hidden sides earlier in the game. And part IV, "Ending It," is about how to end things consciously, if ending turns out to be the appropriate course of action. When you know how to deal honestly with this issue, you can move on without bringing your old baggage along with you.

If you are reading this book to help you find true love in your life, I want you to know that true love is possible for you — if you are willing to revise your approach to dating using the truth skills I'll be describing. In these pages you will learn how to take emotional risks — to say what's so without knowing how others will react to you. This is essentially what it means to "Get Real."

In Getting Real (the title of my previous book), you accept certain realities about how life is and how other people are, such as the reality that you cannot control whether another person likes you or not, and the reality that sometimes you will feel pain about this fact. Getting Real is about getting to an awareness that emotional pain will not kill you, that being liked is not necessary for your survival, and that by really feeling your pain (without making it more or less than it is), you can heal the old business from your past. (Chapter 10, "What to Do When Your Buttons Are Pushed," tells you how.) The goal of Getting Real is to get to the place where experiences like rejection and criticism no longer have power over you. You become free of the need to control your world to prevent your buttons being pushed. This will enable you to live in the present in a state of love.

As you get more real, the love in your heart will grow. As you find out that you can deal with things you used to avoid, your trust in yourself and in life itself will be growing. As your self-trust grows, you will not need to go through life with your defenses activated — watching out for the possibility of someone upsetting or offending you. You won't go around fearing other people, so you'll be able to connect to your essential loving and self-loving presence. Then your relationships will work — because you won't be looking for the other person to make you feel okay. The reality is that they're not going to do that. If you're still holding on to the idea that there's someone out there who can make you feel okay or that you'll feel better when you have someone who loves you, I urge you to give up that hope right now. Relationships are a wonderful vehicle for healing and transformation, but they are not about finding someone who will make you feel whole and complete. As you learn to risk being transparent in relationships, you will discover that feeling okay comes from being honest and real. It does not come from receiving someone else's esteem or respect.

> As you find out that you can deal with things you used to avoid, your trust in yourself and in life itself will be growing. As your self-trust grows, you will not need to go through life with your defenses activated.

Honesty is the only hope for relationships. Honesty can be difficult, and it can trigger pain, but if it does, this old buried pain needs to come to the surface so it can be seen, felt, and healed.

There are many others like you in the dating world who want to get real in their relationships. These are people who have already tried and given up on: getting the other person to stop pushing their buttons, telling the other person what they wanted to hear, or compromising their integrity to avoid being alone. The number of people who practice Truth in Dating is growing every day as more of us learn to Get Real.

Assumptions of the Truth in Dating Approach

This book is based on the following assumptions:

- Intimate relationship can be a wonderful vehicle for inner development, and you don't have to be married to enjoy its benefits as a spiritual voyage.
- No other person is ever going to meet all of your unre-solved childhood needs. Yet these unresolved issues will come up in an intimate relationship or a potentially inti-mate one — even on a first encounter. This fact makes intimacy an excellent context for uncovering those unfinished emotional needs that still need to be felt and healed.
- While the truth sometimes hurts, when it does it's because there's emotional pain buried inside you that needs to be acknowledged, felt, communicated, and so healed.
- Most singles would be more honest if they had the req-uisite honesty skills and if they had someone they trusted who agreed to practice Truth in Dating with them.
- Honesty does not come naturally to most adults, but the skills for becoming more honest, conscious, and respon-sible can be learned.

PART ONE

Why Truth in Dating?

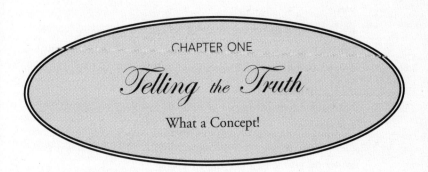

CHAPTER ONE

Telling the Truth

What a Concept!

Truth in Dating is about using honesty as a "practice."
A practice is a discipline that you take on intentionally
in order to expand your awareness and enhance your
capacity to experience life to the fullest.

Have you ever

- said yes to someone when you wanted to say no?
- lied to someone in order to protect his or her feelings?
- wondered how the person you're dating feels about you, but didn't want to ask for fear of appearing insecure, needy, or pushy?
- had your feelings hurt but didn't admit it?
- felt angry but acted like everything was fine?
- been jealous about your date's attention to another person, but acted cool?
- pretended to like someone more than you really did?
- pretended to like someone less than you really did?
- wanted to be physically affectionate, but didn't want to appear too eager, easy, or horny?
- wanted to express appreciation, but held yourself back?

- pretended to be more sexually turned on than you really were?
- had sex with someone in order to avoid conflict or confrontation?
- agreed to go out with someone and then called later to break the date?
- felt nervous or inhibited with someone you're especially attracted to?
- wished you could be more spontaneous and natural with someone you're just getting to know?

If you answered yes to any of these questions, rest assured that you are not alone. In my workshops and conversations with research participants, almost everyone answered yes to most of them. Telling the truth is not easy. Yet when you do allow yourself to be real and spontaneous, you're more radiant, alive, and attractive.

Sharing Self-Talk Right Away

In my Truth in Dating seminars, I'll frequently encourage two people who have never met to simply share "what I was thinking as I noticed you from across the room." I call this inner conversation "self-talk." When they share these thoughts, they become delightfully spontaneous, interesting, and funny. It is amazing how a person who at first may seem shy or inhibited suddenly comes alive when he stops trying to do things right and simply shows up real. In a recent seminar, I asked Ted, one of the men in the group, to pick out a woman he found attractive and then whisper to me the thoughts he was having as he noticed her across the room. He said, "I'm thinking that someone as cute as her would probably not be interested in me." So I asked him, "What if you were to go up to her and tell her that you noticed her and then tell her what you just told me? Would you be willing to try that?" He accepted the challenge, walked over to where she was seated, and told her, "I have been watching you for a while, and I wanted to come over and say that I think you're really cute…and I was also thinking to myself that someone as cute as you would probably not be interested in someone like me…but then again, who knows?" The other workshop participants who were watching cracked up! Then I coached the woman, Cherie, to tell me what she was thinking to herself at this point: "I've never been approached quite like that before. I'd like to be able to say I'm attracted to Ted, but at this point, I'm not.…And yet, because he was so open and funny, he certainly got my attention. I like how spontaneous he is, and I think I'd like to spend more time getting to know him." After only a slight bit of encouragement, she was able to share all of this with him. And again, the audience got a real charge out of it — as did Ted! Several of those watching the interaction commented about how radiant the two of them became as they were sharing what they were really feeling and thinking. One witness remarked, "As they got more spontaneous, once they got going, they seemed to shine more brightly. It looked like they were lit up by some inner source of energy. It was amazing!"

When people take risks and show up real, they get lighter, brighter, more radiant, and more magnetically attractive. This is one of the rewards of practicing Truth in Dating.

I have observed this phenomenon myself many times. When people take risks and show up real, they get lighter, brighter, more radiant, and more magnetically attractive. I imagine it has something to do with the fact that when you are not trying to hide or impress, you are more relaxed, and the life force moves through you more easily. This is one of the rewards of practicing Truth in Dating.

What's at Stake?

Why can't we be more relaxed and free? What are we afraid of? What danger do we seek to protect ourselves from? From my research conversations, I have found that most singles give entirely too much weight or meaning to the outcome of each dating interaction.

Ron was wildly attracted to Maya. On the second date, Maya told Ron, "I like you as a person, but I'm not sexually attracted to you." What Ron concluded from this was: "I'll never have what I want. I'm just not that attractive. The ones I really like never feel the same about me." This is sad, but typical. One disappointing conversation gets magnified and becomes a sweeping generalization about "the way my life is going to be forevermore."

Harvey had been talking with Maureen at a party for about fifteen minutes when she confessed to him, "I'd really like to take you home to meet my mother. I think she'd like you as much as I do." Since he already knew that he was not very attracted to Maureen, he immediately panicked, thinking to himself, "Oh my God, now I have to act like I feel the same about her. And she'll get the wrong idea…and I'll be trapped and unable to say no to her. I just can't stand hurting a woman."

Why can't we be more relaxed and free? Most singles give entirely too much weight or meaning to the outcome of each dating interaction.

In the above two examples, both Ron and Harvey had an automatic fear reaction to what the woman said to them. Instead of simply being present in the moment, their minds went racing off into the future in an unconscious, patterned way.

Old Tapes and Buttons

Generally, most of us are not very good at simply being in the present moment — since we're quite vulnerable to automatic fear reactions. When I notice such reactions in myself or others, I see them as evidence that an old fear has been triggered. Metaphorically speaking, a button has been pushed. Ron walks around with an "I'm not good enough" button always there waiting to be pushed. When Maya said what she said, the tape that played in his mind was, "I'm not good enough to ever have what I want." Harvey lives constantly with a fear of "the woman's" reaction. When Maureen said what she said, his "it's not safe to say no to a woman" button was triggered.

Buttons are those little things we wear around our heart and solar plexus area. If someone pushes one of these buttons, a familiar tape begins to play. Your date calls at the last minute and says he's too tired to come over, and the tape that plays in your mind is, "He's losing interest. This is the beginning of the end. I'd better start withdrawing in order to protect myself." A person you've just met, but are hoping to connect more intimately with, tells you, "I'm not looking for long-term intimacy. I just want to get to know you as a friend." The tape that plays in your head is, "If I were more attractive, she wouldn't be saying that. That's a rejection if I ever heard one!"

> Dating can be a journey toward consciousness and love, toward overcoming our dependence on the illusion of control to help us feel safe.

One reason we can't be present in dating interactions is because we still have unfinished business or baggage from our past. We may wish this were not the case, but it is. You can make it your aim to be present or "in the now," but it's impossible to be present if you are "under the influence" of an unconscious fear reaction. When this happens, our best shot at being present is to notice that we are not. This noticing will, in itself, bring about a degree of present-time awareness.

We all use certain thinking or behavior patterns to avoid discomfort or control anxiety. In a dating situation, our anxiety might be about not knowing where we stand, not getting what we want, or just generally not being in control. Ron doesn't know what the future of this relationship will be, but instead of simply feeling his discomfort about that one thing, he reacts automatically, making a prediction about how his whole life is going to be. This is one of the patterned ways he deals with feeling not in control. Somehow, pretending to know the future gives him some semblance of control — even if the prediction is an unpleasant one.

Dating as a Journey toward Consciousness

How does this relate to Truth in Dating? Dating can be a journey toward consciousness and love, toward overcoming our dependence on the illusion of control to help us feel safe. Or dating can be a series of strategies to help us maintain a false sense of security and control. To put this another way, dating can enhance our self-awareness and self-trust in facing unknown outcomes, or it can keep us on a never-ending search for the perfect partner (as a distraction from simply feeling our vulnerability to things we cannot control). Dating can expand our capacity for love and acceptance of what is, or reinforce our fears that we are not okay if things don't turn out according to our hopes and plans.

The idea behind Truth in Dating is that we don't need to wait until we get into a committed relationship to use our relationship life as a vehicle for personal and spiritual development. We can start right where we are! We can use our dating experiences as a practice.

At present, most people still seem to favor dating as a strategy for staying safe over dating as an awareness practice. But I think the tide is turning. Many people I talked with said they realize that trying to find someone who doesn't push their buttons isn't working. This is a good sign — a sign that people in general may be getting less addicted to comfort and control. It is my hope that if we can admit that we all have automatic patterned reactions based on our unfinished business from the past, then we can enter the dating arena with the aim of becoming more conscious of when our buttons are being

What a relief this might be — if we would stop strategizing about how to create the desired impression.

pushed. We can let go of trying to pretend to be cool or hot or whatever we think is expected of us. We can stop pretending and start being more transparent. What a relief this might be — if we would stop strategizing about how to create the desired impression. Maybe then we could relax enough to be present and awake to our experience of the moment.

I have been helping singles and couples show up real for many years, and I know that honesty does not come easily for most people. For most of us honesty feels risky. So to Get Real, that is, to relax into just being present to whatever you are thinking or feeling, will require setting your intent to make honesty a "practice." A practice is something that you take on in order to expand your awareness, to enhance your capacity to experience life to the fullest, to express your maximum potential. So dating can be a practice for you in which you come to value noticing when you are present and when you are caught in a reaction.

Of course, you may still choose to approach dating using all the strategies you have learned during your life to help you stay in control. The choice is yours. If you want to use dating as your awareness practice, then this book is for you. Even if you are not completely sold on Truth in Dating, you might still find value in these pages if you have a sincere desire for more honest relationships. Learning the Truth in Dating skills will still make honest communication easier and less scary.

Truth in Dating Is Good Practice for Marriage

Not everyone wants to get into a marriage or long-term partnership. But if you do, you probably know that a marriage-type commitment cannot thrive without honesty. Your level of honesty and mutual trust will determine your level of intimacy and fulfillment. Yet, as we know, most marriages are not based on complete honesty. The main reason for this is that married people are just as unlikely to have the requisite honesty skills as single people. Practicing the truth skills while you are dating, when the stakes are presumably lower, can help you develop the tools you will need to make a future long-term committed relationship work. We all need a lot of "practice relationships" before we are ready for lasting love.

An important skill that you'll need if you intend to be in a long-term relationship is the ability to navigate change. Otherwise, you may outgrow your relationship. The best way to learn about dealing with the reality of constant change in relationships is by communicating honestly at all times, especially when it's risky. Honest risk-taking teaches you how to deal with the unknown, an essential skill for going through changes with another person. When you are honest, you never know for sure what the other's reaction will be. It's as if you are stepping into the unknown together. As you get more comfortable and skillful at moving into the unknown, your capacity for navigating change grows, as individuals and as partners.

Here's another way truth-telling can help you learn to cope with constant change: it gives you plenty of experience with the almost universal phenomenon that after you fully express a feeling, it changes. Shining the light of consciousness onto a once hidden feeling brings you to a new relationship with this feeling. Here is an example: Let's say I feel anger at my boyfriend for something he did. I express my anger to him — as a self-disclosure, not as a control strategy. And in the next moment, we are laughing and hugging again. My anger is gone. If it comes back, I'll express it again when it does; and once again, it'll probably change. Expressing feelings freely in the interest of transparency allows us to experience the natural fluidity, the ebb and flow, of life. Life is change. So it's healthy to allow your inner state to change rather than holding rigidly to a position.

> Shining the light of consciousness onto a once hidden feeling brings you to a new relationship with this feeling.

The more truthful we are on the dating journey, the better we will be prepared for a long-term relationship. Truth in Dating teaches us how to be skillfully honest; it teaches us how to surf the waves of change; and it allows us to get more mileage out of our dating relationship. If dating is preparation for longer-term intimacy, it's good to have more rather than less experience.

Truth in Dating Adds Meaning and Purpose

Truth in Dating is a personal awareness practice and a spiritual practice, as well as a way to be more juicy and attractive. As a practice, it's like doing yoga — a yoga of communication. People practice yoga to expand their capacity for feeling and experiencing life. It hurts sometimes, but the pain is good for you. It's meaningful pain. It's not masochistic. The practice of Truth in Dating can give your dating activities a purpose beyond finding a mate — that of finding love, the kind of love that resides in your own being. This love is something that you can enjoy whether you are partnered or single. It's something that no one can ever take away from you. The sub-title of this book, *Finding Love by Getting Real*, has a double meaning: finding others to love and be loved by; and the higher purpose of redis-covering our essential nature, which I believe is love.

> Truth in Dating can give your dating activities a purpose beyond finding a mate — that of finding love, the kind of love that resides in your own being.

The journey home to our natural capacity for loving is the mythi-cal hero's journey. Our ability to let down our defenses will be tested each time we experience hurt, disappointment, or betrayal; every time we meet someone we don't care to spend time with, every time someone tries to dominate or control us. These are some of the hurdles we will inevitably encounter on the hero's path. That path, the path of being consciously human, offers us a chance to peel away the layers of social and family conditioning; to burst the illusions that dictate our attempts to be socially acceptable, to be right, to play it safe, and to appear in con-trol; and above all, to free ourselves of the illusions that create our dependency on someone else's love or acceptance in order to feel okay.

As we learn to let down our guard and show up real, whether oth-ers love us for our realness or not, we become higher order human beings. We have nothing to prove, nothing to hide, and nothing to defend against. We risk losing favor with others, but in the process dis-cover the love for self and others that has always been at our core.

If this seems like a lofty aim, it is also quite a hedonistic one. Life feels better — we experience more pleasure and less frustration — when we stop controlling so much. It feels good to love, to tell the truth, and to operate according to the principle of mutual benefit. If you conduct your dating and friendship relationships with an eye toward spotting the addictions and control patterns that cloud your ability to be open and loving, you will eventually find your way home to that inner peace that is beyond understanding. On the other hand, if you persist in trying to get life to agree to your terms, the experiences of love and trust that you long for will probably elude you.

Chapter Summary

- Truth in Dating is both a way to become more conscious and present and a way to develop deeper self-trust.
- When people take a risk and enter "the unknown" together, it is a bonding experience. And they often appear lighter and more radiant.
- Most people are vulnerable to having old fears restimulated in new relationships, but when this occurs, it allows us to notice our automatic reactions so we can heal them.
- Truth in Dating is a practice for overcoming our illusions about life and relationships — particularly the illusion that being in control will make us safe and secure. Control is an illusion.
- Truth in Dating is a journey toward greater consciousness. It offers a chance to peel away the layers of social and family conditioning so we can relate to others from our essential being — that is, so we can be real with one another.
- If honesty is necessary to make a marriage-type relationship work, then Truth in Dating gives you the skills you'll be needing in the future. It's good practice!

CHAPTER TWO

Honesty

The Only Hope for Relationships

Everyone values honest communication,
but how many have the necessary honesty skills?

Since my book *Getting Real* was published a few years ago, one of the most popular applications of the Getting Real work has been my Truth in Dating seminars for singles and pre-committed couples. In my work with hundreds of truth-seeking singles from New York to California, one conclusion is inescapable: almost everyone seems to value honest communication, but very few have the skills or the confidence to practice it consistently.

According to most of the singles I have met in my travels, the typical dating situation is fraught with fear. It seems that when people believe there's a lot at stake, they get nervous and instead of being their creative, delightful selves, they resort to various anxiety management strategies.

Lois met Jeff at a friend's birthday party and felt immediately drawn to him. But instead of spending time talking with him at the party, she found herself flirting with other men in hopes that Jeff would notice her. She left the party that night without having spoken a word to Jeff.

Lois's behavior is an example of what I call a "control pattern." A control pattern is anything you do automatically, without awareness, to manage the anxiety of feeling "not in control." A favorite pattern of many people is to be overly nice or agreeable. Others try to appear cool or indifferent, as Lois did. Some try to impress by acting superconfident. Others shrink into the woodwork and try to remain invisible. When you're in your control pattern, you are usually "on automatic," acting from habit rather than choice.

People resort to such behaviors because they cannot tolerate the uncertainty or anxiety of the typical dating encounter. Lois felt attracted to Jeff, but she had no idea how he felt about her. She wanted him to be as attracted to her as she was to him, but since she was not able to control the situation to insure her desired outcome, she tried to stay in control by playing it cool.

> When people believe there's a lot at stake, they get nervous and instead of being their creative, delightful selves, they resort to various anxiety management strategies.

Truth in Dating focuses on noticing and learning to live without these habitual patterns. It is about learning to express yourself authentically — to say what you really feel and think, or to simply be silent and listen.

Today's Dating Landscape

With the advent and increasing popularity of personal ads, matchmakers-for-hire, and on-line dating services, it's easier now than ever before to be introduced to a large number of potential partners with a minimal outlay of time and energy. Whether you actually use any of these services or not, you know they're available to you, so you know that you could at least be having a lot of first dates if you really wanted to. You are no longer dependent on getting invited to parties, going to bars or nightclubs, or introducing yourself to strangers at the supermarket. That's the good news.

The bad news is that many of these newer dating venues emphasize the checklist approach to dating. You are asked to make a list of what you ideally want, what you might settle for, and what you have to offer in exchange. This tends to foster the illusion that if you and another person match up in terms of traits and preferences, you're well on your way to successful relating The problem with the checklist mentality is that there is so much more to people than the generalizations they make about themselves. Generalizations like "I'm the kind of person who...loves the outdoors... enjoys parties...needs a lot of alone time...feels things deeply" tell nothing about a person's capacity for relating. It is your ability to openly relate to another person that spells the difference between success and failure in relationships. Most singles (and couples too) do not relate very well. They are too focused on feeling in control. Relating is the opposite of controlling.

In my thirty-five-year career as a relationship coach and seminar leader, I have found that the capacity to relate is the one essential quality that enables a person to enjoy satisfying interpersonal/intimate relationships. Without this capacity, you're doomed to keep repeating the same old script over and over. This capacity is rarely mentioned in personal ads. It is not something you can glean about a person by reading his bio. It is not something you can tell by watching her from across a crowded room. It is not dependent on body type or physical beauty. It is something that anyone can learn, if he or she is willing to practice ten fundamental "truth skills." All ten of these will be described in detail in the next chapter, but the most basic of them is the ability to notice whether the intent of your communication is to control or to relate.

Relating vs. Controlling

When you are relating, you are simply open and present to whatever is — whether this is pleasurable or painful or somewhere in-between. When you are controlling, you are trying to make something happen; for example, you may be trying to appear confident, keep yourself from looking foolish, get others to like you or pay attention to you, avoid confrontation or conflict, make sure the other person is not uncomfortable, get your own way, keep things from getting too intense, or manage the anxiety of simply being present.

When you are relating, you are curious about the outcome, instead of trying to control it. You're more interested in discovering and experiencing what's so, rather than trying to manipulate things to come out as planned. If Lois had known how to relate to Jeff, she might have gone up to him and told him she was feeling drawn to come over and talk to him. Then she would have listened openly to his response, whether it was what she was hoping for or not. It is your skill and confidence in dealing with unknown, unplanned outcomes that make you good at relating. If you lack such skill and confidence, you'll be more apt to resort to control patterns. A control pattern is any automatic, patterned way of thinking or behaving that keeps you from feeling what is really going on inside you and instead helps you appear more comfortable and in control than you actually feel. Practicing Truth in Dating helps you outgrow this need to protect yourself from reality. Through this practice, you develop the inner strength required to deal with what is really going on. You learn to accept the fact that you cannot control how others feel toward you.

It is your skill and confidence in dealing with unknown, unplanned outcomes that makes you good at relating.

If you are dependent on your control patterns to help you cope, you'll be less confident and more fearful, less spontaneous and more rigid, and just generally less resourceful. You'll also be less attractive to conscious, aware people who are seeking to pair with other conscious, aware people.

When you are caught in a control pattern, you cannot be present. When you learn to pay attention to what you're really feeling, authentic, present-centered relating becomes more natural. You learn to free yourself from the patterned ways you overprotect yourself, the ways you try to impress, and the ways you cover your true feelings.

Most singles report that they catch themselves trying to impress and appear in control more often when they are fearful, nervous, or uneasy as compared to when they are relaxed. It is this need to impress, this worry about the outcome of the interaction, that blocks your capacity for "presence." Presence is the ability to feel and sense yourself and your surroundings in the here and now. Presence disappears when you focus on the outcome, as in "If I do this, will he still like me?" or "How can I get him to ask me out again?" Presence is critical in a relationship because if you're not present, there's "nobody home" to relate to the other person, and neither of you will get the benefit of learning from your experiences. We learn by paying attention. Presence allows you to pay attention.

Some control patterns that are familiar to most of us are: over-talking, explaining; judgmental self-talk, self-congratulatory self-talk, fearful self-talk; looking intensely into someone's eyes in order to impress, not looking into someone's eyes in order to avoid too much intensity, waiting to speak until you are sure you'll be well received, impulsively speaking up before you know what you want to say. Control patterns arise whenever you are fearful about being rejected, controlled, attacked, criticized, abandoned, judged, ignored, frustrated, or shamed. Most singles have felt at least one of these familiar fears. How can a person with these normal dating fears ever get relaxed enough to experience truly fulfilling relating with another human being? How can we develop the necessary skills so that we can trust ourselves enough to let down our defenses — trusting that even if things don't turn out so well, we will still be okay?

> Control patterns arise whenever you are fearful about being rejected, controlled, attacked, criticized, abandoned, judged, ignored, frustrated, or shamed.

The ten truth skills described in chapter 3 are a curriculum for presence. They can help you trust yourself enough to approach your dating encounters openly and without defenses. They can help you come back to being present whenever you get lost in one of your unconscious patterns. Remember, the reason we use control patterns is because we are afraid. We are afraid to feel what we feel, say what we feel, or hear what someone else feels about us.

Buttons Reveal Your Fears

Having a button pushed means having an unconscious fear triggered. This leads you to react in an automatic, unconscious way. During one interview, a fiftyish single man named Bruce asserted matter-of-factly, "I consider myself to be very honest, but there's one thing I won't tell a woman I'm dating. I never disclose how little money I have."

"And why is that?" I asked.

"Because women will stereotype a man who lives the way I do. They will automatically rule me out. So I like to wait until after they get to know me before I talk about my net worth . . . or lack of it!"

What do you think about Bruce's statement? Can you put yourself in his shoes? He has probably been rejected more than once, and this has probably been painful for him. He understandably wishes to avoid this pain in the future. But the next woman's rejection of him has not even happened yet. He is imagining this rejection happening in the future. So he's secretive and defensive about his money situation — just to be safe. He is not present. He is engaging in two fairly common control patterns: avoiding a particular feared topic, and rationalizing his reason for doing so.

> Having a button pushed means having an unconscious fear triggered. This leads you to react in an automatic, unconscious way.

I believe he is also deceiving himself when he assumes that his lack of financial means is the reason some women won't date him. Any time you have a standard, one-size-fits-all reason for why something happens to you, this is simply another symptom of lack of presence. If Bruce were present to his actual feelings, he would be feeling his feelings — not thinking up reasons why he might be rejected. Explaining "why" is usually a control game. It's a way to avoid the discomfort of not knowing or not being in control of the outcome.

Feeling Leads to Healing

From knowing Bruce as I do, I imagine that the dating rejections he has experienced in the past have more to do with a core belief about his own unworthiness. His financial situation may be a symptom of deeper self-doubts. Bruce has a deep-seated fear of rejection related to this unconscious sense of unworthiness, which he has played out in different ways all his life. He has defended his self-image by finding reasons why he keeps getting rejected, instead of allowing himself to feel the pain of each rejection experience. If he were able to be present to his experience, he would simply feel his pain, frustration, and anger. This would offer him an opportunity to heal. Feeling your feelings gives you a chance to comfort and heal yourself. If you hide your real feelings from yourself, you will not heal.

> Often a current painful experience will trigger old wounds. To heal wounds from childhood, a person needs to allow himself to experience as an adult what was too intense or painful to feel as a child.

Often a current painful experience will trigger old wounds, such as, for Bruce, the times in his childhood when the kids at school refused to play with him during lunch hour. If he were willing to feel his feelings about this, he would have a chance to heal his old wounds. To heal wounds from childhood, a person needs to allow himself to experience as an adult what was too intense or painful to feel as a child. By using his "adult reasoning," he stays stuck in an old pain management pattern. His current "reason why" has to do with money. But such reasoning is nothing more than a mental construct. As such, it is not real. Until he connects with and feels his pain about the unfinished emotional business from his past, he will continue to be vigilant and fearful about being rejected. And, as long as he avoids handling the real source of his pain, he will keep getting triggered any time a woman asks him about his financial situation.

Control Patterns in Action

Let's consider what might happen when Bruce gets triggered in a dating situation. A woman he likes inquires, "Do you invest in stocks or mutual funds, or do you just keep it all in a money market fund?" (She's indirectly trying to find out how much money he has.) At that moment, Bruce's gut tightens and his throat constricts, but he hides his feelings and replies casually, "Oh I have a little here and a little there." From this point on, the relating between these two is compromised. She did not openly ask for what she wanted, and he got his "not good enough" button pushed, tried to hide this fact, and gave her an evasive answer. A wall begins to grow between them. Neither of them notices this because both have gotten accustomed to such inauthentic relating. They continue to date for several months, but the indirect communication and evasiveness continue until finally something happens that brings things to a head, and they stop seeing each other.

In the dating world interactions like this occur all the time. People go momentarily "unconscious" when their fears come up, and they don't even realize this is happening. When Bruce hears a woman's question about the state of his finances, his automatic fear reaction is, "She'll think I'm not good enough." The woman in this example happens to have unconscious fears about "not being cared for." So when he gives her an evasive answer, she imagines that he's distancing himself from her. The tape she hears is, "He doesn't care enough about me to be open with me."

In dating, unconscious fears can wreak havoc with people's interactions. When two people are intent on avoiding the pain associated with their core fears, they just keep on doing the same dance with one partner after another — secretly hoping to find someone who won't push any of their buttons! Of course this never works. They may find new partners to date, but sooner or later if a fear is there, it will get triggered.

From Getting Triggered to Being Present

Truth in Dating is about adopting a set of attitudes and practices that will help you notice when you become afraid and then help you come back to being present. You become familiar with all your feelings, including fear, anger, and hurt, instead of pretending these don't exist. Once you accept yourself as you are, it's easier to be present all the time. For most people this is an ideal they hardly dare to dream about. Yet when you learn to live in the present, your fear of others' reactions disappears. You discover that fear is usually a head-trip about the future — about your not wanting the past to repeat itself in the future or not wanting the future to turn out wrong. When you are able to notice your internal state of agitation, you have a way to bring your attention back to the present moment. You can be openly available to the actual possibilities of your situation. This is a big part of what love is — being open to each moment with all its possibilities.

In the next chapter, I'll be sharing with you the ten truth skills that I teach in my Getting Real and Truth in Dating workshops. If you want to get a solid foundation in this work, and you haven't already read *Getting Real,* you might want to do so, as that book provides a very helpful background. It shows how to speak your truth with awareness and compassion using the ten truth skills. Here we'll spend less time explaining the skills and more on applying them in new relationships.

> Truth in Dating is about adopting a set of attitudes and practices that will help you notice when you become afraid and then help you come back to being present.

Truth in Dating involves practicing the ten truth skills with people you are just getting to know as well as with people you already know. You may be a bit reluctant to suggest such a radical practice in the dating arena, but this book will show you how to do so. In the chapters that follow you'll find numerous examples of how to initiate a conversation about Truth in Dating with a new acquaintance.

Chapter Summary

- Most singles find it difficult to be honest because they give entirely too much weight to the outcome of each dating interaction. They imagine their self-worth is at stake.

- People go momentarily unconscious when they fear that some painful past experience is about to repeat itself. Then they can't hear what the other person is actually saying. This causes all sorts of confusion and unnecessary pain.

- Unfinished business from the past always crops up and messes with us. When you find it hard to stay present, it's probably a sign that one of your old fears or negative beliefs has been triggered. This means that there's some buried pain inside you (pain that was perhaps too much for you to experience as a child). This pain is something that you now need to fully experience and deal with consciously.

- When we learn to tell the truth to ourselves about our fears, then we can recognize when our buttons are being pushed and come back to being present.

- The ability to relate is the essential skill for successful relationships. Relating means being present to and being willing to reveal what you are experiencing in the moment — your feelings, your wants, your intentions.

- Most people are addicted to control and don't even know it. Controlling is the opposite of relating.

- Truth in Dating can help you learn to simply notice your fears, and not identify with them, so you can stay open to your essential loving and self-loving essence.

CHAPTER THREE

The Ten Truth Skills

Honesty does not come naturally to most people,
but it is a skill that can be practiced and learned.

I feel a deep sadness when I hear people tell me how much they have been hurt in their dating relationships and how this has caused them to approach each new relationship with fear or to give up on relationships altogether. Given such past experiences, singles need a recovery program — a way to reconnect with their open, undefended, essential nature; a way to build inner strength so that when things don't work out, they can use the situation for learning and growth instead of as an excuse for giving up or playing it safe. This is where the ten truth skills have an important role to play. The truth skills are actually life skills. They involve awareness practices and communication tools that, when combined and practiced together, allow people to feel more grounded in their actual here-now experience. By using these skills people learn to be more present and aware of what they are sensing, feeling and thinking in each moment, instead of getting caught up in fears about the future and regrets about the past.

Some of the truth skills are most useful in the beginning stages of meeting and getting to know someone. Most apply to all stages. All of these skills assist you in learning to trust yourself to be more honest — to trust that whatever the outcome, you will be able to handle it. Below is a list of the ten truth skills. The rest of this chapter will consider how each of these skills applies to Truth in Dating.

1. Experiencing what is
2. Being transparent
3. Noticing your intent
4. Giving and asking for feedback
5. Asserting what you want and don't want
6. Taking back projections
7. Revising an earlier statement
8. Holding differences or embracing multiple perspectives
9. Sharing mixed emotions
10. Embracing silence

Truth Skill #1
Experiencing What Is

Experiencing what is helps you make the distinction between what you actually experience (see, hear, sense, feel, notice, remember) versus what you imagine (interpret, believe, assume) to be true. This enables you to notice and comment about what you see or hear your date doing instead of jumping immediately to conclusions about what this behavior means. For example, you notice your date is not looking at you when he speaks. Instead of assuming you know how he feels, as in, "I see you're uncomfortable with this topic," you'd say, "I notice you are looking at the floor as you speak, and I'm thinking that maybe you're feeling uncomfortable. . . . Are you?"

Experiencing what is teaches people to "stay on their own side of the net," that is, to speak only about what you see, hear, feel, or think and to refrain from telling the other person what he or she is feeling. "I see you looking at the floor" is an example of staying on your side of the net. That's your own *experience*. "I see you are uncomfortable" is getting over on the other person's side. That's your *interpretation* about the other. Can you see the difference?

If you get caught up in believing your interpretations about another person's behavior, this will interfere with your ability to experience what actually occurred. And when you respond to this other person, you'll be responding to your interpretation about what she did instead of what she actually did. This can cause all manner of misunderstanding and needless pain.

Noticing vs. Interpreting

To get practice with this skill, think of something someone did or said that triggered in you an automatic reaction of hurt, anger, fear, or judgment. As you think back to this, notice if you are having trouble recalling exactly what was done or said. Often when a negative reaction is triggered (when a "button" has been pushed), we tend to remember our interpretation about the other person's behavior, but not the behavior that gave rise to the interpretation. If the behavior was something like the person saying, "I have to go now," interpretations like, "He's bored with me," "She doesn't have time for me," or "He's losing interest" are quite common.

> If you get caught up in believing your interpretations about another person's behavior, this will interfere with you ability to experience what actually occured.

See if you can recall the other person's actual words. Now reflect back on the interpretation you gave to the words. When my colleague Simone did this exercise, she recalled an attractive man named Dirk addressing a sentence to her that began with the words, "At your age . . ." Simone did not hear anything after that. She assumed she knew what he was going to say — something that implied that she was too old to be attractive to him. She remembered her reaction, which was a tightening in her belly and some self-talk: "He's not interested in me as anything other than a friend. Better give up any ideas about having a romance with this guy." So she concluded right then and there that she and Dirk would be friends and nothing more.

Can you see how Simone jumped to a conclusion — how she went immediately over to Dirk's side of the net? She did not tell Dirk what she heard or what she felt, and she didn't ask him what he meant. If she had, she might have learned something about him and his feelings toward her. As it was, she stayed safe from the truth by using her protective control pattern. The truth might hurt, so she didn't take any chances.

As witnesses to Simone's little drama, we know that the truth from Dirk might not have hurt. She might have been pleasantly surprised. Or once Dirk learned that she had romantic feelings toward him, he might have taken a more romantic interest in her. Such things do happen! But the natural course of events was not allowed to unfold. By interpreting Dirk's behavior, instead of experiencing what is, Simone "took control," and short-circuited the real possibilities inherent in the situation.

Most people become more appealing when they reveal their sensitive, vulnerable sides.

Truth Skill #2
Being Transparent

To be transparent is to be willing to be seen, warts and all. Many singles imagine that if they let a date or potential date know their vulnerabilities, they will be rejected. Yet my experience as a dating person and a dating coach has shown that most people become more appealing when they reveal their sensitive, vulnerable sides. It isn't your competence or attractiveness that creates an emotional bond between you and another person. Your needs and your vulnerability do that. Most people like to feel needed, so when you reveal your needs or insecurities, people feel there is a meaningful role for them to play in your life.

By this, I am not suggesting that you present the story of your wounds and misfortunes in vivid detail. I am talking more about being open about your feelings, impressions, wants, and self-talk related to your interaction with the person in front of you.

Noticing What You Avoid

Are there certain things you tend to hide from others? Are there things you know you could never say on a first date, for example? These represent areas where you do not feel safe about being transparent, about being seen. Take note of these areas or topics, because they reveal areas where you have unfinished emotional business. One man I interviewed told me he could never tell a woman that he was nonmonogamous until after he had been dating her for at least a month. When I asked why, he explained that he felt vulnerable about this since in his past, he had often been criticized and put down for his sexual lifestyle. He wanted to feel he really could trust the woman before telling her about this aspect of himself. I felt empathy for this man's position, but I also thought about how the woman might feel. Some of the women in my study said they felt manipulated when a man saved such news until a sexual bond had already been formed. These women said that if they had known sooner about the man's sexual lifestyle preference, they probably would have ended the relationship sooner. As it was, these relationships did eventually end.

> Even if telling the truth does lead to the early demise of a potential relationship, there is likely to be more warmth and respect for someone who tells the truth right away vs. someone who waits too long.

Being transparent does not guarantee that people will always love you or that they will always want to stay with you. But even if telling the truth does lead to the early demise of a potential relationship, there is likely to be more warmth and respect for someone who tells the truth right away versus someone who waits too long.

Transparent Talk

Here is an example of how you might practice being transparent on a date. Let's imagine for a minute that your date has just said something that hurt or offended you. Instead of hiding the fact that your feelings are hurt, you might say, "Hearing you say that, I notice I'm feeling hurt" or "I notice I'm shutting down." Can you see yourself doing this?

Truth Skill #3
Noticing Your Intent: Is It to Relate or to Control?

Do you communicate to relate or to control? Do you know the difference? When your intent is to relate, you are most interested in revealing your true feelings, learning how the other feels, and connecting heart-to-heart. When your intent is to control, you are most interested in getting things to come out a certain way — avoiding conflict, getting the person to like you, being seen as knowledgeable or helpful, et cetera. Communication that is controlling aims at creating a favorable impression. Communication that is relating aims at knowing and being known, seeing and being seen. Relating uses the first two truth skills, experiencing what is and being transparent, to connect with others.

Most people are not aware of their intent. They may be aware that they want to be understood, but that's about all. Even the intent to be understood can be controlling. So instead of thinking that all your communications are simple and transparent self-expressions, I urge you to humbly acknowledge the fact that sometimes you are trying to get the other to understand you the way you wish to be understood, trying to create a certain impression, or even attempting to manipulate the other person into giving you what you want. Controlling is not a bad thing when it is done candidly and with awareness. But it is destructive to trust when it is done covertly or unconsciously.

> When your intent is to relate, you are most interested in revealing your true feelings, learning how the other feels, and connecting heart-to-heart.

Are You Ready to Relate More and Control Less?

Learning the difference between relating and controlling can help you deal better with unpleasant emotions such as anger. Let's say your date just showed up an hour later than agreed, and you are upset. You have several options:

- You can express your feelings in the interest of transparency, with the intent to reveal yourself in a nonjudgmental way (relating);
- You can act like it doesn't matter — even though the truth is that you are feeling upset (controlling);
- You can be cold and distant as a way of punishing him for being so thoughtless (controlling);
- You can tell him you're upset and ask him what happened (relating);
- You can tell him that you notice one of your childhood fears is being triggered — e.g., the fear that he doesn't really care about your feelings (relating);
- You can tell him that if he is ever an hour late again, and doesn't call, you'll probably stop seeing him (controlling).

Can You See the Difference?

Can you see the difference? Relating involves self-disclosure, curiosity about the other person's reality, a willingness to be vulnerable enough to allow yourself to be affected, and an ability to step back and notice your reactions. Controlling involves one-way communication, an attempt to get the other to feel bad, or an attempt to look good or appear on top of the situation. Relating grows out of the desire to be real, to be transparent. Controlling arises from the need to be right, to play it safe, to punish, or to avoid feeling vulnerable or uncertain. Relating builds trust and intimacy. Controlling leads to mistrust and defensiveness.

Truth Skill #4
Giving and Asking for Feedback

Giving feedback is the act of verbally letting the other know how her actions affected you. Being open to receiving feedback means you are curious about and willing to hear how your actions affect other people.

In a relationship, your honest feedback or response is one of the greatest gifts you can give to the other. Most people don't get very much valid feedback in their daily lives, and they long for it. If you decide to take on Truth in Dating as a practice, you are committing to being an instrument for helping others become more conscious. Of course, some will not want your feedback. It's important to establish up front in any new relationship whether or not the two of you are going to practice Truth in Dating. One way to establish this is to tell the other about the concept as described in this book, and then ask if they are interested in this type of relating. Or you could simply tell your date that you are seeking friendships where people agree to tell the truth about their feelings and give one another honest, uncensored feedback.

How Does It Look?

Here is an example of when this skill might be appropriate: If you imagine you just said something that was offensive to your date, you might ask, "I'm wondering how that remark came across to you. I got the impression that you didn't like what I said."

Or what if you were feeling upset about the other's remark? Then, you might offer feedback saying, "When you asked me why I didn't go to work today, I felt a tightness in my chest and a flush of anger in my face. I didn't like you asking me that. I imagine I took it as an attempt to control me."

Be Specific

Feedback is most useful when it is specific — that is when you use Truth Skill #1, Experiencing What Is, to help you name and describe what the other did or said. Be specific about what was actually done or said, not what you imagined or interpreted. Otherwise, the other doesn't know what you are responding to. Instead of saying, "When you didn't listen to me, I felt hurt," say, "When you walked away while I was talking about our vacation plans, I felt hurt." Can you see the difference between being specific and making an interpretation? "When you didn't listen to me" is an interpretation. It's you getting over on the other person's side of the net and telling him what was going on inside him. You can't know whether or not he was listening. All you know is that you observed him walking out and you felt something in your body as a result.

Hearing You Say That, I Feel...

Another sweet and useful way to use this truth skill to help you maintain and deepen your here-now contact with another person is to use the phrase, "Hearing you say that, I feel..." If my date tells me I look beautiful, I'd reply, "Hearing you say that, I feel a rush of energy in my body." Or if he said he was planning to go out with a friend at a time when I was hoping to see him, I might respond, "Hearing you say that, I feel disappointed." After giving feedback, it's really important to use Truth Skill #10, Embracing Silence. I'll describe this more fully below, but in this context, to embrace silence means to stop talking after you have said what you feel, rather than explaining yourself. To speak a simple feeling and then to be quiet allows a deeper contact than if I said I felt disappointed and then went on to explain or justify why I felt this way. It takes fewer words to speak the truth.

Truth Skill #5
Asserting What You Want and Don't Want

Expressing what you want and don't want is a wonderful way to be open and transparent. Many people are afraid to ask for what they want in a dating relationship for fear of either not getting it or of having the other person give it to them out of obligation. When we express what we want we make ourselves vulnerable. Asking to have our wants and needs fulfilled reminds us of when we were little and helpless and dependent. If we cried for attention and didn't get it, we felt lost, lonely, or afraid. Now, as adults we may be reluctant to risk doing anything that might remind us of that very vulnerable period of life.

Asking for what you want is an act of trust. You are taking a step into the unknown — not knowing how the other may respond. At times, your mind may go to the thought, "What if he feels controlled by my request?" I have heard several of my male friends say that they have a hard time saying no to a woman, so they'll give a woman what she wants and secretly resent her for asking. This thought can interfere with my spontaneity, so my practice is to notice when such an idea gets in my mind and clogs up my ability to perceive reality.

Asking for a Second Date

Imagine that you are enjoying a first date with someone you are very attracted to, but you are not sure how she feels about you. You could try to indirectly draw out her feelings about you, or you could ask her how she feels. Or you could practice being transparent about your wants. In Truth in Dating, the chief goal is to communicate from the most real, most transparent and undefended place you can come from. Your focus would be on stepping into the unknown by revealing your innermost thoughts and feelings without knowing how you will be received. This generates a special type of excitement and aliveness between two people. You might say something like this:

> Asking for what you want is an act of trust. You are taking a step into the unknown.

"I'm sitting here thinking about how much I'm enjoying being with you. And I'm wondering how you are feeling. I hope you'll want to see me again. I'd really like to spend more time with you." Then listen to what she says and notice what she does.

Remember, the important thing about asking for what you want is the act of asking, not the outcome. The very act of asking is an act of self-support. You are affirming your worthiness to receive. If you do not get what you want, you will be okay. This lesson will become apparent as you get more relaxed about asking. The more you ask, the less important it becomes to get everything you want. It's when you don't ask very often, and only ask for a few really big, important things, that you tend to put too much weight on getting what you ask for. It's important to learn to ask for what you want easily and often. This will help you become free of the attachment to getting everything you want.

Truth Skill #6
Taking Back Projections

The phenomenon of projection explains why opposites attract and later repel. If some aspect of my own personality is unconscious or suppressed, I may find that I have a pattern of being attracted to men who exhibit this quality in spades. For example, I was conditioned to see myself as competent, strong, independent, and responsible. I tend to be less aware of and comfortable with my weaknesses and vulnerabilities: my self-doubts, my fears, my insecurities. So what kind of men am I attracted to? I am attracted to men who have overlearned the very qualities that I have under-learned — men who seem more comfortable with their own dependent feelings, men who allow their emotions to overtake them at times.

If some aspect of my own personality is unconscious or suppressed, I may find that I have a pattern of being attracted to men who exhibit this quality in spades.

Opposites attract, but then after a while those very qualities that drew me to a particular man may become quite unappealing. At first, I liked how open he was to his emotions. But now, I find he is so overcome by his fears and insecurities that I wind up having to handle more than my share of the worldly responsibilities.

Have you ever been attracted to someone for some wonderfully appealing quality only to discover a few months down the road that this very same quality turned you off? That's the first half of the projection process — the way that you're attracted and later repelled by someone who is your opposite personality type. The second half of the process involves taking back or rediscovering your hidden or suppressed quality. You notice that quality in the other, and now, instead of criticizing him for this, you recognize that "dependency" (for example) is a hidden aspect of yourself. Now, from this more enlightened perspective, being in this other person's presence can help you connect to this less conscious aspect of your own being and perhaps find value in it.

How Projections Affect Attractions

The dating game offers many opportunities for projections to operate. Most of our attractions are based on projections. A supermasculine male is attracted to a superfeminine female. He has disowned his softness and his nurturing side. She has disowned her ability to take power in the world and make things happen. They get together, and if things continue for a while, each learns from the other something about his or her hidden or less developed side. Or a high achieving woman is attracted to a sensual, feeling-oriented man. Through the relationship, just by being around each other, she gets more in touch with her sensuality, and he gets to connect more fully with his ability to get things done.

Truth Skill #7
Revising an Earlier Statement

Revising an earlier statement is also known as "going out and coming in again." This means giving yourself permission to revisit a particular interaction or moment in time if your feelings change or if you later connect to some deeper feelings or afterthoughts. For example, after telling your date that you'd be interested in going out with her again, you later realize that you aren't attracted to her, but were afraid to hurt her by telling the truth. So you decide to revise your original statement. You call her up and tell her, "I realized after you asked me about getting together again that I didn't feel safe about telling you the truth about my feelings. I was afraid of hurting you. What's true for me is that I'm not feeling attracted to you. I want to respect you by being truthful with you."

This truth skill can be useful any time you realize later on that your feelings have changed. You simply let the person know, "After I said such and such, I later realized there was more to it than that. What I now feel is_____." Or, "When I said such and such, I realize now that I wasn't very present or aware. If I had it to do over, I'd tell you_____." As we consider various dating challenges in later chapters, we'll see many other applications for this truth skill.

> The reason many people fear intimacy is that they fear losing themselves in a relationship. If you know how to practice holding differences, you won't need to fear losing yourself.

Truth Skill #8
Holding Differences or Embracing Multiple Perspectives

The reason many people fear intimacy is that they fear losing themselves in a relationship. If you know how to practice holding differences, you won't need to fear losing yourself. Holding differences refers to the ability to listen to and empathize with opinions that differ from yours without losing touch with your own perspective. For example, imagine that you and the person you have been dating disagree on whether to tell your children that you two are having a sexual relationship. In holding differences, you might tell your partner, "I respect that you don't think I should be completely honest with my kids just yet, while I, on the other hand, want to tell them anything they ask about."

Active Listening Helps

If you and a person you are dating encounter a difference of opinion or values, a good way to practice holding differences is by using active listening. In active listening, you listen to the other's viewpoint and then, before you state your own view, you restate what you just heard the other say, and ask if you have heard it correctly. Then you state your view or position.

Active listening can also be used if you find yourselves in a really tough conflict situation. Let's imagine, for example, that you believe in sharing the details of how intimate you are being with the other people you are seeing; but the other person does not want to talk about such details, even though she has agreed to practice Truth in Dating. It's a common occurrence that when two people commit to truth-telling, they will eventually encounter differences in how they define the concept. Rather than trying to get the other to change her mind, this truth skill would counsel you to both practice holding differences. You would each take a turn expressing your feelings, views, and wants, while the other listens and then repeats back what he hears. Make sure both people get a turn — or several turns, until each feels heard. Do not attempt to reach agreement. Simply feel into and hold in your awareness your own view, and alongside this, your partner's view. See if you can take the position that you really want your partner to get what she wants, but at the same time you really want to have what you want. Often simply holding the two positions in your consciousness side by side allows for an interesting transformation to occur. People report that somehow their positions mysteriously shift, or their fear of not getting their way dissolves. This is not a logical process, but rather some sort of emotional alchemy.

By holding differences over a period of time, you learn to be less resistant to the discomfort associated with differing positions. As you learn to relax into rather than resisting such discomfort, your resistance to your partner's position also relaxes. You learn to bind tension better. ("Binding tension," or the ability to contain conflicting feelings, has long been seen by psychologists as a sign of emotional intelligence.) Thus, you becoming a "bigger," more emotionally mature, person.

> See if you can take the position that you really want your partner to get what she wants, but at the same time you really want to have what you want.

Truth Skill #9
Sharing Mixed Emotions

This truth skill comes in very handy when you want to tell someone the truth but at the same time are concerned about her feelings. If you are like most people, you can probably think of at least one or two people in your life with whom you're afraid to say something for fear of hurting their feelings or offending them. Take some time right now to think of such a person. How do you feel as you consider telling this person your feelings or thoughts? Do you notice any mixed feelings — such as the desire to clear the air alongside a fear of being misunderstood? If you do have mixed feelings, expressing both feelings can add depth to your communication. This type of communication can also help the other see your humanness and your positive intent.

If you do have mixed feelings, expressing both feelings can add depth to your communication. This type of communication can also help the other see your humanness and your positive intent.

Mixed Emotions on a First Date

I have used this skill often on a first date when I want to tell a man that I do not want a second date with him. Here's how it might go: One of us raises the question, "How are we feeling toward each other, and is there enough interest to want to see each other again?" Sometimes, before responding to this question, I'll just be silent with him for a while. I want to establish a nonverbal connection before I start talking about such a potentially sensitive subject. Then I might tell him that I'm willing to share my thoughts and feelings if he wants to hear them. At that point I might look at him and say, "I'm having a mixture of feelings. I know I need to be completely honest because I respect you so much. At the same time, I'm afraid of hurting you. I'm pretty sure I don't want to see you again, and as I say this I'm concerned that this will hurt you. You see, I have come to care about you as we've been getting to know each other."

This scenario is only one of many possible ways to express mixed feelings. I never do it the same way twice. But the time when I did express myself using those words, my date told me he was very touched and felt very close to me. He said that my words did hurt him some, but he also said it was the sweetest rejection he'd ever experienced!

Truth Skill #10
Embracing Silence

Authentic communication depends as much on silence as it does on words — the silences between your words and the silence you leave after you have spoken as you await the other's response. Silence is required to allow your words to sink in. As you speak, you hear yourself better when there are silences. Listening to yourself is an essential ingredient for presence. Silence between words also provides room for new ideas and feelings to gestate and take form — yours and the other person's.

> Authentic communication depends as much on silence as it does on words — the silences between your words and the silence you leave after you have spoken as you await the other's response.

When you can embrace silence, you do not need to know everything in advance or have all the blanks filled in. You understand that there are many things that cannot be known all at once or once and for all. These things emerge gradually as we get to know the other person.

Avoiding the Silence of Presence

Have you ever noticed yourself asking a question and then, before the other person has had a chance to respond, answering it yourself? When I notice myself doing this, I know it's an indication that I'm avoiding the discomfort of simply being present with the other person.

Just the other day when I was with my boyfriend, I noticed a pain in my hip that I wanted him to massage. I started to ask, but as soon as I asked the question, I felt anxiety about how he might react. I had the impression from a previous conversation that he had other things on his mind, so I began to imagine that my question was an imposition. The truth was I had no idea how he would respond. And there was really no reason to be anxious. But I was. So instead of allowing him to respond, I said something like, "Oh, I don't really need this right now," thus staying in control and avoiding the silence, the experience of not knowing. This mundane example shows how the ego mind works. If it gets the tiniest bit uncomfortable, it initiates a control pattern — in this case the pattern of filling the silence to manage my anxiety.

The most important thing about embracing silence in a human interaction is that it allows for feelings to be fully experienced — your inner feelings and the feelings being exchanged. This helps you develop your ability to notice what is and prepares you to communicate with more of your whole being, so you're not just coming from your head or your automatic control pattern. I recommend that you pause before speaking — to check in with yourself, to get grounded in your bodily sensations, and to connect with the other. This takes a few seconds of silence. During this silence, energy is building to support the contact between you and the other person.

Chapter Summary

The ten truth skills in a nutshell are:

1. Experiencing what is (You can sense and identify your present feelings and sensations. You can notice and not identify with your assessments, projections, and interpretations.)
2. Being transparent (You can disclose to others what you are feeling, sensing, imagining, or saying to yourself.)
3. Noticing your intent (You can consciously reflect on the intent of your communication: is it to relate or to control?)

4. Thriving on feedback (You are open and curious about others' impressions and reactions to you. This is different from being dependent on others' reactions.)

5. Asserting what you want and don't want (You can express a desire clearly and with full contact, without expecting to get everything you ask for.)

6. Taking back projections (You understand that you may be attracted to someone who has overlearned the very qualities that you tend to deny in yourself. You know how to use this understanding for self-awareness and healing.)

7. Revising an earlier statement (You can revisit an interaction if your feelings change or if you later discover a deeper level of expression.)

8. Holding differences (You can hear and empathize with someone else's feeling or viewpoint while at the same time holding a different feeling or viewpoint.)

9. Sharing mixed emotions (You can communicate your multiple feelings about an issue or situation.)

10. Embracing silence (You can allow empty space between your words or between your words and those of another person. You can acknowledge the nonverbal emanations in the silence. You can tolerate uncertainty, ambiguity, and not knowing.)

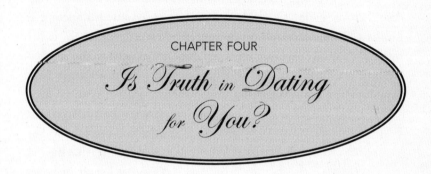

CHAPTER FOUR

Is Truth in Dating for You?

Truth in Dating is not for the fainthearted.

When some people hear the phrase "Truth in Dating," they come back with, "Telling the truth can be dangerous," or "I'm too honest already, and it gets me into trouble." When I hear these words, I am likely to ask, "Can you tell me about a specific situation when you got in trouble for being too honest?" (I prefer specific examples to generalizations.) Then I listen. The stories I have heard from people who say they are too honest have never, not once, been about the person saying what she was actually feeling in the moment. Usually, what I have heard is a story about the person engaging in an unconscious control pattern and then wondering why he didn't get better results. In all of these cases it was not their honesty that got them into trouble but rather their inability to express themselves authentically. One woman told about numerous dating encounters in which she thought she had been too honest. To her, being "too honest" was telling her date a lot of personal information about herself, including information about a health condition that she felt shame about. She

then felt hurt because the man to whom she told her story did not "vali-
date" her for sharing so openly and did not reciprocate her attempt at
intimacy by offering similar disclosures of his own. "Too honest" to her
meant, "I tried to disclose a lot about myself hoping he would appreciate it or offer a similar type of disclosure, and I didn't get much back
from him, so I wound up feeling disappointed. I guess I'm just too honest." In Getting Real terms, what
she did was not honest. She
never told him that she was
disclosing herself in hopes
that he would appreciate her
and feel closer to her. And she did
not tell him that she wanted a similar depth of
disclosure from him! Her "being too honest" was actually a manipulation to get something from him without making herself vulnerable by
asking for what she wanted. This is a typical control pattern.

> Communication that is controlling usually backfires sooner or later.

Controlling Is about Being Right, Safe, or Certain

Remember, a control pattern is anything you do to

1. act more knowing or in control than you really feel;
2. justify your actions;
3. convince yourself or the other that you are right;
4. play it safe in order to prevent an unwanted outcome;
5. manage or manipulate the other person to behave in a way that serves your interests, but not theirs;
6. avoid feeling what you want or what you feel (e.g., anxiety about whether you are accepted); or
7. avoid saying what you feel or want (e.g., "I want you to tell me something personal about yourself").

Communication that is controlling usually backfires sooner or later.
Relating leads to trust and openness between yourself and others.

Anger in Disguise

The other type of situations where people said they were too honest have usually been when they were angry but tried to cover this up. Instead of expressing their anger in a self-revealing way, they would express a judgment, a "helpful" suggestion, a penetrating insight, or a veiled criticism. Such indirect expressions of anger are not honest. People do this type of thing quite frequently. Have you ever been in a situation where someone was giving you seemingly helpful advice, but the advice seemed self-serving or even hostile, and you got the impression that this person had a hidden agenda? An example would be when your boyfriend tells you that you need to reorganize your priorities, rather than telling you that he feels angry about how little time you spend with him. This is controlling, not relating. It's not honest. It's a way of protecting himself rather than revealing himself. If he were to express his anger in a way that is relational rather than controlling, he'd do it as a self-revelation. He could simply say, "I'm angry that you chose to work last night instead of being with me." It's controlling to say, "You need to get organized so your time isn't taken up with useless busywork." Can you see the difference? In relating you speak your feelings, not your judgments. And you do so in the interest of transparency — not to get the other to change.

Often, people think they are being honest in the way they express anger or displeasure when, in fact, they are being manipulative.

The Truth in Dating Quiz:
How Safe Do You Feel to Show Up Real?

Here is a short quiz to help you assess your ability to relate versus your tendency to use self-protective control patterns. To the left of each item, using a scale of 1 to 5 (with 1 meaning "generally not true of me" and 5 meaning "generally true of me," place the number that represents how you see yourself.

___1. After a first or second date, if my date asks, "Do you want to get together again soon?" and I do not want to see this person again, I would probably say "Yes," and then call later to cancel.

____2. If someone asked me (after we'd been on a few dinner dates) to describe my ideal mate in detail, I would give a detailed answer, even if my answer included qualities that this person did not possess.

____3. If I'd been on a few dates with someone whom I otherwise found very attractive, and this person had consistently had bad breath, and it was really unpleasant for me, I would find a way to tell the person directly and gently that their breath odor bothered me.

____4. If my date shared derogatory gossip about a mutual friend, I would tell him that I was feeling uncomfortable, angry, or whatever I was actually feeling rather than remaining silent.

____5. If I were attracted to someone, but had no idea how this person felt about me, I would play it safe. I'd wait to find out how the person felt about me before disclosing my feelings of attraction.

____6. If my date told me I had a nice body, I would probably either say something nice about him, or offer some other comeback (rather than simply receiving the compliment).

____7. If someone whom I like put pressure on me to spend time with him at a time when I really wanted to do something else, I would not mention that I had wanted to do something else, even though I still preferred to do this other thing. I would give up my other plans.

____8. If my date cancelled on me at the last minute, and I was really hurt or angry about it, I would tell him or her about my feelings.

____9. If my date was talking nonstop on a topic that did not interest me, I would try to act interested.

____10. If my date felt hurt feelings about something I said and he told me about it, I would appreciate it.

___11. If, on a first date, my date asked me, "Do you have any health problems?" and I had herpes, I would not tell him at that point.

___12. If my date told me he or she was seeking a sexually monogamous relationship, and I knew I did not want that, I would say so.

Scoring the Quiz

Add up your composite score for items 2, 3, 4, 8, 10, and 12. Higher numbers on these items indicate a high aptitude for relating, i.e., for Truth in Dating. This is your "relating score." The highest possible score here is 30. Now add up your composite score for items 1, 5, 6, 7, 9, and 11. Higher numbers on these items indicate a low tolerance for open, honest relating. This is your "controlling score." The highest possible score here is also 30. Now subtract your controlling score from your relating score to get your final score. Here is what your final score might mean:

As you read further in this book you will learn there are compassionate ways to deliver bad news.

- Minus 24–0: You tend to sugarcoat, pretend, or avoid discomfort quite often; you probably have a lot of fear about telling the truth.
- 1–10: You are learning to take risks and tell the truth sometimes, but you still need plenty of practice.
- 11–18: You make it a practice to tell the truth even if it is uncomfortable, but you do withhold or shade the truth sometimes.
- 19–24: You value telling the truth over staying in control. You are impeccably honest. (Or you are lying to yourself.)

Now, let's take each item in turn and examine what your answer might indicate about you.

1. A high number (3–5) reveals a difficulty speaking the truth when you imagine it might hurt someone's feelings. You probably use a number of control patterns to protect others' feelings, or to protect yourself from having to deal with other people's feelings. As you read further in this book you will learn there are compassionate ways to deliver bad news. Even if the other does feel hurt, you can show empathy and caring for the other's feelings while still being true to yourself. This is an example of Holding Differences, Truth Skill #8.

2. A high score here reveals that you are willing to speak your true thoughts even if this might not be what the other wants to hear. This is a good measure of your capacity to relate.

3. If you answered that you would tell someone you found her breath offensive, this shows a willingness to take a risk in order to keep yourself present. Perhaps you realize that if you withhold this, you are likely to be distracted by it and therefore not present.

4. Here is another item about your willingness to risk having the other person get uncomfortable. A high score means you are willing to take such a risk in the interest of transparency. Remember, saying you're uncomfortable or angry is not the same as judging or criticizing the person. You're not telling the person there's something wrong with him. You are saying what you feel. This is relating.

5. A high score here indicates a tendency to play it safe — not revealing your feelings until you know what the other person feels. What is the worst thing that could happen if you revealed your feelings or self-talk first? And what is the best thing that could happen? Do you perhaps have a number of strategies to avoid exposing yourself, appearing foolish, or sticking your neck out?

6. A high score here indicates difficulty simply receiving a compliment. Some people are just generally uncomfortable "receiving." Instead of simply taking in a compliment, they always have a ready comeback to deflect or manage whatever they are feeling. Their feelings might be comfortable or uncomfortable, but instead of feeling and expressing what they feel, they "take control" of the situation by coming back quickly with a scripted remark. Just feeling and expressing feelings would be more real. Using a comeback is a control pattern.

7. If you would abandon your own plans and not mention this, you may have the "people pleaser" control pattern. Pleasers often put themselves second. They would rather harbor anger toward someone than risk having someone angry with them. While they may look easygoing and adaptable, pleasers are just as much control freaks as those who are pushy about getting their own way.

    > While they may look easygoing and adaptable, pleasers are just as much control freaks as those who are pushy about getting their own way.

8. A high score on this one indicates a willingness to tell the truth even at the risk of not looking good, appearing "too sensitive," or creating a hassle. This is what Truth in Dating is all about!

9. A high score here means you are playing it safe in order to avoid conflict or trouble. You might feel angry, irritated, or judgmental (usually a cover for anger). If you knew how to express such feelings more skillfully, you could be more courageous and honest.

10. A high score on this one shows you are open to hearing potentially uncomfortable feedback, preferring the truth over what's comfortable for your ego.

11.   One could argue that information about a sexually trans-
      mitted disease is not relevant unless you plan to have sex
      with this person, but I'd call that a rationalization. If you
      are withholding this sort of information, are you pro-
      tecting yourself from possible rejection? Some single
      people are so afraid of herpes, for example, that they will
      not even date anyone who has it. If you had a high score
      on this item, what are you afraid of? Would you try to
      get this person to really fall for you before you tell him
      or her, hoping the person may relax his standards if he
      really loves you? (This point could be made for a num-
      ber of other secrets: other health problems, financial
      problems, illegal activities, a criminal record, unusual
      sexual practices or preferences, et cetera.) Do you tend to
      withhold the truth when you imagine that speaking
      honestly might interfere with getting what you want?

12.   A high score here means you are willing to risk losing the
      relationship rather than compromise your integrity. Even
      if you did lose the relationship, you would probably gain
      in self-respect and respect from the other person. And
      sometimes after a person expresses an honest feeling,
      these feelings change. Telling the truth paves the way for
      deeper communication, which often leads to a change of
      heart.

What Blocks Intimacy?

Intimacy is a mixed bag for most people. We wish for it, and we fear it.
If we are going to be open to love, we need to identify and let go of the
fears that stand between us and what we most deeply want.

Why do we fear intimacy with another? Based on our past experiences, we probably associate intimacy with pain. We think that being
close to people will lead to being hurt.

How can people hurt us? They can do things that remind us of the

hurtful things that our early childhood caregivers did — they can criticize us, shame us, reject us, ignore us, judge us, smother us, abandon us,
or control us.

When we were small, those things hurt a lot. We were really sensitive back then and really dependent on the good will of the big people
for our survival. But we're not little anymore. We're big now. We are not
dependent on anyone for our survival or well-being the way we were as
children. So if someone I'm really attracted to tells me he does not want
to see me again, I'll be okay. I may get my feelings hurt, and I may cry.
I may not be able to hide my feelings from him, so I may feel a bit
exposed or vulnerable. But I'll get over it. What is wrong with feeling
emotional pain for a little while? Most people will go to great lengths to
avoid this sort of pain. Because of the beliefs they carry about emotional
pain, they create a lot of unnecessary suffering for themselves.

Fear of emotional pain blocks your openness to love. If you have
been hurt in the past in a relationship (and who hasn't?), your mind
will store this memory. When you start
getting close to someone in the
present, this painful memory
is triggered, and the mind
goes into action to protect
you from "danger." The
ancient wisdom traditions,
which deeply understand how the
ego-mind functions, counsel us to detach from
believing the fears and scary stories our minds tell us.

It's time to wake up to the
difference between how things affected
us as sensitive, vulnerable little people
and the actual effect of similar events
now that we are big.

The mind does have important evolutionary significance in that it
does store memories that are useful in protecting us from real danger —
like recording memories about why it's good to look both ways before
crossing a busy street. But if a person you are dating criticizes you, rejects
you, abandons you, or tries to control you, this is not real danger. It's
time to wake up to the difference between how things affected us as sensitive, vulnerable little people and the actual effect of similar events now
that we are big. Dating can seem scary because we forget that we're big

now. Certainly, our past wounds will get restimulated in a dating relationship, and this will hurt; but now, this is an opportunity to feel the things we were too fragile to feel when we were small. With the help of a conscious partner, someone who agrees he or she wants to practice Truth in Dating, we can move beyond our stuck places — the places where we stop relating and start controlling. We can open up to the possibility of real, grown-up love.

Does Honesty Ruin Your Chances?

If you have some hesitation about telling the truth about yourself or your feelings, what might you be avoiding? For many people the answer has something to do with the belief that "if I'm honest, let's say about the fact that I might be nonmonogamous or bisexual or have a health problem or a problem with the IRS, that'll ruin my chances with a lot of people. It'll narrow my range of options." Yes, this may occur in some cases. But why would you want to develop a relationship with someone who is not accepting of your chosen lifestyle or your health issues? Many single people knock themselves out trying to be acceptable to everyone and wind up with people falling for them whom they wouldn't want to be with anyway! That's the reward you get for trying to please everybody — you get to deal with a lot of unwanted attention!

What's so bad about limiting your options earlier in the dating process rather than later? And who's to say that a particular disclosure will, in fact, limit your options?

Ward was a well-known multimillionaire. After spending an evening with Linda, he knew he wanted a second date. He also knew that he would probably have to tell her that he was deeply in debt to the IRS for back taxes. He was afraid to tell her, but he did not want to begin their relationship holding back such a secret. As they were driving to the restaurant for their second date, he told her his whole financial story. Then he asked how this affected her and her feelings for him. Linda was candid. She asked some hard questions about how he was planning to handle his problem. At the end of the conversation, she told him how much her respect for him had grown. He had taken a risk. He had trusted the unknown. He had allowed her to see that his financial situation was not as "together" as people imagined. She later told him that she had fallen in love with him that evening — as she watched him struggle to find the words to be honest with her.

Obviously, you can never be sure about what will happen when you share one of your secrets. But the important thing to remember is that even if a certain disclosure does lead to losing someone's favor, you'll be okay. And isn't it better to know sooner rather than later? Remember, you're not a dependent little kid anymore. You're big now. You may get upset;

> She had fallen in love with him as she watched him struggle to find the words to be honest with her.

you'll perhaps feel the pain of loss. Hopefully, you'll find ways to support and comfort yourself in your pain, and then you'll recover. Usually a person's ideas about a potential loss cause more pain and suffering than the actual loss.

Taking a Risk and Surviving

Martin and Vicki met and discovered their mutual attraction on a singles hiking event. They decided right from the start to practice Truth in Dating. Right away, after only two all-day dates, they discovered that while he saw himself as "not willing to commit to monogamy," she saw herself as "definitely monogamous." But, contrary to what one might expect, this did not abruptly end the relationship. They talked about the issue almost every time they were together, Martin expressing fear about losing her over this issue, and Vicki saying that she was disappointed, and at times very angry, about this difference. They kept expressing their feelings and clearing the air regularly. Sometimes the topic led to painful conversations; other times they could laugh about it; but they just kept expressing whatever came up for them. After dating each other for about a month, they decided to go ahead and start having sexual intercourse.

Becoming more sexual seemed to intensify their fights, but they continued to enjoy each other's company. And although Martin said he wanted to be free to have other lovers, he never actually did so. The two have been partners now for over four years. They consider themselves very compatible and very much in love. Martin still insists he's not willing to call himself monogamous, and Vicki still isn't happy with this. But overall, she's happier with him than she's ever been with anyone.

So does honesty ruin your chances? Who knows? For many people, people like Vicki and Martin, it appears that the ability to be honest with one another may actually strengthen the bond between them. As Martin once said to me, "I know I can be myself with her totally. I can express whatever I'm feeling and trust that she'll do the same. This type of relationship is not easy to find. I'm not about to give that up!"

Chapter Summary

- Truth in Dating is not for everyone. But even if you're not ready to commit to total honesty, the skills in this book can help you become more confident and present.
- Truth in Dating can also help you recognize your control patterns — the automatic habits you use that interfere with being present.
- Dating seems scary when you forget that you are no longer little and fragile. You will survive if someone rejects you.
- Finding someone to practice with can help you get past the place where you usually get stuck in a relationship.

PART TWO

Dating 101

CHAPTER FIVE

Getting Clear about What You Really Want

What would you ask for if you didn't put limits
on your sense of what's possible?

I f you want to meet the woman or man of your dreams, it's a good idea to know what those dreams are. Do you dream about snuggling by the fire night after night, or are you more drawn to the fantasy of traveling the world together? Do you long for days and nights of non-stop lovemaking, or would you sooner spend your free time in intelligent conversation? Or do you want all of the above?

The question "what do you want in a relationship?" requires that you ask yourself these sorts of questions. Many singles resist targeting their talent search for fear of winding up with too few possibilities to choose from. Instead they conduct themselves so as to attract the widest possible range of eligibles — only to discover that they've attracted a whole bunch of people that they don't enjoy spending time with!

Wanting Is Uncomfortable

What do you really, truly want? Many people are uncomfortable with this question. From my interviews with singles, I found that most people know what they want but don't believe they can have it. Often, I heard the response, "I know what I want, but I don't think it exists." Some have experienced having what they want for a short time and then lost it. Others say they want one thing, but always seem to wind up with something else.

The Many Dimensions of Wanting

Do you have trouble feeling, expressing, or getting what you want? If so, this chapter will help you get clarity about how to communicate your wants more clearly and powerfully, while at the same time placing less significance on the outcome of your requests.

Remember it's not so important to get everything you want. But it is very important to be able to know, feel, and express your wants. Truth in Dating is about being honest with yourself and others about your wants, doing what you can to get what you want, and then letting go of trying to control the things that are not within your control. Many people let go of their wants far too easily. Others are so attached to the outcome of their requests that they either ask only infrequently or they feel devastated when they do not get what they want.

> Most people know what they want but don't believe they can have it.

Lara had grown up in a family that adored her, but as an adult she had never been able to get that same feeling in a relationship; that feeling of being adored and cherished. She kept finding herself relating to men who couldn't give her what she wanted. She wondered, "I grew up in a loving family. Why can't I attract a loving mate?" When she and I looked more deeply into her childhood story, she discovered that although she had been given a lot of praise and attention by adults, she had never felt safe to ask for what she wanted. Her family gave her what they could, but they also let her know that the family finances were tight and the parents were stressed to the limit providing for their five children. In this way, her parents gave her the subtle message, "It's not okay to ask for material things because that would make us too uncomfortable. Try to be happy with praise and affection, but don't ask for anything else." To most of us reading this, Lara's situation sounds pretty good. She got plenty of love, and was only lacking material possessions. Why, then, does she seemed blocked in finding a loving relationship?

The answer to this question lies in the fact that Lara grew up with the unconscious belief that if you want something (in this case, things that cost money), you should suppress those wants and be satisfied with what you have. So, although she thinks of herself as someone who is unblocked in the area of wanting, she actually has some serious mental blocks in this area. She unconsciously assumes that she must "take potluck," even though her conscious self-image tells her, "I deserve the best."

Many singles are puzzled about why they keep taking potluck instead of really going after what they want. Limiting beliefs may be one factor, but an even more common cause is the fear of feeling too vulnerable. Feeling your wants passionately and deeply makes you vulnerable to being disappointed if you do not get them. Many singles can't tolerate feeling vulnerable, so they lower their sights and go after what they think they can have instead of being honest about what they really want.

If you wish to explore this issue, here is an exercise: Try seeing if you can allow a true want to arise from the depths of your being. This may take some time, so be patient with yourself. Then ask yourself, "What do I fear might happen if I really went for it? Is there some negative consequence that I'd prefer to avoid?" Once you can be simultaneously aware of what you want and what you fear, then a healing can take place.

Bonnie admitted to me that she was confused about what she wanted. She had been to numerous workshops that promised to help her manifest the man of her dreams. And although she had done all the exercises carefully, she realized that she lacked faith in her positive declarations. On paper she said things like, "I want someone who makes me laugh, someone who likes himself, someone who is financially stable, someone who loves to travel." But the men she met rarely fit any of these criteria. Bonnie's experience is a common one. Many people say they know what they want, but yet they always attract something else.

When I hear about this sort of thing, I wonder if Bonnie has a wish and a fear pulling in opposite directions. If you think this might be true of you, use the exercise above to see if you can become conscious of both the wish and of the fear. Wants and fears often go together. For example, people often wish for success and fear success at the same time. Or they want intimacy, but also fear it. This is normal. It's important to accept that two seemingly contradictory things can both be true. If you can become conscious of "the two sides of wanting," an inner shift occurs. The two sides no longer cancel each other out. Instead, they come into relationship with each other. It's as if an inner conversation between your two sides can now occur.

Getting Complete Is Important

Many people are so afraid of rejection that they have a tendency to play it safe by accepting less than what they really want. They assume they'll have a better chance at success with someone if their fears of rejection or abandonment aren't running quite so strongly. But there is a fallacy in this assumption. If you lower your aspirations without reality testing the belief that you couldn't attract what you really want, this creates an incomplete situation in your mind. Such unfinished business will make it difficult for you to focus your attention on the person you are with — because some part of your mind is still incomplete about the question, "What would happen if I really went for what I want?" This incomplete agenda will make it impossible for you to truly connect with the person you have "chosen" to be with. The mind works this way: When you feel or want something, but try to pretend that you don't, this feeling doesn't just disappear. You may try to push a troublesome feeling out of your mind's foreground, but it won't go away that easily. You'll always be thinking somewhere in the back of your mind about what you really want but didn't have the courage to go after. If you are going to get free of "incompletes," you'll need to take action on your wants. That's the best way to resolve that very important question, "What would happen if I really went for it?"

I meet many singles who say they want something, but do not take action on it. When I asked the question, "What do you want in your relationship life?" these individuals would give an answer that they believed in their minds but did not support with their actions; for example, "I want a cocreative partnership with someone on a spiritual path"; or "I want someone who's stable and loving I can have two or three children with." Then I would ask, "What are you doing to help make this happen?"

> To get free of "incompletes," take action on your wants. That's the best way to resolve that very important question, "What would happen if I really went for it?"

The most common answers were, "Nothing," "Nothing at the moment," or "Not very much"; or "I have my mind on other things right now; it's not the time for me to have what I want."

After seeing all the ways that people tend to play it safe or avoid being conscious of their wants and fears, I conclude that wanting is an area where many people's actions are ruled by automatic, unconscious patterns. For that reason, before we focus on clarifying what you want, let's look at the ways people tend to go unconscious around the whole notion of knowing, expressing, and fulfilling their wants.

What Gets in the Way of Fulfilling Your Wants?

Two things can prevent you from having what you really want. One is a lack of alignment between what you want in different aspects of your life. The other is the fear that you simply cannot have what you want. Let's consider these two issues in turn.

Lack of Alignment between Wants

Often we say we want one thing, but our actions speak differently. There is a lack of alignment between our actions and our stated intentions or between our various wants in the different domains of our life.

What do you want in your relationship life, your creative or work life, your fun and recreation life, and your spiritual life; what do you want health-wise? Do your wants in these various aspects of your life support each other? It is important to consider the degree to which your differing wants interact. If you want something in your career life that contradicts what you want in your relationship life, this will sabotage your ability to be clear and focused about your wants. For example, perhaps you want lots of leisure time for loving, and you also want a high-powered job. This could reveal a lack of alignment among your wants.

Lonnie wanted a traditional marriage to a family-oriented man who had a good job but wasn't wedded to his work. She was a single parent of two young boys and wanted someone to help her raise them. But as the marketing manager for a well-known women's magazine, she had little time for either family life or dating. Her dating life consisted mostly of conversations conducted on the cell phone in her car with men she met through internet dating services. Whenever a man wanted to meet her for coffee or dinner, she would allow only a minimum amount of time for the meeting, and then she'd have to rush off to an appointment or to chauffeur her boys to their after school activities. Still, she insisted that she did want to get married again. There was an inconsistency between what she said she wanted and what she was willing to make time for.

I've spoken with many singles like Lonnie — people who said they were ready to make someone else significant in their lives but who seemed to have little or no time for a day-to-day relationship. Many singles, especially those who use the internet or answer personal ads, think they want a full-time relationship but may not be willing to set aside even a few hours per week to actually get to know someone. If this

> I've spoken to many singles who said they were ready to make someone else significant in their lives but who seemed to have little or no time for a day-to-day relationship.

sounds like you, perhaps the truth is that you want an occasional play-
mate, or maybe a sexual friend, rather than a life partner. Whatever you
want, it's okay. No one says you have to want what you imagine most
other people are looking for. Just be honest about it. You may find out
that there are many more people than you thought who want the same
thing.

Fear of Not Being Able to Get What You Want

Most people have experienced so much frustration of their wants
and needs early in life that they harbor unconscious self-defeating beliefs
that they will never get what they want or that it's not safe to go after
what they want.

For example, I recall an experience I had when I was a youngster
that helped to instill a deep-seated belief that I could not get what I
wanted, no matter how hard I tried. World War II was going on, and my
dad was called into the army. As my parents prepared for his departure,
I could sense tension in the atmosphere of our home. I imagine I was
also sensing my mom's sadness as she anticipated my dad's departure.
Then, on a gray day in November 1944, the three of us drove to the train
station to see my dad off. I was pretty silent until the very last moments
before he got on the train. At that point I put all the pieces together and
realized what was happening. As he slowly walked away from us, I
started screaming, "Daddy, don't go! Daddy, don't go!" But in spite of
my protests, he was on his way, and I didn't see him again for a year.
From that experience (and others like it), I acquired a belief that no matter how much you want something, even if you holler about it, you
won't get it.

This experience is part of the conditioning that has shaped my personality. When I'm under the influence of this conditioning, I unconsciously assume that saying what I want will have little effect or will lead
to pain and is therefore something to be avoided. Now that I know
about this pattern, I have learned how to make a conscious effort to get
in touch with my wants — but this still does not come easily to me.

Most people have felt frustration like mine at some time during their childhood. Now, as adults, they may have trouble asserting what they want and don't want. Often they'll be quite expressive in some areas, but in other aspects of their lives, perhaps in the sexual arena for example, they'll find it very difficult to freely express their wants.

If you are someone who has difficulty expressing wants, there's help available. Let the person (or people) you're dating know that you sometimes have trouble connecting with or speaking about what you want. Ask for help, as in, "I know from past experience that I am sometimes not aware of when I want acknowledgment or affection. I'd like your help in getting in touch with my wants; so if you ever get the impression that I'm not telling you what I really want, I'd like you to give me a little nudge — like maybe asking me, 'What do you want right now?' I forget to ask myself that question, so I'd love some help from you. Are you willing to do that for me?"

People who expect to be disappointed often are. I have seen time and again how whatever you unconsciously fear tends to follow you around.

We all need a little reminder now and then to pause and check in with the question, "What do I want right now in this situation?" Follow this with, "What am I willing to do to get it?" Try teaming up with a friend, perhaps someone you're dating, and agree to ask each other these two questions from time to time.

Does Your Communication Reveal Negative Expectations?

People who expect to be disappointed often are. I have seen time and again how whatever you unconsciously fear tends to follow you around. If you fear disappointment (which is the same as expecting it), that's what you will attract. The way to reverse this self-defeating pattern is to become conscious of the fear and then allow yourself to feel what you feel rather than using your control pattern to avoid feeling fear or discomfort. Marilyn had a pattern of nodding her head when listening to someone. It was her way of creating the impression that she was connecting to this person — and avoiding feeling her fear that people weren't paying attention to her. The fear of "not feeling connected" (or attended to) was something she felt far too often. With some coaching help, she came to realize that nodding was a way to avoid "not feeling connected." Rather than simply feeling her fear consciously, she was "acting out" her fear; she was also avoiding feeling how much she wanted to feel connected. As long as she employed this head-nodding strategy to avoid feeling the fear and the want, she would not be able to heal her sense of alienation.

Her coach taught her to be aware of when she was nodding her head as a control pattern. This was her signal that she was not present, and her cue to tune in to her discomfort. She learned to be more present to herself when she wasn't feeling connected rather than pretending to feel otherwise. In this way, she learned to use her awareness of a control pattern to become more present.

One of the best ways to become aware of your own control patterns is to pay attention to your speech patterns and gestures. Here are eight of the more common unconscious speech patterns that can block you from feeling your wants.

Unconscious Speech Patterns

1. Asking a Question and Then Answering It

Do you ever ask a question and then before the other has had a chance to answer, answer the question yourself? When you notice yourself doing this, use Truth Skill #7, Revising an Earlier Statement. Even if you are in the middle of answering the question, stop and say, "I just noticed I'm starting to answer my own question. I'd like to start over...." Simply repeat the question and then keep quiet, allowing the other person to do whatever he does with your question. Usually, we answer our own question because we are trying to avoid the anxiety of not knowing whether we'll get the answer we want.

2. Beginning with a Disclaimer

Do you ever begin a request with a disclaimer such as, "I know this is probably too much to ask, but..." or "I'm not attached to this, but..." or "I hope you don't think me pushy or rude, but..."? These apologetic preambles indicate anxiety about what you're requesting. What are you afraid of? What if that happened? It's useful to identify your fear and recognize that a fear is usually just a thought about what could happen. These kinds of fears are not real.

3. Using Manipulative Phrases

Some people unconsciously add phrases like "don't you agree?" or "isn't that so?" at the end of a sentence. This is another speech pattern designed to get someone to agree with you when you fear that they may not. You want agreement, but are not taking responsibility for wanting this. When you notice such a pattern, use your noticing to become aware of what you are trying to avoid. What if this person doesn't agree with you? What painful consequences do you imagine? Usually when you see yourself trying to get agreement by using such a phrase, you'll wake up and realize that you actually don't need this person to agree with you. You're just operating from a pattern you learned a long time ago.

4. Laughing or Giggling

Have you ever found yourself laughing or giggling when speaking about your wants, or when feeling a want that you don't dare speak about? Laughing can be an unconscious way to mask feelings that you don't want to feel — for example, to avoid feeling how much you really want something. If you know that you sometimes do this, be mindful of this tendency and when you notice it, stop and feel your feelings.

5. Explaining and Justifying

Some people cannot ask for something without explaining or justifying why they have a right to ask for it. Example: "I washed the dishes, so now it's your turn to dry them." (Instead of "I would like you to dry these dishes" or "Will you dry the dishes?") Justifying your request is another way of trying to control the outcome or your anxiety about asking. If you catch yourself doing this, simply revise your initial request. Start over. Some people imagine that a clear, direct statement of a want will come across as controlling. But actually, a simple, direct expression is more relational. You're saying what you want and letting the other respond however he responds. You're not manipulating him by telling him how reasonable or how justified your request is. When you add an explanation, rationale, or justification, this is controlling. Controlling comes from fear — the fear that if you are simply open to whatever happens, you might not be able to handle it. The fear of disappointment is just part of your conditioning. You didn't always get what you wanted as a child. It hurt to feel frustrated or disappointed. Now, to ward off the possibility of more pain, you go around fearing that you'll hear bad news and trying to make sure that you don't.

> A fear is usually just a thought about what could happen.

6. Saying "We Need To..."

Have you noticed yourself or another starting a request with the words, "We need to..." or "You need to..." Instead of saying "I want us to..." or "I want you to..."? You avoid making a request in favor of the subtly manipulative "We need to..." An example would be saying, "We need to get this issue out in the open," rather than "I want to talk with you about this issue." When you find yourself making a statement like this, restate it as a direct want. Some people fear sounding pushy, but in truth people are more apt to give to you if you can be open and responsible about saying what you want.

7. Embedded Requests

Here's another subtly manipulative strategy that comes from an experience I have had with a woman I'll call Fran. Her control pattern works this way: whenever she wants me to do something with her or for her, she'll start out her request by saying, "I'll do such and such for you, and then you can do thus and so for me." She has not asked me if I want her to do that for me; nor have I ever given her any indication that I'd be open to doing thus and so for her. Her language assumes I'll do what she wants, but she never asks me. Then when I do not do it, she's disappointed — thus confirming her unconscious expectation that no one will give her what she wants.

8. Threats

When all else fails, there are always threats — direct threats and covert threats. A threat is any statement or behavior that signals "If you don't do what I want, you'll be sorry." Nan told Jacob, "If you start going out with other women, I'll need to keep things balanced by dating other men." Can you see how Nan avoids asking for what she wants? This is controlling. She doesn't say, "I don't want you to go out with anyone but me" (which would be relating). She masks her vulnerability by using a threat.

> Some people cannot ask for something without explaining or justifying why they have a right to ask for it.

We have just considered eight ways of avoiding asking openly for what you want. If you saw yourself in any of these examples, you have just taken the first step in getting free of the control pattern. Becoming aware of a pattern will help you let it go. Now that you see it, you can probably also see how unnecessary it is.

What Do You Want?

Now that we have considered the unconscious patterns and avoidance strategies typically associated with wanting, let's focus on clarifying what you want.

When considering the question "What do you want?" it's useful to create a detailed and specific vision of how you want your relationship life to look, feel, smell, and sound. Start by creating a picture of your ideal day with another, from the time you wake up to the time you go to sleep: Do you wake up together or at different times? Do you sleep in the same bed? Do you have breakfast together? What activities do you engage in together and separately? How much talking versus silence is there between you? What sorts of things do you talk about? How much touching occurs between you? How does your body feel being with this person? How spontaneous and uncensored do you allow yourself to be?

Then, create a detailed picture of an experience you'd like to share with this person — an intimate day together or perhaps an adventure you'd like to have.

Imagine taking this person to meet your family and friends. How would that go?

Imagine you and this person having a disagreement. How would you deal with differences or conflicts?

Imagine yourself bringing up a topic that is difficult or sensitive to talk about. Picture in detail your ideal scenario.

Picture yourself making love with this ideal person. How does that feel? What does the other do that turns you on? What do you do to pleasure your partner? How much verbal communication is there? What's the emotional tone like? What's the setting like? Are any drugs or alcohol involved in your scenario? What about chocolate?

If you really put some time into answering these questions, you will learn a lot. You may find, for example, that the people you have been meeting do not fit with your stated values. Or you may realize that you have never in your life experienced safety or fulfillment in the presence of another person. Or you may discover that you have never considered the possibility that you and this ideal other could have conflicts or disagreements. If any of these things are true, you will find more useful material in chapter 16, "What Can You Really Expect in a Relationship?"

Exercise Your Vision

Getting specific about what you want is extremely important. When most people make a list of qualities they seek in a partner, they don't get specific enough about how they want things to look and feel. They never get down to the nitty-gritty of relating. Remember it is how people relate that is the crucial ingredient for relationship success — probably more important than what they like to do for fun, what they look like, or how much money they have.

If you have trouble creating a really clear and specific vision of yourself having what you want, then the following exercise will help you: Recall a time in your life (from childhood to the recent past) when you felt fulfilled and happy in the presence of another person. That person could be male or female; it doesn't matter. What was it about the interaction or about this situation that contributed to your feeling so good? Was this person paying attention to you in a particular way? What was this person doing or how was he being? Take notice of anything that seemed to contribute to your feeling fulfilled. Now envision yourself sharing a similar type of peak experience with an ideal partner. How would this person need to be or behave in order to fit into your vision? What other experiences would you like to share with this person? Now see if you can envision yourself experiencing these things with this ideal partner.

Clarifying Your Values

The best way to get clear on your values is to look at which life experiences bring you joy or fulfillment: What peak experiences have you had? How do you choose to spend your free time? What was the best vacation you ever took? Recall a day that felt truly nourishing to you: What were you doing? Who were you with? Take time now to reflect on these questions and perhaps write your answers down in a notebook or journal. Many singles find that keeping a personal journal is very helpful. Journaling helps you get to know yourself more deeply.

Monogamy vs. Open Lifestyle

What do you want in a relationship with respect to sexual boundaries? Most of the people I surveyed for this book said they were "basically monogamous," meaning they prefer to be sexually monogamous once they have committed themselves to someone, although they might not be so while they are dating. Others told me that they can only date one person at a time, which means they are not only sexually monogamous but perhaps emotionally monogamous as well. From my observations of our culture over the past few years, I have concluded that an increasing number of people see themselves as nonmonogamous. Terms like "open lifestyle," "polyamorous," and "swingers" might apply to these folks.

> What do you want in a relationship with respect to sexual boundaries? It is very important to know and accept your own unique values and boundaries regarding this question.

Still others refuse to be given any label or definition at all. They say it all depends on the circumstances. I think it is very important to know and accept your own unique values and boundaries regarding this question.

Unfortunately there tends to be a good deal of dishonesty, confusion, and self-deception around this topic. I was amazed to discover from my interviews that many people do not talk about this question with people they are dating for fear of making the other person feel uncomfortable.

I urge you to be honest with yourself and others about where you stand on this issue. Of course, you cannot force someone to be honest with you, but eventually anything that is hidden will come to light. When you're ready to bring the topic up for discussion, ask the other if he is open to having a talk about the issue. Then take turns asking whatever questions you have about the other person's values, behavior, and lifestyle preferences. If you are one of those people who fear bringing this issue up "too early in the game," try to identify what inhibits you from asking for the information you want. Are you perhaps afraid of hearing "bad news?"

Notice and accept what is, and if you do see any tendencies in yourself toward wishful thinking or conflict avoidance, just be aware that such avoidance has consequences. Don't blame the other person for misleading you or deceiving you if you have not made your wants and feelings clear on the matter.

In my twenties I sometimes found myself in situations where the man I was dating did not disclose the fact that he was being sexual with other women. In retrospect, I can see that he was giving me a lot of hints and clues that I chose not to notice. If I could go out and come in again, I would have asked for more detail when a man told me he spent the weekend at his former girlfriend's house, for example. The reason I overlooked such remarks was that I was deceiving myself with thoughts like, "Now that he's with me, things will be different. He may not be monogamous now, but after being with me for a while, he'll realize what a good thing he has, and he'll give up the other women." I smile now as I reflect on my tendency in those days to see things as I wanted them to be rather than as they really were. If I'd been open to seeing *what is* early on, I could have saved myself a whole lot of heartache.

> Try to identify what inhibits you from asking for the information you want. Are you perhaps afraid of hearing "bad news?"

How to Communicate Your Wants

It's important to communicate your wants without apology — without diluting your impact with giggles, explanations, or justifications. Then you will be more apt to get what you want. But direct, open communication is not a technique for manipulating the outcome. It is the natural result of allowing yourself to feel what you feel and experience things as they are. When you get good at feeling whatever you feel, you won't be afraid of not getting what you want. From this place of open presence, you trust that whatever happens, you'll be okay.

If Nan, in the example above, could tell her date Jacob, "I want you all to myself. I don't want you dating anyone but me," she might or might not get what she wants. She's making herself more vulnerable to disappointment by asking. But she is also being more transparent — which often helps the other feel more connected to you and responsive to your needs. Asserting your wants can feel like a risk. Any time you express a deeply felt want, you are risking the experience of hearing "no." Yet the best way to get over your fear of being told no is to hear it and realize, "Wow, my fear came true. He said he didn't want to see me again, and I'm actually okay!" If you think you're not okay, take another look. You're probably not in touch with reality. Your feelings may be hurt, and you may be giving surplus meaning to these feelings — such as "this must mean I'm not lovable" — but the meaning you give to an experience is not the reality. It's just how your mind responds based on old fears and beliefs.

Below is a three-part process for communicating your wants to another person clearly and powerfully:

1. Paint a picture. Create a specific scene with your words. And put yourself and the other person in that picture. Don't use generalizations or abstractions. Instead of saying, "I want you to be more romantic," which is too abstract and general, say (for example), "I want you to pick me a bouquet of roses from your garden." Can you see the difference? Or instead of saying, "I want more special time with you," try being specific about something you want right now. For example: "I'd like us to make a fire in the fireplace and build a nest of pillows and blankets and just lie together cuddling, listening to our favorite music.... Would you enjoy that, too?"

2. Acknowledge the other. Acknowledge the other on the spot when he is giving you what you want. When you are feeling pleased about something he is doing or saying,

tell him so right then and there. Say, for example, "I love how you're massaging my feet. That feels wonderful the way you squeeze and pull my toes."

3. Time your request. When you want something such as help around the house, ask for it at a time when it could actually happen. For example, if you want his help on a repair project, don't tell him that when he's watching the football game. Make the request at a time when you are actually free to show him what you want, and he is free to pay attention. Many people sabotage getting what they want by asking at a time when it's unlikely to happen, e.g., asking for help in the kitchen when he's in the middle of another project. If you find yourself doing this, notice if you are angry at him about his not helping in the kitchen on previous occasions. Often, people instigate a fight by asking for the impossible instead of expressing anger directly and responsibly. Chapter 12, "Conflict, Disappointment, and Anger," describes how to clear anger and disagree constructively. In addition, my book *Getting Real* offers more suggestions for preventing and resolving conflicts.

Wants, Boundaries, and Buttons

Most people can make a list of the qualities they value in a partner. Here is a way to help you decide which of these are *preferences* and which represent *boundaries* or standards that you are not willing to compromise. Draw a large circle on a piece of paper (or in your journal). Inside of the circle write all the valued qualities that you'd ideally like to find in a significant other — things like "enjoys water recreation," "loves to cuddle," "has a retirement plan." Enter the things that are most important in larger, bolder letters, or in a different colored ink. On the outside of the circle, write the things you do not want, such as, "I don't want someone who has kids." Then, in the area farthest from the circle, write all the things you absolutely would not tolerate, such as: "smokes cigars," "owns a gun," "makes his living illegally." After you have done this, look at the things you have written inside the circle and ask yourself if there is anything there that you believe you absolutely must have for your well-being or happiness. Underline these things. These are the things that really need to be scrutinized to identify any items that are based on false or outdated beliefs about yourself. But first identify these items without censoring. Then look at each of them asking the following questions (each with an example).

> The meaning you give to an experience is not the reality. It's just how your mind responds based on old fears and beliefs.

- Is this item on the list because of something I'm trying to avoid experiencing? (Did I write "anticipates my needs" to avoid having to ask for what I want?)
- Is this item connected to any of my "favorite fears," like the fear of abandonment or rejection? (Did I write "is nonjudgmental" to be sure I don't get my "fear-of-criticism" button pushed?)
- What life skill might I be forced to learn if I were not able to have this? (Let's say your list of "must haves" included "able to support him- or herself financially." What might you be forced to learn if you were paired with someone who could not do this? Perhaps your boundaries around sharing or generosity would be stretched. Or perhaps you would be challenged to set limits on how much you are willing to take care of another person.)

Mapping your wants in this way is a very important exercise. It can help you accept that it's okay to have wants. It might help you see that some of your wants are based on false or outdated beliefs, and it can help you become more honest about expressing what you want — even if you imagine you won't get it. It may even reveal that some wants are intended to help you avoid getting a button pushed. The Truth in Dating approach counsels that expressing what you want is much more important than making sure you get what you want. When you focus your energy on honest self-disclosure instead of trying to control the outcome, you will be happier and more self-confident, regardless of whether or not you get what you want. And strangely enough, people who express themselves honestly without being manipulative are the ones who seem to get what they want most often.

Where Are You Heading?

The question of where you are heading in life suggests that it is important to be around people who support your life's purpose or destiny — people who are headed in the same direction as you are. To live authentically requires clarity of intent.

Serena was a belly dance teacher and performer when she met Ned, a surgeon. Her passion in life was to help women and men reclaim a sensual relationship with their bodies. She fell for Ned before she realized how intensely jealous he got every time she performed in public. Before and after every performance, he would complain about how he imagined the other men lusting after her. He asked her to confine her belly dance activities to teaching, and to teaching women only. Serena refused. She was clear that teaching and performing were inseparable for her. She told Ned how much sorrow his attitude and jealous behavior brought her. She loved him, but she was not willing to change for him. He fussed and fumed and went away for a while, but eventually he did learn to deal with his jealousy and accept her dancing in public. He still needs to vent his frustrations at times, but Serena and Ned have learned that just because he doesn't like some of the things she does, it needn't stop them from loving each other. Serena

> People who express themselves honestly without being manipulative are the ones who seem to get what they want most often.

was able to communicate her feelings to Ned in a way that he could eventually accept. It wasn't the words she used. It was her clarity of intent and the self-trust she conveyed in her attitude. She knew she had to remain true to herself on this one. Even though Ned was used to getting what he wanted in relationships with women, he was eventually able to accept Serena's position and not take it personally. Perhaps it was her clarity about her life purpose that made this possible.

How Much Do You Compromise?

A truthful, real relationship is cocreated moment by moment. If the question of a particular (i.e., specific) compromise is "up" for two people, the thing to do is for each to express what he or she wants and to acknowledge that he or she also wants the other to feel satisfied. This is Truth Skill #8, Holding Differences or Embracing Multiple Perspectives. In other words, start with the belief that somehow, with enough good communication, both people can be satisfied. Differences are often scary. We imagine that having conflicting wants may destroy the relationship or at least do a lot of damage. So we don't give ourselves a chance to really express our wants, feelings, and fears. If we did, we'd learn how to do this while maintaining a spirit of good will. We'd learn that we can be committed to our own wants while still being committed to helping the other feel satisfied.

In the case of Serena and Ned, while Ned did feel angry and frustrated with her decision, he never felt disrespected or unloved. And eventually, after he saw that Serena's clarity of intent was not about him or her love for him, he accepted the situation and even welcomed it as a useful learning opportunity. He learned some important lessons that were far more valuable than getting his own way. For example, he learned that getting someone to conform to his wishes has nothing to do with being loved. In fact, Ned found that he felt more trusting of Serena's love when she did not conform to his wishes. He learned that he could tolerate frustration and still feel okay, and he learned that he could express his frustration and anger to her and the relationship would be okay. I knew Ned before he met Serena. He had always been able to get women to give him his way by using a variety of well-honed power tactics. He had confused "getting his own way" with being loved. Through holding differences Ned and Serena came away with a sense of empowerment and love that does not come cheaply. Rushing to compromise is what most lovers do because the anxiety associated with conflict is too uncomfortable. Instead, Ned and Serena chose to stay connected in a way that did not deny or downplay their differences.

Chapter Summary

- Many singles aren't clear about what they want because they fear that they could never attain it.
- To help in clarifying and communicating your wants, it's useful to paint a specific picture, putting yourself and the other in that picture.
- Going after what you want is more important than whether you actually get it.
- It's good to ask for help in getting in touch with your wants. Ask a friend to remind you frequently to check in with yourself about the question "What do I want right now?"
- It is important that your wants in the various domains of your life be in alignment with one another.

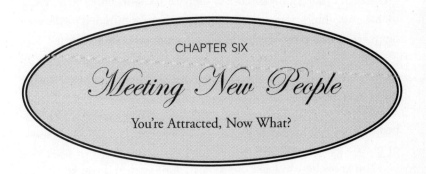

CHAPTER SIX

Meeting New People

You're Attracted, Now What?

*When you make it your intent to simply be present,
fears about the outcome disappear.*

Tom thought of himself as shy. He felt butterflies in his stomach whenever he entered a roomful of people he didn't know. He felt awkward starting a conversation, but if someone else made the first move to get to know him, he had no problem keeping the conversational ball rolling. Tom's story is a common one. From my interview conversations, I have learned that many singles feel relatively confident as long as they don't have to be the initiator.

For some of us, just going up to someone we have never met and beginning a conversation is the hardest part. They don't call it "breaking the ice" for nothing!

When I asked people, "What could go wrong? What are you afraid might happen if you went up to someone and tried to initiate contact?" the answers went something like this: "I could wind up feeling so uncomfortable that I'd freeze. Especially when I'm attracted to someone, I sometimes get so nervous that I don't know what to say." When I hear such an answer, I feel empathy. I have certainly felt something similar at times. But now that

I have been making it my practice to simply be present, letting go of trying to make sure things turn out well, I find I'm much more relaxed — whether I'm meeting new people or just moving through my daily activities.

You Already Have What It Takes

Most people already have all the skills they need to be real with new people. And you probably do, too. It's when they try to be scintillating or make a good impression that they get into trouble!

You know how to make eye contact, don't you? And you know how to ask questions, right? And you can listen, can't you? And, unless you have a particular physical challenge, you are able to walk over to someone. I imagine you know how to say, "Hello, my name is____." And I'll bet you have given your phone number to people numerous times in the past. Okay, so you have the basics. The question remains: How would you do each of these things from an authentic place inside yourself rather than from the desire to impress or the need to play it safe? And how might you use the very act of meeting someone as a way to increase your present-time awareness? For me, viewing everything as a practice, instead of focusing on whether or not I get a favorable response from a particular person, takes the pressure off. Whatever I do, I view it as an exercise in being authentic. So all I have to do is say what I'm feeling or thinking or wondering. Then the interaction is a success. If I do get nervous, then I try to notice what thoughts took me into the future and away from present time. Then at least I learn something about myself. Either way, I can't lose!

> It's when they try to be scintillating or make a good impression that they get into trouble!

Noticing

The first step is noticing. What do you notice in this moment? To get practice with this skill, stop reading for a moment when you reach the end of this paragraph, and look around at your surroundings. What do you see? Check in with your body. What sensations are you aware of? As you do this, notice your breathing. Now you have a basic experience of what it is like to be present. Can you feel a wave of relaxation come over you as you become aware of your breathing? Allow yourself to really connect with this sensory impression. What would it take to transfer this experience to a social situation? Maybe all you need to do is tune in to your bodily sensations and breathe. For many, that's all it takes.

View everything as a practice, instead of focusing on whether or not you get a favorable response.

Now imagine yourself in a roomful of people — at a party, a meeting, or a lecture hall. Imagine that you are standing or sitting next to someone you would like to meet. Now imagine paying attention to your bodily sensations as you notice your thoughts. Imagine speaking out loud about something you see, something you feel, or something you are thinking. Here are some examples:

"I'm noticing that I'm feeling warm. Are you feeling warm too, or is it just me?"

"I notice you're wearing blue. I think it looks really nice with your blue eyes."

"I notice I'm getting hungry. Would you like to get out of here and get something to eat?"

Starting a conversation based on present-time noticing is a good way to keep yourself from becoming nervous. Remember, you don't have to be scintillating or entertaining. Just be simple, direct, and present. And remember to breathe.

Asking Questions

Another good way to initiate contact with someone is to ask a question — if it's a sincere question and you really care about the answer. Forget about trying to be cute, to provoke a reaction, or to shock.

In preparation for writing this section, I brainstormed with a couple of friends about all the questions we have ever been asked by someone who just walked up to us with the intent of getting to know us. Here are some of the questions we have heard that we liked:

- What's most important to you in your life these days?
- What's going on in your life these days?
- What's your story?
- How is it in there?
- Do you feel like talking?
- Do you feel like talking with me?
- Do you feel like talking about yourself?
- What's up for you these days?
- Do you want to have a conversation or would you rather just stand here and people-watch?
- Do you want to know what I'm thinking right now?
- Do you want to know what I'm thinking about you right now?
- Do you play tennis?
- Do you believe in love at first sight?
- Are you open to having a conversation?

You may be surprised to know that there are many people who can just go up to a stranger and start a conversation like that. If you're saying to yourself, "I could never do this," what are you afraid of? Of course, it's natural to have fears. In fact, knowing your fears and allowing yourself to feel whatever you feel will help you be more present. I remember one of the most satisfying exchanges of my life was when I went up to a strange man whom I found attractive and confessed, "As I was coming over to approach you, I wondered if you could see how my body is shaking."

> Starting a conversation based on present-time noticing is a good way to keep yourself from becoming nervous.

This particular man happened to love it! Not everyone would. And after I confessed my shakiness, I began to relax.

What is the worst thing that could happen if you went up to someone and asked a question? Most people have two main fears in this instance: looking foolish or being rebuffed. What do you fear? Is this the same fear you tend to carry into any new situation? Just be aware, and use this awareness to know and accept yourself better.

The Dance of Contact

Making contact with a new person is like a dance. You look at her. She either looks back at you, or she looks away. You take a step in her direction. She either stands still, moves a bit toward you, or moves away. You touch her lightly on the shoulder. She leans into your touch, or she pulls away. These are some of the dance steps of a typical first encounter. Paying attention to what you are doing and how the other is responding will keep you present. Try not to analyze why the other does what she does. Just notice how you feel when she looks at you or looks away, when she moves toward you or moves away.

> If you can stay aware and present to what is actually going on, your words and actions will have a quality of depth and groundedness.

Noticing your feelings and bodily responses to her behavior is a wonderful awareness exercise. Make it your goal to accept what is — your feelings and her actions — without trying to control the outcome. Notice also when your body gets tense, or when you want something different to be going on. If you can stay aware and present to what is actually going on, your words and actions will have a quality of depth and groundedness. You won't need to plan out your every move. Pretty soon, with practice, the appropriate response will be there when you need it.

There is something quite wonderful about allowing yourself to simply do what you feel like doing, trusting yourself to do the right thing. If this sounds difficult, it will become less so as you learn to value entering each new social situation with the intent of being present to what is rather than the intent to get a particular outcome. Most people will find that even an awkward attempt to be real is more attractive than the most polished attempt to impress.

Asking for the Order

Okay, but you do want a particular outcome much of the time. I'm not telling you to hide this. Wanting something and asking for it can also enable you to be more present. This is relating. Wanting it is different from being three steps ahead of yourself worrying about whether you will get it or strategizing to make sure that you do. This is controlling.

In selling, there comes the moment when the salesperson needs to find out if the prospect plans to buy. This is called asking for the order. In dating, there's the moment when contact has been made, perhaps some interaction has occurred, and now you begin to feel the need for something more explicit. Perhaps you want to know if there is enough mutual interest to continue the conversation. This is a time where words are usually necessary. You've danced the dance. Now it's time to talk the talk.

> Most people will find that even an awkward attempt to be real is more attractive than the most polished attempt to impress.

You know how you feel, but you don't know how the other person feels. Let's imagine that you are clear that you'd like to continue getting to know this person. How do you find out how she feels? How do you ask for the order? In keeping with Truth in Dating's emphasis on present-time awareness, here are some ways that other singles have found to articulate this:

- I don't know how you're feeling, but I'm enjoying talking to you very much. (Then wait and see what she says. Don't rush to fill in the silence. Just be quiet for as long as it takes.)

- I'd like to go over there and sit down together so we can continue this. What about you?
- I'm feeling I'd like to get to know you better. Is the feeling mutual or not?
- I'm amazed at how easy it is talking to you. Are you up for continuing this?
- I like talking with you. (Then be quiet and let her respond or not. Then notice how you feel. Stay aware of your bodily sensations.)
- I hope we can keep getting to know each other this way. Are you available for that or not?

Each of these statements is based on a simple, authentic expression of a feeling or a want. There is no intent to be cute or to impress. There is no attempt to pressure the other into anything. If you ever notice yourself putting pressure on someone to conform to your wishes, stop and say something like, "I need to start over. I wasn't very present. I was getting ahead of myself. What I meant to convey was..." This is an example of Truth Skill #7, Revising an Earlier Statement.

I hope we can keep getting to know each other this way. Are you available for that or not?

Planning Ahead

Many people are reluctant to ask for the order for fear of not knowing where to go next. What if she says something that catches you completely off guard? What if she says nothing at all? What if she says "No"? What do you say then? You don't have to plan out what to say next, but there is something that might help. You may recall in chapter 3, in the section on feedback, I introduced a sort of one-size-fits-all phrase. That phrase is, "Hearing you say that, I feel…" This phrase is a good way to keep yourself in present-time contact with the person you're speaking to. Practice using this phrase with friends in situations where you feel safe. Then, after the phrase begins to feel natural to you, it will be available to you anytime. Even when the unexpected happens, you can use this phrase as a way of staying present with yourself and the other.

> "Hearing you say that, I feel…" This phrase is a good way to keep yourself in present-time contact with the person you're speaking to.

Listening

Another basic skill that you already have is the ability to listen. Of course, you may need to do something (such as the suggestions above) to get things started, but then being a good listener can do wonders for building connection with a new person.

If you have ever taken a communication workshop or been to couples therapy, you have probably been exposed to the technique called "active listening." This is a technique first popularized by psychologist Carl Rogers back in the early 1960s. To actively listen to someone, you look at the person and listen attentively to both the words and the feeling tone. Then you say, "Let me see if I got what you said… what I heard you saying was…" and repeat what you heard to the best of your ability. This is a wonderful practice for being in present time and not getting ahead of yourself. (There is additional discussion of active listening in the context of holding differences in chapter 3.)

Many people cannot listen because they are so focused on what they want to say next or on the interpretation they are giving to the other person's words. Active listening helps you stay focused on what's real. Just say what you heard, without interpretation. Active listening not only keeps you present, it also helps you stay on your own side of the net. It keeps you out of the realm of interpretation and surplus meaning.

Here is an example of a recent exchange I witnessed between two people who were meeting for the first time:

RANDALL: I really enjoyed her lecture. What did you think of it?

ZARA: I liked it too. I especially connected with what she said about loving our desires more than the object of our desires. I think I do that a lot in relationships.

RANDALL: So you're saying you do that a lot in relationships... you love your desires more than the object of your desires? (He does not have any idea what she is talking about. But active listening keeps him present and gives her a chance to clarify what she means.)

ZARA: Yes, I think so. By that I mean when I am in a relationship, I love the feeling of wanting someone or the feeling of loving someone. Maybe that's what the songwriters mean when they talk about being in love with love.

RANDALL: So you're saying that when you're with someone, you love that feeling of wanting them or of loving them. But the actual caring for the person himself is not as important. Did I hear that correctly?

ZARA: I couldn't have said it clearer myself.

In this example, we see Randall actively listening with someone who may have never heard of this technique. It only takes one person to do this practice. But it benefits both. It seemed to help Zara keep in touch with what she had just said and to hear herself better.

Can you imagine yourself using this technique with a new acquaintance? Sometimes it helps to practice it first with someone you know pretty well so you can get comfortable using it. Of course, you do not need to repeat what the other said exactly, word-for-word. But do watch out for any tendencies you may have to show off how insightful you are. Presence is simple. It does not try to impress.

Watch out for any tendencies you may have to show off how insightful you are. Presence is simple. It does not try to impress.

Humor

Humor usually works best when it is spontaneous. But you can learn to develop your humor muscles. Try observing the events of your daily life with an attitude of amusement. Cultivate the ability to comment playfully to yourself about unexpected or even frustrating situations. Soon you will discover yourself sharing this humorous self-talk out loud. When you exude a spirit of lightness, people often feel drawn to you; whereas when you have a complaining attitude, you're not as appealing. To become more self-aware in this area, make it a point to notice how often you complain. Many people in social situations use complaining as a way to begin a conversation. The energy of complaining is revealed any time you want something to be different from what it is.

I was in a very long line at closing time at the post office the other day. There were about fifteen of us standing there in line for about thirty minutes — because only two windows were open at that time, and the two customers at both these windows had many large packages to mail. Standing in line is a great place to practice meeting new people. Knowing that I'd be coming home later to write this chapter, I observed how different people handled the situation. Most of them were frustrated, and after a while, presumably in order to let off steam, some people began complaining. One man said to the woman next to him, "Why isn't that other window open?" She said nothing. Then another man complained, "They should know to have more people working on the day after a holiday!" Of course, these two men were not trying to meet anyone to date, but what if they had been? Would you be attracted? Would you want to join them in that type of energy?

I decided to express myself by picking up on the humor of the situation, so I remarked to the person next to me, "I think we've been here

> Make it a point to notice how often you complain. The energy of complaining is revealed any time you want something to be different from what it is.

for over thirty minutes. Next time I'll bring my sleeping bag." I noticed after I said this that several people began smiling and making eye contact with me. A few began to engage me in conversation. Perhaps my humorous remark helped people relax or maybe it helped them recognize and accept our common plight. For whatever reason, after I said that, people started giving me more of their attention.

To develop your own humorous side, notice when something unexpected or frustrating happens. Notice your self-talk. If you're complaining, what is the want underneath the complaint? Can you be compassionately amused with yourself for wanting things to be different from the way they are? Try making fun of yourself out loud in a good-natured, light-spirited way.

> Can you be compassionately amused with yourself for wanting things to be different from the way they are?

Practice this in situations where you feel safe and accepted. As you develop your humorous side, it will begin to come out when you are meeting new people.

Good Places to Meet Like-Minded People

If you want to find people who might be interested in conscious relationships, a good place to meet them would be workshops or lectures about relationships. Look in the paper or call your local bookstores for a list of their book signing events. Local colleges always have various lecture series going on. And many larger churches now sponsor singles mixers and singles-only recreation events. Pick a church whose beliefs and teachings resonate with your values, call the church office, and get on their mailing list.

Conferences are another great venue for connecting with people of like mind. You can learn about upcoming conferences by consulting publications on subjects of interest to you.

Meeting people via the internet is also a possibility. Every year there are more and more internet matchmaking or meeting services that cater to singles on a conscious path.

Teleclasses are a wonderful way to connect with people — although these people may be spread far apart geographically. A teleclass is usually done in a once-a-week conference call, where all class members call in to the same bridge number and have a focused conversation about a pre-arranged topic. I lead teleclasses for small groups of six to eight people on such topics as sexuality, relationship as a spiritual path, and the ten truth skills. If you sign up for a teleclass partly to meet people, be sure the class size is small and the format is interactive. I personally have made lifelong friends through teleclasses. And now when I go to New York City, Paris, or London, I'll have a place to stay with one of these friends — some of whom I have never met in person. Appendix B includes information about teleclasses.

Chapter Summary

- Meeting new people with the intent of simply being present can actually be easier than doing so while trying to insure a certain outcome.
- You probably have most of the basic skills for meeting new people already — skills like making eye contact, asking questions, and listening.
- The most basic skill for keeping yourself present is the ability to notice your feelings, sensations, and thoughts.
- Once you learn to notice *what is,* it is a short step to commenting on what you notice.
- If you are afraid of getting tongue-tied, or not knowing what to say next, get in the habit of replying to feedback with the phrase, "Hearing you say that, I feel..." This phrase will bring your attention back to your experience and keep you in present-time contact with the other person.

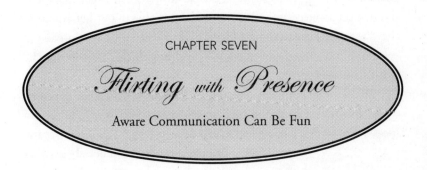

CHAPTER SEVEN

Flirting with Presence

Aware Communication Can Be Fun

Flirting isn't serious, but many people have forgotten how to play. Playing is present-centered.

nnette walked into the hotel conference room knowing she had missed the first speaker's presentation. Seeing the roomful of people engaged in animated conversation, she was relieved to find that she had gotten there during the morning coffee break. As she scanned the sea of faces looking for someone familiar or at least friendly, she spotted a man with wavy black hair and deep-set eyes, wearing a light gray sweater. As she looked at him, he noticed her and smiled. Her eyes felt drawn to continue looking into this man's eyes. She felt almost hypnotized as she smiled and continued their eye gazing. At the same time her mind was chattering away, "This is not appropriate — I don't know this person — I came here looking for a job, not a mate — he could be married — he could be an ax murderer — or worse, he could get the idea that I'm lonely, horny, or desperate!" As her self-talk continued, she began to move toward the coffee line, which also happened to be in the vicinity of the wavy-haired stranger, "I just like the feeling I get looking at this man. I don't know what it is about him.

Okay, he's looking around at other people now, so I can forget about him and just get some coffee." But Annette wasn't able to put her attention elsewhere. She kept wanting to look back and see if he was looking at her again. She thought of going over and introducing herself, but she didn't have the courage.

After standing in line a few more minutes, she was able to get some coffee and find a seat. She tried to concentrate on what the second speaker was saying, but she had a hard time focusing. Her mind was full of questions and fantasies about what she might say if she ran into "him" during the next break. But the second speaker's talk ran over time, and the second morning break was cancelled. Annette never saw the wavy-haired stranger again.

Many people appear to be seriously challenged in the flirting department. They put too much importance on the outcome of each potential flirting encounter — so the actual encounter never happens.

Have you ever seen a person who was really attractive to you but not had the courage to do anything about it? According to my research conversations, this is an extremely common occurrence. There's even a section in the classifieds of most larger newspapers for Lost Opportunities: *You were sitting at an outdoor table at Whole Foods with a golden retriever next to you. I was the gray-haired forty-something man in the red minivan. You smiled. I waved. I wish I'd stopped to get your name. Call me if you are reading this....*

Many people have had the experience of being attracted to a stranger and not knowing what to do about it. In fact, most of the singles I have met appear to be seriously challenged in the flirting department. They put too much importance on the outcome of each potential flirting encounter — so the actual encounter never happens.

What Is Flirting?

Flirting is supposed to be lighthearted, not serious. It's a low-stakes, low-pressure bid for contact where it's understood that the other person may pick up on your overture or not. But most people do not view flirting that way. They take it personally if they make a bid for more connection and the other does not respond in kind. Annette is such a person — so she avoids flirting. She told me that she kicks herself for days after every missed opportunity, but she just can't seem to get past her worries about the outcome.

Flirting gets easier and less scary once you learn how to be present. When you are aware of the sensations of your body and can objectively notice the thoughts running around in your mind, that's a big part of presence. Your attention is on this moment, not on the future — which helps you feel more confident, and less worried about how things will turn out.

Flirting gets easier and less scary once you learn how to be present. When you are aware of the sensations of your body and can objectively notice the thoughts running around in your mind, that's a big part of presence.

The Benefits of Risk-Taking

From my experiences as a dating coach, I have concluded that the most authentic and engaging type of flirting involves sharing your self-talk — going up to that stranger and sharing with him exactly what you have been saying inside your own head. This gets you out of your head and into action!

If Annette's story seemed familiar to you, here is an exercise for you to try: Think back to a time when you noticed and felt attracted to someone in a crowd. What did you say to yourself about this person or about the idea of striking up a conversation? Let's outline some possible conversation that might go on in your head, such as:

- Someone as attractive as that is probably not available.
- Maybe I'm not his type.
- I find him attractive, but if I said this he might think I was pushy or rude . . . or desperate.

- I'm way too shy to just walk up to someone. I'd rather wait for the other person to make the first move — even if he never does.
- I find him attractive, but I'm not sure that I want anything from him.

Now imagine yourself approaching the person to see if he or she is available for contact, introducing yourself, and saying your self-talk out loud. What do you feel as you imagine doing this? Just notice your feelings. Whatever they are, let them be. Doing this in your imagination can give you practice feeling uncomfortable — which is a good thing! There's a sense of inner strength and power that comes from consciously stepping into the unknown — consciously taking a risk without knowing the outcome.

> There's a sense of inner strength and power that comes from consciously stepping into the unknown — consciously taking a risk without knowing the outcome.

Now, just for practice, imagine and list some of the things you would hope he might say or do in response, such as, I hope he'll

- smile.
- move toward me and touch my shoulder.
- say, "I noticed you, too."
- say, "I'm glad you came over."
- say, "I'm here with someone, but I still think you're great to approach me like this."

Now imagine and list all the things you fear might happen, such as, I fear she'll

- just look right past me.
- say, "I'm not interested."
- say, "I'm here with someone."

- ask, "What do you want?"
- act uncomfortable and turn away.
- say, "Pardon me, but I have to go now."

Most people find it helpful to list their most hoped for and most feared responses. What they find is that even the feared responses, when seen in black and white, are not as painful as they'd imagined. People realize that if the person says, "I'm not interested," they are actually better off knowing this than if they wasted their attention harboring a fantasy about someone who is not interested in them.

So ask yourself: What if I decided to simply share my self-talk with anyone I find myself gazing at from across a crowded room? How dangerous would that be? It might seem risky, in one sense, but is it actually dangerous? I imagine the biggest risk for most of us is the fear of looking foolish. In my opinion, to be willing to be a fool is to be free. Freedom is a choice: do you choose to risk looking foolish and possibly damage your ego — or to live in fear of looking foolish and dampen your aliveness? Flirting is a foolhardy thing to do. You don't know the outcome. You could be perceived as inappropriate. You might get rebuffed. But whatever happens, you will survive just fine. Flirting is a low-pressure type of risk-taking. Every time you take a risk and survive, your self-confidence is strengthened — and your trust that no matter what life deals to you, you can deal with it.

> The most authentic and engaging type of flirting involves sharing your self-talk.

One Man's Risk

After considering his hopes and fears and self-talk, a man in one of my seminars, Dirk, decided to walk across the room and share with an attractive stranger exactly what he had been saying to himself: "Hello, my name is Dirk. I noticed you from the other side of the room. I noticed your smile and how easily you seem to laugh. I was hoping if I came over here, maybe you'd smile at me . . . or laugh at me — either one would be great." Actually Dirk had only said to himself the first statement about her smile and her laugh. He had other things ready to say, but he felt so freed up by just going over to her that he threw away his script and began to improvise. What he discovered was, "Every encounter with a new woman is an opportunity to learn to become more comfortable with spontaneity. Now that's becoming a bigger goal for me than actually getting a date."

Uncovering Outdated Beliefs

You can use the exercise above, where you list your hoped for responses and your most feared responses, to uncover any old beliefs about how you expect to be treated or how you think you need to be treated. If you were afraid to hear the words, "What do you want?" notice the emotional charge linked to these words. If these words trigger a reaction in you, it's very important to know this about yourself. Being conscious of your triggers or buttons is a prerequisite for being real.

Let's imagine that you have a fear of someone saying, "What do you want?" You hate being rejected, and you'll do almost anything to avoid it. You are wired up to watch out for the slightest sign of rejection. When you think you see such a sign, your body and mind go into a heightened state of arousal. You're prepared for danger. You're ready to fight or flee — just like your primitive ancestors. So you automatically use one of your control patterns: Before the other person has a chance to say anything, you say, "I can see you're busy," or "I'm sorry to be a pest, but . . ." or "Hi gorgeous, how's it goin'?" Even this last statement is a control pattern because it's designed to protect your ego. It is an attempt to look cool rather than revealing

"Every encounter with a new woman is an opportunity to learn to become more comfortable with spontaneity. Now that's becoming a bigger goal for me than actually getting a date."

your feelings. Can you see why I call these control patterns? They are patterns because they are automatic and repetitive. And they are controlling because they are intended to protect your ego from pain or discomfort rather than risk revealing your real feelings or thoughts. The statement, "I'm sorry to be a pest," is like saying, "I'll call myself a pest before you have a chance to." "I can see you're busy," is like saying, "I'll reject myself from the conversation before you have a chance to."

When you have an automatic, knee-jerk reaction, this signals that one of your old fears has been triggered. This can be a wake-up call telling you that your ego-mind is working-ing overtime to protect you from something that probably does not exist in the present. Like the famous fool in classic literature, Don Quixote, you're tilting at windmills. Windmills are not dangerous. They are part of your everyday landscape. But based on past conditioning, you view them as threatening.

Almost everywhere you go there will be many good-hearted, sensitive people looking for permission to be open and loving and honest. But they may be waiting for someone else to make the first move.

Most people in most social situations have some degree of fear of other people. Usually this fear is not conscious, but it creates a low-level tension that you can feel if you tune in to it. The aim of Truth in Dating is to show you that in most social situations, you have nothing to fear. The windmills are not going to harm you. Remember that almost everywhere you go there will be many good-hearted, sensitive people looking for permission to be open and loving and honest. But they may be waiting for someone else to make the first move. Will you be one of those who make the first move? Or will you be one of those who wait?

Total Body Self-Awareness

There's active flirting and there's receptive flirting. So far, we have been talking about active flirting — taking a risk and sharing your self-talk. Receptive flirting starts with becoming aware of the physical and energetic sensations in your body. As you feel your breath going in and out, your feet on the ground, and your body in space, you exude a more powerful energetic presence. You can just stand there against the wall, and people will be drawn to you. When you are aware and present in your body, your gaze will be more relaxed and focused. The simple act of making eye contact will draw others to you.

The next time you go out to a social gathering, make it your intention to be aware of your physical presence at all times (except when you're not!). Notice how others respond to you. Don't try to flirt. Don't try to make anything happen. Just feel and sense and notice. When people do this in my dating seminars, they report feeling more confident, less worried about the outcome, and more warmth toward other people. My theory is that they feel more warmth first because they are relaxed and present in their bodies, which allows their energy to flow more freely; and second, by focusing attention on the here and now, they are less attached to the outcome, and not so worried about how other people could hurt them. Less fear leads to more love, openness, and warmth.

> By focusing attention on the here and now, they are not so worried about how other people could hurt them. Less fear leads to more love, openness, and warmth.

Once you learn how to receptively flirt, try combining this with active flirting. Share self-talk and then just relax and breathe and notice your sensations and your surroundings. This will take your mind off of worrying about results.

Become a Truth in Dating Ambassador

If you are intrigued by the idea of practicing Truth in Dating when first meeting someone, there are seven steps to be aware of. I call them The Seven Steps of Conscious Flirting. These steps occur whether you are just seeing someone for the first time or are connecting with someone you have known for years. Flirting happens throughout a relationship — not just in the beginning. In any shared moment between two people, the life of the relationship moves through seven subtle steps. Being aware of these steps can help you stay present to what is going on between you and the other. The seven steps occur as these seven questions arise and are answered:

1. What am I feeling and thinking right now?
2. What do I want?
3. What am I willing to risk?
4. Can I now speak the truth that is calling to be spoken?
5. Can I now listen openly to the other's response?
6. What am I feeling and thinking now? Do I still feel and want the same thing?
7. Do I stay or move away? (And do I do this openly or not?)

Let's consider each of these steps in detail.

1. What am I feeling and thinking right now? This might also include the things I was saying to myself about the person or the fantasies I was having a few minutes ago. Joe sees Mandy sitting at a table talking and laughing with a couple of friends. He feels attracted. He likes how she looks and how she pays attention to her friends when they are talking. He imagines she is a good listener and that she knows how to draw out the best from people. (As he thinks this, he pays attention to the difference between what he actually sees and what he imagines about her. He uses his fantasy about her as a working hypothesis — something he'll want to gather more data about.)

> What am I feeling and thinking right now? What do I want? What am I willing to risk? Can I now speak the truth that is calling to be spoken?

2.   What do I want? Joe wants to go over and be in her presence. He wants to find a way to have a conversation with her.

3.   What am I willing to risk? He imagines that if he simply walked over and told her that he noticed her, she might be put off. Then again, she might like it. Either way, he'll get to talk to her and get a sense of how it feels to interact with her. Joe decides to go for it.

4.   Can I now speak the truth that is calling to be spoken? He walks up to Mandy's table slowly, feeling his physical sensations and the movement of his body, looking at her as he walks. He also looks at her friends and acknowledges them with his eyes. When he gets close enough to start a conversation, he waits for Mandy to look at him. Then he says, "I was watching you from over there" (looking at Mandy), "watching all of you laughing and talking" (looking at others one-by-one), "and I was noticing" (said to Mandy) "how you pay attention to your friends. I said to myself, 'I bet she knows how to bring out the best in other people.' I wanted to come over and say this to you, and to introduce myself. I'm Joe."

Can I now listen openly to the other's response? What am I feeling and thinking now? Do I still feel and want the same thing? Do I stay or move away? (And do I do this openly or not?)

5.   Can I now listen openly to the other's response? This is the step where most people blow it! They don't stay in the receptive mode long enough. They can't be quiet and give the other person a chance to digest what was just said and to respond. They may imagine that the person in Mandy's position is getting uncomfortable, so they rescue her with some quip or other control pattern

(as in "You're probably too busy anyway"). In Joe's case, he waits for what seems like five minutes but is really only about five seconds. During these five seconds Mandy looks away from him, first at her teacup, then at her two friends. Finally, without smiling, she looks him in the eye and says, "I'm in the middle of something here, and I'd rather talk to you some other time."

6. What am I feeling and thinking now? Do I still feel and want the same thing? When Joe checks in with himself now, he feels a mixture of things: he's pleased that he said what he said and he likes how clear Mandy seems to be about her wants. So on the one hand, he's feeling warm and happy. On the other hand, he's still not sure if she really wants to talk with him, and he feels disappointed that he's apparently going to have to wait to find this out. He takes a deep breath to help him connect with his total body self-awareness. This brings him back to presence.

    > When you are aware and present in your body, your gaze will be more relaxed and focused.

7. Do I stay or move away? (And do I do this openly or not?) Joe feels like staying close to her so he can perhaps continue talking with her after she finishes the conversation she is involved with. He tells her, "I appreciate you for how you said that. I'll be over there under the clock for a while if you want to come over when you're done here."

After this, he's back to the first step. These seven steps will start all over again (for both Mandy and Joe) if and when she comes over to talk with him.

Can You Imagine It?

As you put yourself in Joe's shoes, how are you feeling about what you just did? Would you be pleased with yourself for taking the risk? Or would you be telling yourself something like, "You just made a fool of yourself. Couldn't you find a more casual, less direct way to approach her?" Or how about, "This type of thing always happens. The ones I'm attracted to aren't attracted to me"? If this last sentence sounds like you, you are "filling in the blanks," assuming you know how the story will end when you really do not. People fill in the blanks to protect themselves from the anxiety of not knowing. They imagine they do know, and as a result, they never find out the truth.

> People fill in the blanks to protect themselves from the anxiety of not knowing. They imagine they do know, and as a result, they never find out the truth.

Try This Scenario

When you flirt with someone, do you control or relate? Here is a typical first meeting scenario. Put yourself into this scene and imagine how you would handle it.

You are at a singles party talking to someone whom you find very attractive. The two of you have been in conversation for about ten minutes, and you're feeling warm and excited about getting to know this new person. For the past few minutes you have had the mysterious feeling that you and he (or she) are the only two people in the room. Then, after a pause in the conversation this person says to you, "I am enjoying talking to you, but I need to go to the bathroom. I look forward to continuing this afterwards." The person walks away and you go over to get something to drink. Then, after about ten minutes, you notice this person having a very animated conversation with an attractive person of your gender. Both seem to be enjoying themselves immensely. What do you feel and think, and what do you do? Would you go over and join them? Would you wait and see if the person approaches you? Would you assume he or she was insincere and just using the bathroom as an excuse to exit the conversation?

Your (imagined) way of dealing with this scenario says a lot about your ability to relate, i.e., to be open and communicative about what's true for you versus your tendency to control, i.e., to behave strategically in order to play it safe or avoid discomfort. Can you imagine yourself going over to join the pair and practicing the seven subtle steps of conscious flirting? And then perhaps telling the person that you had enjoyed meeting her and you'd like to continue talking later if she wanted to? Would this occur to you?

Or are you more likely to tell yourself, "*C'est la vie* — it doesn't matter — it's no big deal"? This might be your way of avoiding discomfort. If you use this strategy, you would probably leave the party with unfinished business.

What if you were to share your self-talk in this imagined scenario? What might you say? Is this something you can actually imagine yourself doing? If not, why not?

Here's How Relating Can Work

Here's how one woman handled an actual situation very similar to this. Adele decided to go over and join the man, Ron, and the other woman in conversation. When there was a pause, she told Ron that before he had gone off to the men's room, she'd been about to tell him something, which she'd still like to do when the time was right for him to resume their conversation. She stayed in conversation with Ron and the woman, and soon the other woman left to get a drink. Ron told her he was glad she had come over and really wanted to hear what she had to say. She told him that she had been feeling an attraction for him. He loved hearing it, and they went home together that night.

When you let someone know you find him attractive, you don't need to be sure that he is going to respond in kind. If you treat yourself as too fragile to handle unintended outcomes, then you don't develop

the resilience that human beings need to cope with a world full of unpredictability and change. On the other hand, if you take a risk, you may
learn that you cope rather well with uncertainty. And sometimes, you'll
get lucky like Adele did!

Chapter Summary

- Sharing your self-talk with an attractive stranger is a very
  effective flirting practice because it brings you into the
  present moment with the other. It also gets you out of your
  head and into action.

- Imagine yourself taking a risk and approaching someone.
  This can help you become more comfortable with discomfort — so you don't waste your life avoiding being uncomfortable.

- The seven steps of conscious flirting are actually seven questions that can be asked of yourself progressively, They are:

  1. What am I feeling and thinking right now?
  2. What do I want?
  3. What am I willing to risk?
  4. Can I tell the truth to the other?
  5. Can I be open and receptive to the other's response?
  6. What am I feeling and thinking now? Do I still feel
     and want the same thing?
  7. Do I stay or move away? (And do I do this openly
     or not?)

- Knowing these seven steps can make you more aware of
  your feelings, your wants, and your intentions. This will
  help you approach each interaction with more confidence.

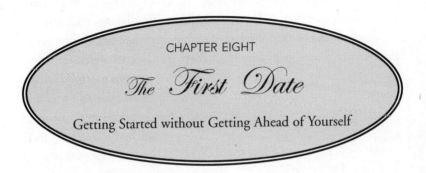

CHAPTER EIGHT

The First Date

Getting Started without Getting Ahead of Yourself

There are a lot of unknowns at this point.
See if you can consciously embrace the unknown and
at the same time embrace your need for information.

Janine was eagerly anticipating her first date with Eric. They were planning to go for a walk on the beach and then perhaps have dinner — if things went well. Otherwise, they had already decided, they would just shake hands and wish each other a happy life. The two had met a week before at their kids' soccer game, so they had not yet spent any alone time together. But she knew she liked his looks, his enthusiasm, and the fact that he had a son the same age as hers.

Her mind was racing: "What if he's not really available? I think he has an ex-wife in town. I wonder if he's still hung up on her. What if he wants to go to bed right away? I'll need time to get to know him. What if he turns out to be dominating and controlling like the last guy I dated? What if he has met someone he likes better in the meantime? What if he's wearing cologne? I'll have to ask him to go wash it off. What if he takes offense at that?"

The few days before a first date are a time when your mind can run wild with unanswered questions. Even though Janine and Eric had talked on the phone a few times since their first meeting, there were still a great many questions to be answered. One of the biggest challenges of the first date and the initial stages of dating is the fact that you are probably going to have many questions that cannot be answered until you have spent more time together. In the initial stages of dating it's natural for fears and insecurities to come up because the future is so uncertain. You may be tempted to try to get all your questions answered right away, but don't use your commitment to Truth in Dating as an excuse to grill your date with questions about the future that cannot be answered. Certainly, if you have questions about the possibility of a future together, it's important to reveal them, but that's different from expecting your date to give you information that can only be revealed over time.

> In the initial stages of dating it's natural for fears and insecurities to come up because the future is so uncertain.

The Big Question

One question that you can and should address right away, however, is "How important is honesty to each of us?" I think this is one of the most important questions to cover on the first or second date. If you view dating as a path to self-awareness and your date is seeking someone to feed his or her addiction to comfort and security, the two of you will be at cross-purposes. So why not find this out right away?

In preparing yourself to raise this question, it's good to be ready to explain what you mean by Truth in Dating. Here's one way I have heard people present it: "I'm only interested in dating people who are committed to being completely honest — even if this makes us uncomfortable. To me, honesty means we're willing to talk about whatever thoughts and emotions are coming up between us — what we feel, what we want, and when we get triggered by each other. What do you think of this?" (Then pause and let the other person respond.) There's a book that explains it pretty well called *Truth in Dating*. I can show it to you if you want."

After you introduce the concept, it's really important to listen to whatever the other has to say. Your date might say, "Yes, of course," but really not be capable of this sort of relating. He may say yes and not have a clear picture of what he's saying yes to. He may say no, imagining that he's not very good at this sort of thing or that he won't be able to do it as well as you can. Or he may have had some painful or frustrating experiences in the past that he still associates with truth-telling. Be open to his questions and to whatever resistance he may have to the idea. For most people, Truth in Dating will be a radical concept. They may value honesty in some abstract sense, but not when it comes to actually revealing their feelings and thoughts to someone they are just getting to know. Many of my interviewees said something like, "Sure I value honesty, but only if nobody gets hurt. It's not worth losing a relationship over it!" The fact that this sentiment is so common shows how fearful most people are.

Here's the choice you face: Do you want to start out the relationship by being true to your own values? Or would you rather play it safe and make sure your behavior stays within the other person's comfort zone? Are you ready to break out of the widely held belief that you have to be careful not to upset other people? By making Truth in Dating your awareness practice, you will come to see how many unconscious patterns you have that reinforce the belief that the world is a scary and unfriendly place.

Don't use your commitment to Truth in Dating as an excuse to grill your date with questions about the future that cannot be answered.

What's the Payoff?

Once again I want to emphasize the power of this practice to deepen your own self-trust and openheartedness. The longer I practice the ten truth skills, the more loving and safe I feel. And there are many other singles who share my experience. I know this practice has great potential for transforming the dating scene from one of suspicion and caution to one of caring and mutual support. The reason honesty works this way is this: When I speak my truth, I am affirming that I can trust myself to handle unintended or unpleasant outcomes. I'm reinforcing the belief that whatever life deals to me, I can deal with it. This makes me feel confident and good about myself. If, on the other hand, I try to play it safe and speak only about things I'm sure will not rock the boat, then I'm reinforcing the belief that I cannot handle unexpected or unplanned outcomes. Think about it this way: if your self-confidence or esteem depends upon having things always turn out as planned, then your sense of self is on pretty shaky ground.

As you know, a relationship is a living, ever-changing, unpredictable thing. If you can only handle things that conform to your preconceived ideas and expectations, you're going to be in trouble. Truth in Dating is a wonderful way to train for long-term intimacy because it gets you in the habit of continually stretching your comfort zone, while at the same time having fun with someone you like. You come to really value the growth that comes through relationship challenges.

> This practice has great potential for transforming the dating scene from one of suspicion and caution to one of caring and mutual support.

With Truth in Dating, you win either way: If things develop into lasting love, you're fortunate. If they do not, you're still fortunate because you have used the dating relationship to become a better person.

The Rules

So what are the rules for Truth in Dating? Somewhere during the first conversation you have with someone about this topic, you will need to define your expectations: What does Truth in Dating mean to each of you? Does it mean getting down and dirty with all the gory details of your previous relationships? Does it include sharing your psychological history? Does it mean telling him that you're turned off by how he dresses or how he kisses?

To arrive at your own "rules," do this exercise: Set aside time together to brainstorm and write down all the questions like those above that come to mind. Then, for each item on the list, tell each other about whatever feelings of excitement or fear are coming up as you consider that question. For example, as I look at the items on my list, one of my questions is, "Should I tell him I'm seeing other men, and how much should I tell him?" I have some fear about telling my date that I am dating other men besides him (if I am). In the past, some men have put enormous pressure on me to stop seeing other men. So now I am afraid that if I am seeing other men, and I tell the truth, then this man will have nothing further to do with me. Listing your fears like this is a useful practice. It helps you deal more consciously with fears instead of letting them dictate your choices.

> Deciding to go deep does not mean dumping out a bunch of psychological insights about yourself. It is up to the two of you to define the type of honesty you both want.

Invariably, I find that when I am honest with someone, we wind up feeling closer. Some people think that the first date is too soon to start practicing complete honesty. But if your aim is to get to know someone to see if you're compatible, why not start right away to open up and get closer? Having this conversation is a way to clarify your values about selfdisclosure — about how deep you both want to go in an intimate relationship. Deciding to go deep does not mean dumping out a bunch of psychological insights about yourself. It is up to the two of you to define the type of honesty you both want.

Personally, the type of honesty I prefer includes the following:

- I'd like our conversations to be mostly present-centered — talking about what we are feeling, wanting, or thinking in the present moment, as opposed to talking about other people or past relationships.

- I want us to be free to talk about things that might be difficult.
- I want us both to feel free to ask for what we want.
- I will answer any sincere question honestly.
- I will ask about anything that I am curious about, but I can accept it if the other person does not feel like answering.
- I like to share personal stories. I think telling our stories is an excellent way to get to know each other. (For example: What was your childhood like? Did you have siblings? What jobs have you had? Have you been married, and if so, how did that relationship end?)

Sometime during the first month of dating, if you know you want to keep seeing this person, I think it's good to have a conversation about buttons and limiting beliefs. I'd probably ask my date to read about buttons in chapter 10 first. Then, I might tell him about one or two childhood experiences that have resulted in automatic fear reactions — like the fact that my dad used to pop off in anger, which has led me to have fear about a man's anger coming at me. I believe that if we can talk openly about our patterns, then these things will not have so much power over us.

Sometime during the first month have a conversation about buttons and limiting beliefs. If we can talk openly about our patterns, then these things will not have so much power over us.

What If He or She Is Not Interested?

Melanie decided to introduce the idea of Truth in Dating to Ken on their third date. She did her best to present it in a positive, openhearted manner. But, in spite of her best efforts, Ken's response was, "That'll require way too much processing. I don't want to spend all our time together talking about feelings and fears. I want to just have some fun together for a while and see if it feels compatible. Maybe later, after we've been going out for a while, I'd be willing to try being more open about what I'm really thinking."

Melanie was disappointed. She really liked Ken and didn't want to scare him off. But she also wanted to be with someone who could handle openness and honesty. She was afraid of winding up with someone she would have to protect. Should she call it quits right there or should she pursue the issue a bit further? She decided not to give up. She modeled the Truth in Dating approach by Holding Differences (Truth Skill #8) as she replied, "I'm feeling a lump in my throat listening to what you're saying. I can hear that you'd rather we get to know each other more and see if we're compatible before getting into too much processing. I think there is wisdom in your point of view. I'm not into endless processing either. But I want to be with someone who values open communication the way I do. I don't want to get too far into a relationship if we know already that we want different things in a relationship. That's really what I'm concerned about. I don't want to get into a situation where I can't be myself... where I think I have to hide certain things so my date won't be uncomfortable."

"I don't want to get into a situation where I can't be myself...where I think I have to hide certain things so my date won't be uncomfortable."

After hearing this, Ken paused and thought for a long time. Then, he disclosed that in a previous relationship, his girlfriend had been all over him with questions about what he meant by this or that, and it drove him nuts. She said she was doing this in the interest of honesty. He had felt trapped because there were other things he did like about her, so he didn't want to cut off the relationship. Finally, her questioning got to be too much, and he stopped seeing her, vowing that he would never again get into a relationship with someone like that. After disclosing this to Melanie, he saw more clearly why he was resistant to Truth in Dating. He got some distance from this position and was able to see that Melanie was not like this other woman — even though she did value honesty.

Hearing himself talk about this, he realized, "Maybe I'm not really against telling the truth after all. In fact I was being honest just now when I talked about my old girlfriend. Now I see that the problem I have with Truth in Dating comes from some old fears. I just need to trust that I don't have to get into any processing if I don't feel like it. If you want to practice Truth in Dating, let's do it with the understanding that you can ask me things, and I can tell you if I'm open to talking or if I'm not. That's really all I need — to give myself permission to set some limits when I need to. Can you live with that?"

Don't be discouraged if you get some initial resistance. Share your feelings and your vision, perhaps painting a picture of the fun, learning, and expanded consciousness you hope to have as a result of practicing Truth in Dating.

Melanie liked his response and was glad she had pursued the matter. She saw that he was committed to taking responsibility for himself. Now that she thought about it, this was her biggest reason for suggesting Truth in Dating. She wanted to be with someone who could take care of himself in a conversation, so she wouldn't be worrying about protecting him.

With different people, different issues will surface when the initial question about Truth in Dating comes up. Often it may take a bit of conversation before a person's underlying fears and resistances come to light. The moral of this story about Ken and Melanie is: Don't give up too soon. Don't be discouraged if you get some initial resistance. Share your feelings, ask for what you want in a noncontrolling way, and describe your vision, perhaps painting a picture of the fun, learning, and expanded consciousness you hope to have as a result of practicing Truth in Dating.

The Purpose of Dating

People date for different purposes. Most people over the age of thirty are looking for lasting love — a long-term, committed partnership. But you cannot assume that this is what someone wants until you talk about it and until you know her well enough to see if her behavior is congruent with what she says she wants. Some people in their teens and twenties may also want to find a compatible life partner, but others may still be at the "I just want to get to know myself" stage or the "I just want to have as much sex as possible" stage. No matter what your intentions are, be open to the possibility that there are others who have similar needs. Do not assume that if you just want a lot of sex, you have to manipulate and deceive in order to get that. I found many younger people who were dating primarily to get sex or to get to know themselves. These motives are not unusual. Being honest about these things is what is unusual!

The first date is a good time to consider the question, What is my purpose in meeting and getting to know you, and what is yours? If dating is successful, what will be the result?

From my research and study over the years, I conclude that there are many people who are not conscious about their real motives for dating. They say they want a long-term monogamous relationship, but they always quit at the first sign of conflict, or they do not make time in their schedule for anything deep and lasting to develop, or their needs for control are so high that they are simply not well suited to partnership. If you find yourself with someone who does not seem to walk their talk, disclose your observations and your fears, and see how they respond. At this point try to avoid assessments or interpretations about the other person. That's not the brand of honesty I am trying to promote. There's

> If you find yourself making assessments and judgments about him, you are probably having uncomfortable feelings. Talk about these instead of about your judgments.

a saying: You can only be honest about yourself. All you can really know is what you feel and think and observe. If you find yourself over on the other's side of the net making assessments and judgments about him, you are probably having uncomfortable feelings (e.g., fear, hurt, or anger), and you probably need to talk about these instead of about your judgments. The most real and respectful thing is to talk about yourself and your own feelings. It is disrespectful to tell others what you "see" about them. Relationships simply work better when you make it your practice to speak only about yourself.

What Happens on a First Date?

What you do on a first date depends on what has already gone on between you. If you have spent hours on the phone together, you will have already covered some of the basic questions, such as: Are we both looking for the same thing in a relationship? (Are we both seeking a long-term commitment?) Does he have the personal qualities that I want in a mate? (Can he communicate his feelings?) Are our values and lifestyles compatible? (Do we both want to be sexually monogamous? Do we both want children?) If the first date occurs after only a few minutes or hours together, then you may not even get to those questions on the first date. But you will have questions. On a first date most of your questions will have to do with the issue of compatibility: Do we enjoy each other's company? Do we have enough in common? Do we feel sexual chemistry? Are the feelings mutual? These questions are not strictly "yes"- or "no"-type questions. Often your answers will be "yes and no" — yes I'm attracted, but not as much as I'd like to be; yes we have some things in common, but he doesn't like parties, and I'm a social butterfly. So, unless there are clear "no's" on a number of big questions, you may reach the end of the first date feeling that you will need to see more of each other in order to know how compatible you are. While you may feel love (or lust) at first sight, you will probably also feel some ambivalence for a while about the question of where you want to go with this person. The ability to tolerate

The first date is a good time to consider the question, What is my purpose in meeting and getting to know you, and what is yours?

uncertainty is a sign of emotional health. If you find yourself seeking certainty at this point in the relationship, I suggest you slow down or back up. Imagine you are interviewing this person for a very important job. You have a lot of questions that need to be answered, and they will not all get answered in the first interview. Instead of trying to impress or trying to get your date to like you, focus more on the

If you find yourself seeking certainty at this point in the relationship, I suggest you slow down or back up.

things you want to learn about her or him. This will help you stay centered in your own reality instead of losing yourself in trying to make a good impression.

What about Love at First Sight?

If you think you really are experiencing true and deep love right from the start, notice if this is a pattern for you. Have you often felt this before and only later discovered that it was not real? Or you may have another pattern. Maybe you are so "ready" to be in love that anyone who comes remotely close to being your type will capture your attention. In the early stages of attraction (especially if there is a lot of chemistry), it's easy to deceive yourself, so it's really important to know your patterns. Here are some other questions to ask yourself after the two of you have been out a few times:

- Am I able to look at this person and identify what I like and don't like about him, or am I focusing all my attention on whether *he* likes *me?*
- Have we ever talked about something difficult, or are we treating this relationship as too fragile for certain topics?
- Do I say the things that are on my mind or in my heart, or am I still waiting for "the right time"?
- Am I (or is my date) a sex, love, or relationship addict?

There are many "undiagnosed" relationship addicts out there. They may seem very available — almost too available to be true — but the truth may be that they are dependent personalities who are not ready for grown-up love. If your date showers an excessive amount of attention on you and tries to get you to commit (or have sex) sooner than you're ready to, this could indicate relationship addiction. If you suspect that you or your date have this addiction, Appendix B lists some resources (books, tapes, and treatment programs) to assist you.

- Does my date have an addictive personality? Does he use alcohol, food, work, partying, shopping, gambling, or drugs in a way that I'm uncomfortable with? Am I able to discuss this with him? Does he get defensive if I bring up something I'm uncomfortable about? A person with an addictive personality is often quite charming. Such people may also be good at expressing feelings — which can be quite seductive. If you are bothered by something and feel unable to bring up the topic, this is not a good sign. You may be intuiting (correctly) that this other person would only become defensive if you brought it up.

> If you are bothered by something and feel unable to bring up the topic, this is not a good sign. You may be intuiting (correctly) that this other person would only become defensive if you brought it up.

- Do I have a need to rescue people? The need for love is strong. Sometimes this need eclipses other needs and values so that you sacrifice too much in order to preserve the relationship — even a two week relationship! If you know that you are feeling especially needy, hungry, or lonely, watch out for things like self-deception, denial, and self-sacrifice. When your decisions are colored by extreme neediness, they will be poor ones.

Sex, Drugs, and Rock 'n' Roll

Rock 'n' roll is fine on a first date, but I'd be wary about bringing sex, drugs, or alcohol into the picture (with the exception perhaps of a drink with dinner). Sexual intercourse often creates emotional bonding. If this occurs before you have fully explored your compatibility, you will be short-circuiting your mate selection process. Of course there are many people who date just to get sex, so if that's your situation, being honest about this will help you hook up with others who want the same thing. You may be doubtful that there are others who just want a "sexual play-mate," but let me assure you that there are.

Like drugs and alcohol, sex also tends to alter your per-ception of reality. And like these sub-

Like drugs and alcohol, sex also tends to alter your perception of reality. And like these substances, it can help you deny what is really going on and avoid feelings that really need to be faced.

stances, it can help you deny what is really going on and avoid feelings that really need to be faced. Kissing and sexual innuendos are great on a first date, but if you're committed to truth, you'll need to be mindful of how sex, drugs, and alcohol can alter your ability to perceive, speak, and hear the truth.

I used to work with junkies in jail and on the streets. I'll always remember how different their personalities were when they were "using" versus when they were "straight." Without drugs, they were highly anx-ious — so anxious they could hardly function. With drugs, they seemed pretty normal, even charming. Many people who would not be consid-ered junkies medicate themselves regularly. When a person is using drugs or alcohol (or food or sex) this way, you cannot know who or how they really are. There is no possibility for Truth in Dating.

Drugs and alcohol can also be used to manipulate a date into hav-ing sex. If you are ever manipulated into having sex, contact your date in order to express and clear your feelings. Using the forgiveness process detailed in chapter 12 may help. You may also want to "go out and come in again," telling your date that if you were not loaded, you would not have allowed yourself to go that far with him. Something as serious as unwanted sex should not be passed off without doing some work to resolve your feelings. Otherwise the pain of this unresolved incident will linger, creating mistrust of others and low self-trust.

First Date Dilemmas

What if your first date is an immediate disappointment? What if you can't tell whether your date is attracted to you or not? What if one of you wants to be sexual, and the other isn't ready yet? What if everything goes great until the good-night kiss, and then you discover you can't stand how he kisses? What if he has some other habit or foible that turns you off? What if he says, "I'll call you," but doesn't? What is the best way to find out whether your date has a sexually transmitted disease (STD)?

If I'm preoccupied with my feelings of disappointment, there's no point in trying to hide this. That would interfere with my ability to be present to what is.

These are just a sampling of the types of situations that cause distress during first dates. How would you handle these if they came up for you? To show you how Truth in Dating can help you navigate tough situations, I will consider each of these dilemmas in turn.

What If You're Immediately Disappointed?

Angie's face fell when she opened her front door and saw Ed standing there. His shoulders drooped. He looked tired. And he was more overweight than she had remembered. He looked at her expectantly, as if he wanted a big hug. She turned away and invited him in. Both Ed and Angie felt an immediate sense of disappointment. They had each spent the week in hopeful anticipation of this moment, and now any sense of hopefulness seemed very far away. If you were in Ed's place, what would you do? And what if you were Angie?

Would you speak truthfully about your feelings or just try to get through the evening as painlessly as possible? It's the first date, so you probably don't yet have an agreement with your date about complete honesty. Still, you have a choice.

If I were practicing Truth in Dating in Angie's shoes, I would probably say something like, "Ed, I was really looking forward to seeing you. And now, as you may be able to tell, I'm feeling something I did not expect to feel. I'm not nearly as attracted to you as I was last week when we talked. I'm not sure if this is a momentary thing or if things will change. I do know that often, after I confess a feeling, it will change, and I'll end up feeling closer to the person. I respect you, and I don't think you'd want me to be phony with you, so that's why I'm sharing this. As you may know I'm very committed to honest communication." Then I'd be quiet and pay attention to him with an open heart. I would not try to make light of the situation, nor would I want to make it a big deal. I'd listen to whatever he said, or I'd simply be quiet with him as he took in my words. My only goal is to be as honest and respectful and present as I can be. If I'm preoccupied with my feelings of disappointment, there's no point in trying to hide this. That would interfere with my ability to be present to what is. I am open to being surprised about what happens next.

There have been times when I have expressed something like this, and my feelings actually did change. I wound up really liking the person — dating him and even being lovers. Often things do change, but sometimes they don't. You might wonder, "Why bring it up if it may change anyway?" I bring it up because I am committed to sharing anything that might interfere with being present, and also because, once again, when I trust the unknown in this way (instead of trying not to rock the boat), I learn that I can trust myself to handle unexpected

> When I trust the unknown in this way (instead of trying not to rock the boat), I learn that I can trust myself to handle unexpected consequences. This is one of the main reasons for practicing Truth in Dating — to strengthen your self-trust.

consequences. This is one of the main reasons for practicing Truth in Dating — to strengthen your self-trust.

What if Angie is honest with Ed and he suggests that they end the date right then and there? How should she react to that suggestion? I think that depends on whether both people have really had the chance to say what they need to say. If I'm Angie, and I think that there's even the remotest chance that I could warm up to Ed, I would tell him so. As Angie, I would also want to ask myself the question, "Am I putting too much emphasis on sexual chemistry? Is it possible that someone I'm not immediately attracted to could actually end up being a good match for me?"

I certainly think it is fine to end a first date after thirty minutes if that is what at least one of you honestly wants. Yes, even if only one of you wants to end it right there, it's okay. But I hope if you're Angie, and you're sure you want to end it, that you acknowledge Ed in some way for how he received the "bad news."

How Can You Find Out Where You Stand?

Jan knew she was very attracted to Kevin even before he showed up to take her to dinner. She was hoping he felt the same way, but she had an intuition that he wasn't really available on some level — at least to her. Still, she was going to go for it with all she had.

When Kevin showed up, he seemed distracted. This triggered her feelings of insecurity, but she over- rode these and acted bouncy and cheerful. Behind this façade, her mind was chat- tering away: "I can't tell if he's attracted to me or not. How can I find out?"

> If I'm preoccupied with my feelings of disappointment, there's no point in trying to hide this. That would interfere with my ability to be present to what is.

At dinner, they talked about many things and seemed to have a lot in common. Jan was having a great time, but she was still frustrated, not knowing Kevin's intentions. She watched his body language. When she put a hand on his shoulder, he didn't pull away, but he seemed not to even notice her touch. Often when she looked into his eyes, she noticed that he turned his glance elsewhere. Finally, as their first date was drawing to a close, Jan decided to take a risk and ask Kevin how he saw their relationship — did he see her as a possible romantic partner? Or did he see her more as a friend? She decided to ask her question in this "multiple-choice" format: "Kevin, I have a question for you about what we're doing together. Do you see me as someone you're wanting to date and get to know better in that way? Or are we just friends? I can't tell. I can live with whatever your answer is, but I think you know that I'm attracted to you as more than a friend."

Do you see me as someone you're wanting to date and get to know better in that way? Or are we just friends?

Before Kevin answered, he took her hand. Jan's heart skipped a beat, and she thought, "Maybe he likes me after all." But his words were not what she wanted to hear. "I like you, Jan, but I'm seeing what we have as a friendship. When I asked you out, I wasn't sure, but I'm getting clearer that something that I want in a girlfriend just isn't there with you and me. Thanks for bringing this up because I wasn't sure how to do it."

In the brief conversation above, both Jan and Kevin modeled Truth in Dating as it applies to the sometimes awkward situation of finding out where you stand and telling the other where they stand with you. It's not necessary to offer a lot of explanation. A simple, direct question and a simple, direct response are usually the most real and respectful way to go.

As I mentioned in the previous section, after you express something, it often changes. Often it is the person in Jan's shoes who experiences a change. After confessing her attraction, it mysteriously goes away. She's no longer as infatuated with him. Truth in Dating helps you understand some pretty deep lessons about life and relationships — in this case the lesson that secret feelings often change after being exposed to the light of day.

What If One of You Wants to Be Sexual
and the Other Isn't Ready?

While I have cautioned against being sexual too soon, the issue is often "up" on the first date: Am I feeling sexual desire? Is the other person? How can I get him or her to want me? Do I want to wait until we know each other better? Will my date take no for an answer?

If there is a mutual attraction, some kissing and perhaps some fondling may occur on a first date. (This is not to suggest that this should happen, but it may.) After this, the question of when to have sexual intercourse may come up. If your date wants to be more sexual than you do, it's up to you to assert your boundaries — without making the other wrong for wanting something different. But what if you really like this person and are afraid he'll lose interest if you make him wait too long? Tell him this — that you really like him and are afraid he may lose interest, and you want him to wait. Be sure and tell him what you want. That's really important. Some people are shy about asking the other to wait, imagining this to be an unreasonable request. If he's not willing to wait, this may be a sign that he's a sex addict, he just wants to get laid, or he's a person who is so insecure that he tries to manipulate the other into a premature commitment. So maybe it's good to find this out now.

Before you have sex, you will need to know and trust one another enough to be able to talk honestly about safe sex. If you can't talk openly about it, you're not ready to do it. There are at least three important conversations that need to occur: (1) a conversation about your recent sexual history and sexually transmitted diseases (STDs); (2) one about what turns you on and what turns you off, sexually; and (3) one about what method of birth control, if any, you will use. Talking about these things is an important prelude to sex. Hearing your date talk about her recent sexual history will give you a sense of how she feels about sex. Telling each other what turns you on will help you have a more pleasurable experience together. Chapters 13 and 14 go into more detail on how to talk openly about sex. The final section in this chapter covers how to talk about STDs.

What If Some Habit or Foible Turns You Off?

Many singles report that one of the hardest things to deal with on a first or early date is the first kiss, if they don't like how their date kisses. Other common turnoffs that come up early on are: bad breath, body odor, nervous tics, anxious mannerisms or speech habits, extra weight, and taste in clothes. If you happen to be turned off by how your date kisses (for example), how might you deal with this?

Truth in Dating would counsel you to mention it as soon as you become aware of it or very shortly thereafter. If you don't, you won't be present to whatever else is going on between you. You'll be thinking, "How am I ever going to tell her that her kissing needs improvement?"

Besides this, another reason to mention it soon is: if you do plan to keep kissing her, and you wait six months to let her know that (for all this time) you've been wishing she'd kiss differently, how are you going to feel bringing it up after so much time has passed?

I recall one incident where I decided to talk to my date about his kissing. I asked him if he was open to talking about kissing and to describing to each other how we liked to kiss and be kissed. In that context, I told him that when he put his tongue so far into my mouth right at the start of our kissing, I felt uncomfortable, and that I preferred a tongue action that was more like teasing and less like penetration in the beginning. I then asked if he wanted me to demonstrate what I was trying to describe — which he did. And then he did the same for me. We gave each other "kissing lessons" on how we each preferred to kiss and be kissed. All the while we were talking and joking as we negotiated a compromise that would satisfy both of us.

> I asked him if he was open to talking about kissing and to describing to each other how we liked to kiss and be kissed. If you introduce the topic this way, both people get a turn to share, so it's less threatening.

Issues like bad breath and nervous habits can be dealt with in a similar fashion. Begin by suggesting the topic, saying something like, "Can we talk about whether either of us has any habits or traits that turn the other off?" If you introduce the topic this way, both people get a turn to share, so it's less threatening than if only one person were giving the feedback. One-way feedback is okay too, but after you mention that you'd like to give him some feedback, be sure to ask if he's open to hearing it. After you give someone feedback, ask for feedback in return, as in, "Is there anything like this that I do that bothers you?" Asking for feedback regularly in a new relationship is a good practice because your date may be reluctant to approach certain issues unless you ask.

What If He Says, "I'll Call You" — but Doesn't?

What if he says, "I'll call you" and then you don't hear from him for a week? Should you call him? Should you assume he lost your number? Or would you assume he wasn't sincere in the first place? Truth in Dating would counsel you to not assume anything. The truth is you do not know what his intentions were when he said he'd call. And if it's only been a week, you can't be sure that he isn't planning to call in ten days or two weeks. Uncertainty is uncomfortable for most people. If you can, try using this period of not knowing as a "stretch" for yourself — a conscious exercise in learning to get comfortable with discomfort. But if the lack of closure is interfering with your life, then by all means, call him and ask what his intentions are.

If you decide not to call him, you'll need decide for yourself what you feel is a reasonable time to wait, such as "two weeks max," and then if you do not hear back within that time, let it go.

Talking about Sexual History and STDs

Brandy was nervous, but she knew it was time to initiate a talk with Bret about safe sex and STDs. It was only their first date, but they had been making out for almost an hour, and it was pretty clear that sooner or later they would want to have intercourse. She started out simply: "I'm thinking about the fact that we may want to become lovers at some point, and I'd like to talk about birth control, safe sex, and all that." She didn't make a long speech. She just said one sentence to get the conversation started. Many singles report that they often put off having such a discussion because they feel awkward getting it started. Once it's started, most said they have no trouble with it — unless they have an STD, and then there is the temptation to save that news until later on in the relationship (probably not a good idea).

If the most critical thing is getting the conversation started, the next issue is what information do you need to exchange? You'll need to find out if he or she has any of the following: genital herpes, genital warts, candidiasis, hepatitis B and C, syphilis, bacterial vaginosis (female), gonorrhea, chlamydia, trichomoniasis, and pelvic inflammatory disease (PID). You'll also need

> Talking about sexual diseases and sexual histories can be stressful. But this level of stress is something even a new relationship ought to be able to handle.

to ask if he or she has been tested for AIDS recently and what the results were. Then, even if you both are free of disease, you should use condoms for at least three months before having sex without a condom (if you are being monogamous during this three month period).

Other questions that you may wish to consider are: How many sex partners has this person had in the past three years? What were their genders and lifestyles? Any intravenous drug users? Any anal sex? Were they monogamous? Has this person been in the habit of using condoms, and how does he or she feel about condom use?

Most singles do a poor job of discussing and dealing with STDs. They may ask, "Do you have any STDs?" and leave it at that. This is another symptom of the difficulty people have being comfortable with discomfort. Rather than risk discomfort, they simply go into denial. People need a wake-up call about this very critical topic. Public education is not enough. We need to put a higher value on living in integrity while learning to use the ten truth skills. Talking about sexual diseases and sexual histories can be stressful. But this level of stress is something even a new relationship ought to be able to handle. View this conversation and others like it as a way to build your capacity for being real together. Try seeing it as a way to really get to know the other person better — not just in terms of *what* she says about herself, but also in terms of *how she behaves* under potentially stressful circumstances. If she can't handle hearing that you've had other lovers, for example, she's not a very promising candidate to become your Truth in Dating partner.

Chapter Summary

- The first or second date is a good time to discuss how committed you both are to Truth in Dating.
- There are many more questions on your mind at this time than can possibly be answered. Still, it's normal to have all these questions, and it's okay to admit that you do. Just don't expect definitive answers.
- Each dating pair must decide for themselves their boundaries and expectations around honesty. If you're not willing to be transparent in some areas, be honest about this!
- The first date is a good time to discuss each person's purpose for dating.
- The first date is a time to keep discovering more about your compatibility.
- Sex, drugs, and alcohol do not support truth-telling because they can impair your ability to perceive reality.
- Any awkward situation is best dealt with by sharing your honest feelings and being interested in the other person's feelings.
- If you have begun to share sexual energy via kissing or fondling, it's a good time to initiate a discussion about safe sex.

PART THREE

Advanced Dating

CHAPTER NINE

The Couple's Journey

Romance Is Only the Beginning

Telling the truth will definitely speed things along on your intimate journey, but it's also true that some things just naturally reveal themselves over time.

After a time of dating, unless you have agreed otherwise, the question of commitment will come up. Commitment means different things to different people. To some, it is a thing to be feared because it limits one's options. To others, it means having someone who "will always be there for me." Many people view a commitment as the main goal of dating. They want to find a partner and become committed so their future will be secure. This chapter will help you expand your definition of commitment to include the idea that your relationship (and your commitment) is never secure. Things will keep on changing as long as you live, but the changes and challenges you encounter have meaning and purpose. They also have a somewhat predictable sequence and pattern, just like the hero's journey that mythologists talk about. As a sort of hero's journey for two, an intimate relationship can be a catalyst for self-discovery and a container for your awakening sense of oneness with all that is.

The Five Stages of Relationship

Many people say they want a committed relationship but do not have a realistic picture of what this entails. Chapter 16, "What Can You Really Expect in a Relationship?" will help you decide if you are ready for what Zorba the Greek called "the whole catastrophe." But even if you are not prepared to undertake The Couple's Journey (the title of my previous book), it's useful to know how to navigate the inevitable changes that any relationship will go through.

In the 1970s I did a major research study of relationships based on interviews with one hundred intimate partners and counseling experiences with over three hundred additional couples. I found that a typical relationship will go through five somewhat predictable stages, if partners can hang in there. My study provided further evidence for the maxim that change is the only constant in life. In the box below is the five-stage map of The Couple's Journey. I will discuss each stage, including the "developmental tasks" that need to be accomplished at each step along the way.

Stage 1. Romance: "How alike we are!"
Stage 2. Power Struggle: "How different we are!"
Stage 3. Stability: "We can learn from our differences!"
Stage 4. Commitment: "We are like different parts of one body!"
Stage 5. Cocreation: "We are part of a larger oneness!"

Stage 1: Romance

If the initial attraction is strong and mutual, then the early getting-to-know-you period, perhaps even the first year or two, are a time when people tend to focus on their similarities and the things they like about each other. They may go out of their way to please. This is normal and healthy because it allows a bond of trust to form. At this stage, partners often feel, "Here is someone who will love me as I am. I can feel safe with this person." There is of course a pitfall, too, in this tendency to accentuate your areas of similarity and compatibility: this could lead you to avoid addressing areas of incompatibility or topics that might lead to conflict — like telling him you're uncomfortable with how much alcohol he consumes or mentioning that you've never been monogamous.

Many people who are not familiar with the Truth in Dating approach assume that telling the truth will destroy their romantic feelings. This is not necessarily the case. But for many, if not most new relationships, this is probably what should happen anyway. The romance should end because the two are not compatible enough to go the distance.

> The early getting-to-know-you period is a time when people tend to focus on their similarities and the things they like about each other.

I and most of my friends actually find truth-telling a turn-on. My boyfriend and I have found that we feel closer and juicier after we clear the air, or express our wants or even our frustrations. I recently confessed to him that I was feeling jealous of his attentions to one of his female friends. Instead of getting defensive, he told me that my confession helped him open his heart more deeply to me. He said there was a level of transparency in my sharing that he rarely saw when I was feeling upbeat and happy.

For other people, hearing the truth about someone's upset or anger may be too scary. Some people have never learned to receive feedback about themselves or about someone else's feelings. If you are such a person, you probably need more practice with Truth in Dating before you'll be ready to sustain a committed relationship. But you should begin learning right now to welcome feedback (Truth Skill #4). My book *Getting Real* goes into greater detail on this topic. In addition to the book, you'll need a practice partner and a sincere desire to develop yourself. A good way to find a practice partner is by attending an experiential workshop on communication or relationship skills — such as a Getting Real or Truth in Dating workshop.

As you know, a relationship must sooner or later develop enough strength to contain conflict and differences. You might be surprised to hear that the Romance Stage is actually the best time to begin talking about such differences — like the things you wish you could change about her or the doubts you have about your compatibility. The reason Stage 1 is a good time for such discussions is that this is a period when partners naturally want to accommodate each other. So why not take advantage of the fact that this person is probably more interested in pleasing you now than she ever will be again?

Sharing Your Visions

Romance is a time for talking together about what you each want out of life and partnership. It's for telling each other how you dream of being cared for and how you want to live. It is a time for discovering whether what you want in life is in alignment with what the other wants.

Sometimes partners begin to fantasize about sharing a future together. These "future fantasies" are not plans, and they are not commitments. They are fantasies. But just because they are not yet real doesn't mean they are useless. Fantasizing about a future together is one way partners at this stage can discover whether they have similar enough visions about life, love, and commitment. So the Romance Stage is the time to talk about your visions and values and to perhaps arrive at a shared vision of what you might create together.

> Many people assume that telling the truth will destroy their romantic feelings. This is not necessarily the case. But for many, if not most new relationships, this is probably what should happen anyway.

Bonding

The other developmental task of this stage is bonding. Bonding occurs between infants and mothers during the first few weeks of life. A strong early bonding experience makes for greater emotional and physical resilience in later years. A pair bond between partners has a similar value. It gives your relationship a firm enough foundation so you can better handle your inevitable later conflicts and upsets.

A number of factors contribute to a strong pair bond:

1. Spending time together, especially unstructured time, doing something that brings you pleasure.
2. Speaking honestly about vulnerable, intimate feelings and thoughts.
3. Going through a crisis together. The crisis could be dealing with a major adversity together, such as a dying parent or a sick child; or it could merely be successfully handling a difficult self-disclosure — like telling your partner something he or she does that turns you off.

Connecting with Romantic Feelings

To help you connect with a sense of romance, recall what first attracted you to the person you are dating. Take a few minutes to remember all your positive impressions and feelings, including your excitement about any visions or future fantasies you may have had. Now make this a topic of conversation between you within a few days. It can help to rekindle some of those feelings!

As you recall these feelings, you might notice that some of the attributes that first attracted you have now changed. This fact could lead to disappointment if you focus only on what has been lost. So see if you can think of something that you have gained alongside what has been lost. This helps you recognize that change has two sides: when one thing is lost, this makes room for something new to take its place. For example, when Maureen did this exercise, she noticed that she no longer cancelled plans with her girlfriends whenever Terrance called on short notice to spend an evening with her. Did this mean she loved him less? Had she lost some of her feelings for him? Not at all — she realized this change was a sign that she felt more trusting and secure. She trusted that if she didn't go out with him, he would be okay. She did not need to spend time with him just to make sure he did not go out with another woman that night. She was happy to see this about herself.

Stage 2: Power Struggle

Many people are shocked when they discover that their partner has habits or qualities that did not come to light at first — oftentimes in spite of the fact that there was a mutual commitment to honesty. What they do not realize is that once a strong trust bond is established in a relationship, partners tend to feel safe enough to reveal their darker or more hidden aspects. So if things have changed for the worse, it may not be because you partner was deceptive. It's more likely due to the fact that once a romantic bonding occurs, your partner feels safe and secure enough to let it all hang out. This leads to Stage 2, Power Struggle.

During the Romance Stage, Curt and Vicki seemed to be perfectly matched sexually. They both had similar sexual appetites, and Vicki loved everything Curt did during lovemaking. She would get turned on at his slightest touch. So why, after only a year, is their sex life almost nonexistent? Whenever Curt approaches her, she seems cold and unavailable. And when they do make love on occasion, why does she now complain that he's not "present" enough?

If anything like this has ever happened to you, remember that relationships are characterized by what I call the "tip of the iceberg" phenomenon. When you first meet someone, you'll perhaps get to see about 15 percent of the whole person, the tip of the iceberg. You cannot know this person all at once. Then, if you stay together, you'll see more and more of what was always there. You'll eventually get to see more of what's hiding under the deep, dark waters — the other 85 percent that can only be revealed over time.

The power struggle stage is the stage where formerly hidden differences in wants, needs, and expectations begin to surface — not necessarily because someone was being deceitful, but more likely because this is how relationships unfold. Even a commitment to Truth in Dating cannot prevent the occurrence of a few unwanted surprises.

In Vicki's case, as she came to trust that Curt loved her, she was able to get more deeply in touch with dependency needs that had been with her since childhood — needs that she had never been conscious of before. But now, feeling the safety of her bond with Curt, she began to open up to deeper layers of her subconscious where she discovered old buried pain from a childhood in which her dad had not been there for her. The existence of this unprocessed pain created in her a hypersensitivity to anything that Curt might do that felt similar to how her dad was with her. This causes her to be vigilant about Curt's "lack of presence" in lovemaking, and he can't seem to do anything right.

Truth in Dating can help you prevent much uneccessary struggle by helping you make your unconscious feelings conscious more quickly and easily.

Power Struggles like this cannot be avoided, since everyone alive has unconscious needs and impulses that only come to light little by little over time. But Truth in Dating can help you prevent much unnecessary struggle by helping you make your unconscious feelings conscious more quickly and easily. It speeds up the process of uncovering differences and potential sources of conflict. Truth in Dating makes a constructive game out of digging for hidden, unprocessed emotions. This helps you view the process as something you're in charge of rather than something that takes you by surprise.

Stage 3: Stability

This is the stage where you learn to take responsibility for your own "stuff" rather than trying to get your partner to change so you'll feel better.

As we follow Vicki and Curt into this stage, we find Vicki growing more open to the notion that her struggle with Curt parallels her internal struggle between two aspects of herself — in this case, the needy little girl part and the aloof, too busy parent part. She wants Curt to be more present to her, but what she really needs is to learn to be more present to herself. Because of the type of parenting she got, Vicki never learned to listen to her own needs. It's as if inside of her is a little girl who wants attention and a dad who finds these needs a nuisance. These two internal aspects are in opposition with each other, just as she and Curt are frequently at odds with each other.

The outer struggle mirrors the inner struggle. This means that if your partner's behavior triggers intense anger or hurt, this probably indicates an area where you have unresolved emotional baggage. Truth in Dating makes it normal and legitimate to have triggers or buttons, so there's less shame about revealing them.

Vicki has a tendency to ignore or neglect her own needs — just as her dad ignored her. She also has unresolved anger about her father's neglect, which comes out as anger and blame toward Curt. But once she understands that Curt is only a stand-in for the neglectful part of herself, she can take back the power to heal herself rather than waiting for Curt to treat her better.

> Truth in Dating makes it normal and legitimate to have triggers or buttons, so there's less shame about revealing them.

Using Truth Skill #6, Taking Back Projections, can be very helpful here. Understanding and working with projections is the key developmental task of this stage. Instead of projecting responsibility for "being present" onto Curt, Vicki learns to be present to herself. As part of this process, she learns how to ask for Curt's help at times instead of expecting him to know what she needs and overreacting when he doesn't guess correctly. By asking for what she wants, she is practicing another of the ten truth skills — Truth Skill #5, Asserting What You Want and Don't Want.

Stability is the toughest stage to master. For most people, having a partner provides a ready scapegoat. It's so easy to blame someone else for your pain — all he'd have to do is change one little thing and then you'd feel better! When you let go of blaming your partner, learn to "own" your projections, and take responsibility for your own emotional triggers, then you are solidly in the Stability Stage, and looking forward to Commitment.

Stage 4: Commitment

If you succeed in mastering the lessons of the Stability Stage, the rewards are great. Now, if any of your childhood fears get triggered, and they still will, you can use the occasion to deepen your self-knowledge and self-care instead of thinking you or your partner did something wrong. Practicing Truth in Dating will help you accept whatever is, without judgment or blame, rather than needing things to be the way you think they should be. The ability to accept and deal with things as they are is a prerequisite for commitment.

In the Commitment Stage you can enjoy a genuine sense of safety because there are fewer conditions on your safety. In other words, instead of "I can only feel safe if Curt pays a particular type of attention to me," Vicki learns that her safety is not dependent upon having things go her way. If things don't go her way, she either accepts what is and lets it be, or she looks to change something about her way of responding to the situation. She doesn't demand that Curt rescue her from her own reactions.

Commitment is the stage in which partners learn how to take charge of the things that are within their control and let go of the rest. This gives them the ability to act consistently and reliably on their plans and agreements. Agreements made before this stage are often broken because partners simply do not know themselves well enough. They still have too many skeletons in the closet of their subconscious minds. By this stage most of your hidden stuff has come under scrutiny via numerous episodes of taking back projections. Now that you're being more responsible and less victim-like, your efforts will have more payoff. You can decide to do something and reliably follow through. This further deepens your trust in yourself, your partner, and the relationship.

In this stage you can trust the agreement to spend the future together — "till death do us part," until you mutually agree to end it, or until a certain time has passed where you will reevaluate things. You may decide to "do The Couple's Journey" together, rather than keeping all your options open.

Practicing Truth in Dating at this stage is less about uncovering past wounds and more about creating a future in line with your vision. Once you learn to trust that you can make your visions happen, you naturally want to keep doing this more and more.

Another feature of the Commitment Stage is the increased feeling of unity and interdependence with your partner. You become a "we," where you both naturally consider how your actions will affect your partner. Such thoughtfulness comes not from any sense of obligation, but from a deep connection with and empathy for the other. But you need to go through the other stages together before you can arrive at this sort of commitment. Now your promises to each other are trustworthy. They were not before because you had not yet mastered the basic life task of taking responsibility for your own reactions (the task of the Stability Stage). Until you pass beyond Stability, you are still secretly (or not so secretly) looking to be "taken care of," as in "I want you to stop flirting with other women because it makes me feel insecure." Practicing Truth in Dating will help you get to grown-up love more quickly because it supports you in treating yourself like a grown-up.

Agreements made before this stage are often broken because partners simply do not know themselves well enough.

Many people ask why commitment is the fourth stage in a relationship. Doesn't it take commitment to even get us started on the journey? The answer is yes, it does take a kind of commitment, but the ability to make agreements together that are really trustworthy comes only after your relationship has weathered a number of power struggles and you have uncovered each other's hidden dark sides. Only then do you know yourselves and the relationship well enough to make really trustworthy commitments.

Stage 5: Cocreation

Once two people are aligned in their oneness and feel secure about their ability to make and keep agreements without coming from a sense of obligation, they can create things together with a real sense of partnership — blending both individuals' talents to yield something that neither could do as well alone. They might create simple things like nice dinner parties for their friends. They might coauthor articles or coteach classes. Or they might use their bond to support each partner's individual self-expression in the world. Cocreation is where you reap the rewards of the work you have done in the other four stages, and where you give back to the world from what life has taught you.

It is in this stage that partners connect with their deeper sense of purpose for being together. One cocreative couple, Maddy and Milt, recognized that they had come together to create something of value to themselves and the world.

During the first five years of their relationship, neither of them had been conscious of this. "We fell in love and married for all the usual reasons — sexual attraction, promise of a comfortable lifestyle with a compatible mate, the wish to have children, all of that.

"What we didn't understand until later was that these goals were only the beginning of our reason for being together. When little Milton Jr. entered school, and we decided not to have more children, we began to search together for 'what's next?' There must be more to life than kids, jobs, and sex!

"So we began to look inside ourselves for what wanted to be expressed and to look around us to see what this world might possibly need from us.

"Because we were both interested in keeping abreast of all the new developments in holistic health and healing, and because we and many of our friends had done a lot of writing in this field, we decided to start a newsletter that would focus on new developments in this area.

"Our main worry was not whether we would succeed and make a profit but rather, what would this new work interest cost our relationship?

What sacrifices would we need to make in order to do this project?" This worry points to the main pitfall of the Cocreation Stage — the possibility that so much energy might go into the work project that there might not be much energy left for the tender, nurturing, or sexual aspects of the relationship. In Maddy and Milt's case, they were able to balance love and work pretty well, but this is an issue that needs constant attention in cocreative couples.

The task of the Cocreation Stage is to integrate each person's creativity into a cooperative project in a way that serves the individuals, the couple, and the world.

In the Cocreation Stage partners experience the unity of love for self and love for others. As Maddy told me, partners realize as the journey progresses that "as I know and accept myself more, I become more accepting toward Milt. I discover that there is really no contradiction between self-love and love for others. I think I learned about how to love and accept Milt through coming to love myself, and I'm deepening my love for humanity by coming to know and love Milt." Thus, as the journey progresses each individual's sense of self expands, leading ultimately to a sense of self that is not separate from one's partner or from one's fellow humans.

> When your entire goal is to become more conscious of what has been unconscious, as is the goal of Truth in Dating, you no longer groan when more of that proverbial iceberg is revealed.

It also seems that partners can deepen their experience of love for each other by participating together in a shared creative venture beyond the intimate pair. Differences that once caused stress are now found to be useful — now that partners have learned to use these differences in the service of cocreativity.

This map of The Couple's Journey can help you learn to become more comfortable with change. It can help you avoid needless disappointment over the fact that "you're not the person I first fell in love with." Still, even if you know about the five stages, some disappointment is probably inevitable.

Practicing Truth in Dating will help you flow with and through these changes more easily and quickly. When your entire goal is to become more conscious of what has been unconscious, as is the goal of Truth in Dating, you no longer groan when more of that proverbial iceberg is revealed. You learn to celebrate each upset and each disappointment because with each one of these things, you get to see and accept more of what is.

Chapter Summary

- If a relationship lasts more than a year, it will go through a number of predictable stages, eventually arriving at Cocreation if it endures and matures for a number of years.
- Many people assume that telling the truth will destroy romantic feelings. If this occurs, the relationship should probably end anyway.
- Telling the truth is a turn-on for many people because it helps them show up more transparent and vulnerable.
- Truth in Dating helps you move through the Power Struggle and Stability Stages more quickly so you can sooner reap the rewards of Commitment and Cocreation.

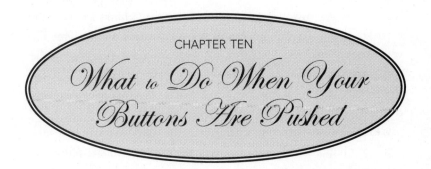

CHAPTER TEN

What to Do When Your Buttons Are Pushed

The truth can hurt, but if pain comes up,
it's pain that was already there.

Dating brings up a variety of fears — fear of rejection, fear of not being good enough, fear of being hurt, fear of hurting the other's feelings, fear of saying or doing the wrong thing, and fear of not being respected. Whatever your favorite fear may be, it will get triggered sooner or later if you are meeting people for the purpose of dating or mating.

Becoming familiar with your buttons is of critical importance in preparing yourself for intimacy and love. We learned a little about this in chapter 3 in the section "Noticing vs. Interpreting."

A button is a metaphor for an unconscious fear that is very close to the surface. It's like a hypersensitive spot on the ego — just waiting to be triggered. When someone does or says something that triggers one of our fears, we go on automatic, and prerecorded self-talk (like a familiar "tape") starts to play.

Here are some examples. Imagine you and your date are cooking a meal together, and your date says, "Why do you have the heat up so high?" The tape in your mind says, "He [or she] "thinks I don't know what I'm doing" (revealing a fear of being criticized). Or, imagine that you have just told your date that you want to take a vacation together and she replies, "Oh, I don't think this is a good time for that." The tape that might play in your mind says, "She doesn't like me enough to spend time with me" (indicating a fear of being rejected).

Have you ever noticed yourself reacting this way? Most of us have more than a few buttons, and most of us don't like it when someone pushes one of them. We don't like it so much, in fact, that we often feel fearful or anxious just knowing that the possibility exists. That's why so many people are fearful or reserved in social situations.

When someone does or says something that pushes one of our buttons, we go on automatic, and prerecorded self-talk (like a familiar "tape") starts to play.

As you practice Truth in Dating, you'll become more conscious of the fears that run your life, and as a result, they'll have less power over you.

Feeling an Attraction Can Push Your Buttons

Heather thought she was pretty confident when it came to meeting men. She felt good about herself and knew that most men found her attractive. One night at a girlfriend's birthday party she met Will, and all of a sudden she didn't feel like her usual confident self anymore. Will's looks and sense of humor reminded her of her high school sweetheart, whom she had broken up with when he went off to college — something she had always regretted. Meeting Will felt like a second chance to her, and from the butterflies in her stomach, she could tell that she was putting a lot of importance on this meeting. She wasn't accustomed to feeling so nervous, and at first she was irritated with herself. He didn't have to say or do anything to threaten her composure. An old fear was being restimulated just being in his presence.

Anytime you find yourself ill at ease, it means a fear has been triggered, and you are not fully present. Heather's "I'm not good enough" fear has been unconscious most of her life, but now it is being brought to the surface. Of course this fear isn't anything real — it's just mind chatter. But most people react to their fears as if they were substantial. When you understand how buttons work, you can learn to notice when an old tape is playing, and this will bring you back to presence.

Getting to Know Your Buttons

You can only be as honest as you are self-aware. We are out of touch with ourselves (and with reality) when we are under the influence of one of our unconscious fears. Practicing Truth in Dating will undoubtedly bring up old fears. This is why truth-telling is seen as dangerous. But it isn't dangerous. It's only dangerous if you consider learning and growth dangerous. Getting your buttons pushed is a normal part of any relationship.

What can you do to become more conscious and responsible around the issue of buttons? First, you can let go of your pride and admit that you do get triggered or overreact sometimes. Then you can take inventory of what your particular fears are. Do you react when you think someone is trying to control you? If so, the "fear of being controlled" is one of your buttons. Are you especially sensitive to hurting others' feelings? If this is the case, you may have a button about "not being seen as a good person." You have an investment in being seen as good — perhaps due to an early experience where someone was mean to you or gave you the idea that you were bad. Are you vigilant about watching for signs that someone doesn't like or value you? Then maybe you have a fear of being rejected, or a fear of being insignificant or worthless.

Many people suffered some type of painful loss early in life, something that felt like abandonment. These people work hard to bind others to them so as to ward off any possibility of future abandonment. Their button is the fear of abandonment. Of course you can have more than one core fear. Most people have several.

Once you are familiar with your buttons and have named them, the next step is being able to tell someone else about your buttons. This is similar to the exercise used in Alcoholics Anonymous, whereby speakers identify themselves with, "My name is _____, and I'm an alcoholic." This helps you get over the tendency to hide your weaknesses or maintain a false self-image. So you might confess to someone, "I want you to know me better, so I want to let you know that I tend to overreact when I think I'm being controlled" (or criticized, or ignored, or rejected, et cetera). Speaking publicly about things you once considered shameful helps you get over the shame.

When you do this, most people won't judge you as harshly as you judge yourself. They will probably feel closer to you for having disclosed something tender and intimate. But remember, Truth in Dating is not about getting other people to like you. It is a practice to help you become more real, more free from fear of how others react to you, and thereby more loving. In the process you usually become more loveable as well, but that's not the point. By talking openly about your fears you are overcoming any shame you might have that you (like everyone else!) have unconscious fear reactions.

> Speaking publicly about things you once considered shameful helps you get over the shame.

Putting Your New Awareness into Practice

Now comes the big question: What do you do when one of your buttons actually gets pushed? Being able to identify and own up to your buttons is one thing, but staying conscious when you are triggered is another matter. Knowing what situations tend to trigger you is an important first step. This helps you relax about the whole idea that you do "go unconscious" sometimes. It also helps you to accept responsibility for your reactions rather than assuming that if someone triggered you, they shouldn't have done it. Armed with this understanding, now when you do get a button pushed and the familiar "tape" starts playing, you'll probably be able to notice what's happening. At first maybe you'll be successful in noticing this one out of every ten times. Then with more practice, it'll progress to one in nine times, and so on.

Pitfalls to Watch For

Many people understand the concept of unconscious reactions, but they still think it's the other's responsibility when they get upset. Brent told Ardis he was prone to jealousy. So when she spent time talking to Manuel at their office Christmas party, he was furious. Brent had expected that speaking about this and making himself so vulnerable should have made Ardis more sensitive to his needs — so she wouldn't do anything to make him jealous. Now that she was aware of his sensitivities, he felt it was her responsibility not to trigger him.

If you find yourself with someone who thinks like this, give him this book, and then ask him what he thinks of the idea that everyone has buttons, and when your button gets pushed, it signals some unfinished business that's keeping you from being present. For example, if your jealousy button gets pushed, like Brent's did, it's because there's something you still need to learn about how to deal with the threat of loss. It's your own responsibility, not your partner's.

What Else Can You Do?

When someone has just triggered you and you are able to notice it at the time, I suggest that you say something like, "I notice I'm getting my button pushed," or "I think I'm having a reaction to what you just said," or "I'm having a fear come up that you don't like me" (or "that you don't think I'm worth paying attention to," or "that you're judging me," et cetera). Name it as your fear without implying that the other did something wrong. Then tell the person that you need some time to get present again. You might disclose that you're in a fear state about some painful memory in your past that is being restimulated. Don't try to give a thorough explanation. Just take some time out and do something to comfort or soothe yourself. You could, for example, talk to yourself in a reassuring way, saying something like, "This is good that you recognized you're getting triggered. Good job! Yeah, it's sad that that happened to you when you were small and helpless. Now just breathe and feel your feelings and know that I am here to support you." When you get good at supporting yourself in this way, you won't need to control how others relate to you. You'll be better able to respect each person's right to be just as he is. And this, too, will win you points with others. You're more loveable when you're not trying to control how others love you.

Giving Yourself a Second Chance

Sometimes you will not realize that you have "gone unconscious" until a few hours or days later. If this happens, it's a chance to use Truth Skill #7, Revising an Earlier Statement. I recently got triggered when my boyfriend mentioned how he wanted to make amends with an ex-girlfriend. Fearing he was going to leave me and get back with her, I criticized him rather than telling him that my fear of abandonment had been triggered. Later that night I realized this, so I called him the next day to let him know that I wanted to revise what I'd said. I told him that if I'd been more present at the time, I would not have criticized him, but instead would have told him I was feeling threatened, that my abandonment button was triggered. He accepted my revision — which gave him the opportunity to reassure me that my fears were unfounded.

Chapter Summary

- To practice Truth in Dating, it's important to be aware that there is the possibility of getting old fears restimulated at any time or any place.
- It's a good idea to do an inventory of your buttons.
- Once you are aware of your core fears and have some language for speaking about them, it will be easier to let others know when one of them gets triggered.
- It is very important to be able to say the words, "I notice I'm getting triggered."

CHAPTER ELEVEN

Deep Dating

Can You Love Your Partner's Shadow?

*If you hope to have a long-term relationship,
you'll need to be able to love your partner's shadow.
Truth in Dating offers a way to uncover people's darker,
hidden aspects earlier in the game.*

A question I hear frequently in my relationship seminars is, "How can I find out if this person is going to become obnoxious or controlling or worse once I get to know him or her? How can I be sure I really know this person's darker side?" The answer I often give, with tongue in cheek, is: "Marry the person!" Of course I'm being facetious, but there is that "tip of the iceberg" phenomenon mentioned in chapter 10. A person's darker side often does not come to light until the two of you have been through quite a bit together. In the beginning he was so deep and thoughtful. Now what looked like depth turns out to be depression. In the beginning she was really spunky and independent. Now these qualities look more like a disregard for his feelings.

In this chapter I'll show you how to speed things up so you can cover more relationship ground in less time, allowing you to get a preview of each other's shadow sides before going too far. I call this Deep Dating.

Deep Dating involves a mutual agreement to voluntarily and consciously talk about things that might trigger your fears. We do this so that we may help one another heal the old wounds that give rise to these fears. I recommend Deep Dating only if you have already done enough work on yourself to know what your buttons are, and only if you have learned how to stay conscious (at least some of the time) while you are being triggered.

After attending one of my seminars, Ruth and Roger decided to try Deep Dating. They thought they were pretty well prepared to take the bumps they might encounter on this path. She was already aware that she had a fear about being ignored, and she knew that when she thought she was being ignored, this triggered a deeper fear that she was unlove-able. Roger knew that he had a fear of being con-trolled, and that whenever he thought he was being con-trolled, this triggered his belief that he was incompetent or stupid. Armed with this self-knowledge they set out on their adventure to intentionally talk about topics and feelings designed to bring up their hidden fears.

> I recommend Deep Dating only if you have already done enough work on yourself to know what your buttons are.

As I relate Ruth and Roger's experiences, I will present exercises and activities that you can try in your dating relationships — if both partners agree that they want to push the envelope of their intimacy and get to know each other's darker sides.

Being Conscious about Ending It

One question that can bring up hidden fears is, "What if things don't work out between us?" Here's how Ruth and Roger dealt with this issue. Early in their dating relationship, Ruth told Roger that she had read the book *Getting Real* and wanted to try some of the things suggested there. Roger responded that he, too, was committed to telling the absolute truth. The first thing they did was to agree that if one or both of them decided they did not want to continue dating, they would not end the relationship without having an honest conversation about why. This deci-sion was arrived at easily, giving the pair a feeling of confidence and trust.

Getting Clear about Buttons

Just having that agreement in place helped Ruth feel valued. Since she was the one who had suggested Truth in Dating, she wondered if Roger was harboring any discomfort that he hadn't voiced. She mentioned her intuition that he might have a button about being told what to do, and asked Roger if he would read the section in *Getting Real* about automatic knee-jerk reactions (buttons). He shared that he knew about his fear of being controlled as well as a few of his other triggers, but he read the section on buttons anyway so they could have a common understanding of this important subject. After that he asked Ruth if she would talk about her own buttons.

If you want to try what Ruth and Roger did, try this paper and pencil exercise: Make copies of the following questionnaire for each of you; fill them out privately, and then discuss your answers.

1. In my previous significant relationships, I have been triggered when my partner...

   (List some specific things that prior partners have done that triggered you.)

2. Now, next to each item listed above, name the fear that was triggered.

   To illustrate how this might look, here's how Roger answered these two questions:

   BUTTON-PUSHING EVENT 1: Sandy said, "Let me handle it." FEAR THAT WAS TRIGGERED: I'm stupid.

   BUTTON-PUSHING EVENT 2: Sandy said, "Isn't that rice overdone?" FEAR THAT WAS TRIGGERED: I'm incompetent.

   BUTTON-PUSHING EVENT 3: Doris said, "Don't ever do that again!" FEAR THAT WAS TRIGGERED: I'm a disappointment.

   BUTTON-PUSHING EVENT 4: Doris said, "You don't get me, and you never will." FEAR THAT WAS TRIGGERED: I'm incompetent and I'm a disappointment.

BUTTON-PUSHING EVENT 5: Molly said, "When are you going
to fix that door?" FEAR THAT WAS TRIGGERED: I'm not capable.

3. If, at the time, I had felt safe enough or been aware
    enough to express my true feelings in each of the above
    instances, here's what I would have said:

    Here is how Roger responded to this item:

    1. I feel irritated hearing you say, "Let me handle it." I also
        feel small and ashamed.
    2. I imagine you're trying to tell me something with that
        question. I want you to say what you are feeling instead
        of asking me, "Isn't the rice overdone?"
    3. I feel a knot in my gut when you say that to me.
    4. I feel sad when you say that I don't get you. I'm thinking
        to myself that I must be a disappointment to you.
    5. I get angry when you ask when I'm going to fix the
        door. I get my button pushed that you're trying to con-
        trol me. It triggers my fear that you don't think I can
        handle this.

4. What hurtful, scary, or disappointing events occurred in
    your childhood that made you come away with the
    beliefs you list in question #2 above?

    *Here is how Roger responded about the first button he noted
    in #2:*

    When I was five, my dad was showing me how to help him put
    together a plastic playhouse he had gotten for me. I was strug-
    gling trying to get two of the parts to fit together, and all of a
    sudden, he grabbed them away from me and said something
    like, "Here, I can do it faster. Just let me do it." I felt extremely
    small and ashamed when he did that. I thought he was saying
    I was too stupid or inept to do it myself.

5. How have you overreacted to getting your buttons
    pushed? List a few specific things you have done or said

that weren't very conscious or appropriate — but at the time, that's how you reacted.

Here's one of Roger's examples:
When Molly said, "When are you going to fix that door?" I said, "Well, I was going to fix it today, but now you've made me so mad I think I need to wait till next weekend. You know I can't stand it when you push me like that."

6. How have you done something to spite another person or get back at them for pushing one of your buttons? List three or four examples.

Here's another of Roger's examples:
When I was married to Lois, she was talking one day about how great her dad was. I thought she was implying that I could never match that; so I started telling her how well my former lover Bonnie had taken care of me, how nurturing she was, how attentive. This was right after Lois had given birth to our second child. She wasn't giving me much attention, and I was pissed. And I was also pissed at her remark about her dad.

When Ruth and Roger shared their answers to this questionnaire, they got to see some of the ways that each had behaved unconsciously in the past. This also gave them the opportunity to see how defensively they had reacted. The ideal Deep Dating partner is someone who can admit her mistakes without blaming or making excuses. It's also great if she can admit to an occasional need to be right, to play it safe, or to appear more certain or in control than she really is.

> The ideal Deep Dating partner is someone who can admit her mistakes without blaming or making excuses.

If I Could Change You...

Most people have a mental picture of their ideal mate. Rarely does any actual person ever live up to this ideal picture. Here is an exercise in which you both get to reveal your ideal pictures — in spite of realizing you cannot make your partner over into that image. In this game, called If I Could Change You, each person takes a turn of about five to ten minutes completing the sentence, "If I could change you I would make you_____." Here are some of Ruth's responses:

If I could change you I would make you

- more self-confident
- work out at the gym three times a week
- feel happier about yourself
- pay more attention to me when I'm talking to you
- not stutter
- not have that little chewing mannerism that you do with your mouth
- never drink more than one alcoholic drink per day

It can be painful or scary to hear things your date would like to change about you if she could. Of course, this is not an exercise designed to make people change. It's designed to help you see how often you take things as critical or disapproving.

Most people feel sensitive about hearing some of these things, even though they know it is just a game. Notice what happens in your heart area when you hear your partner's answers. Does your heart shut down? Do you go numb? Do you get angry or agitated? Do you lose empathy and connection with the other because he or she has hurt you? Do you put up a psychic wall? Can you feel and vibrate with your feelings? Do you act out your feelings by being aggressive or blaming? Do you have to "do something" to get back to a sense of being in control?

Many people who have done this exercise report feeling relieved that the news wasn't as bad as they had feared. Others shut down their feelings and get numb. And others begin to build a case against the other person — perhaps a case about "why this relationship will never work." Try the exercise, and discuss your feelings and reactions with each other. Then, wait two or three days and discuss your reactions again. Sometimes it will take a few days for you both to realize how this exercise has affected you. Share especially any negative self-talk, and notice if this self-talk represents a familiar tape that your mind plays when you feel hurt, fearful, or angry.

Take turns telling each other all the things the other has done so far in the relationship that have created a sense of disconnection or distance.

Being honest about such things can be exciting or scary. Maybe this relationship will endure, and maybe it won't. But finding a Deep Dating practice partner is an opportunity of a lifetime. Don't quit until you learn the truth about how it really is with you and this other person.

I Feel Distant from You When...

Another excellent process for getting down beneath the surface is the exercise "I Feel Distant from You When..." In this exercise partners take turns telling each other all the things the other has done so far in the relationship that have created a sense of disconnection, distance, or wanting to be less close to that person. Partner A takes a turn, and then Partner B does the same, starting from the very first time they met.

Here are some of Ruth's answers:

- I felt less close to you when you talked about your trip to Bali with your ex-wife while you were giving me a massage.
- I felt disconnected from you when you said you'd been at Amy's house last Friday.
- I felt distant from you when you were talking about your feelings for Trina while we were cuddling.
- I felt disconnected from you when you said you'd forgotten

to get the bread from the health food store before our dinner party with the Simpsons.

When you read Ruth's responses, remember she has a button about
being ignored that triggers a core fear that she is not loveable. This exercise can uncover instances when you behaved unconsciously. It gives you
a chance to clear the air. And it reveals how often your unconscious fears
cause your heart to shut down, leading to a sense of disconnection from
the other.

After you have done this exercise on one or two occasions with ref-
erence to past incidents, then look at the possibility of doing this in the
moment when you notice your heart shutting down. Start by agreeing
to be more mindful of the sensations in your body. Make it your intent to
report any contractions you notice in your heart area. So, instead of sharing your list of incidents every week or two, you would speak about your
feelings as you notice them.

Whenever one partner mentions something like this, the other
acknowledges him for doing so, saying something simple like, "I hear
that," "Thank you," or "I appreciate you for telling me." Remember this
is an awareness practice that the two of you are engaged in. It is not an
attempt to change anyone's thinking or behavior.

Did You Feel Distant When I...?

After you have played the I Feel Distant from You When...game for a
while, it's time to probe more deeply into this topic. It's time for each of
you to reflect on incidents in your relationship when you imagine you
might have done something that caused a disconnect. Once you have
pinpointed two or three incidents, ask your partner, "Did you feel distant when I...?" For example: Did you feel distant when I forgot to get
the stamps you asked me to pick up? Did you feel distant when I got up
and left Sunday morning without telling you where I was going? Did
you feel distant when I farted in bed?

Take turns asking your partner this question, perhaps going back and forth a few times. Afterward, talk about how this felt to each of you and how you feel now.

Sharing Your Relationship and Sexual History

Frequently, a dating relationship will trigger comparisons and imagined similarities with past lovers or partners. This is a fertile area for getting one's buttons pushed, so let's use it consciously!

Set aside an hour during the early stages of dating to tell your partner how your past partners have pleased you, sexually and in other ways, being very specific — perhaps even demonstrating. While this conversation is happening, be aware of your bodily sensations, your feelings, and your self-talk, and report these as they come up.

I imagine that some of my readers may be thinking, "I was with you in this chapter until you suggested that! Why would I want to hear my partner extolling someone else's virtues?" The reasons are: (1) You can see if he or she is still carrying unfinished feelings from this relationship into the relationship with you — thus preventing him or her from being fully present with you; this is a part of the relationship shadow that many people do not want to look at; and (2) you can observe your own illusions, attachments, and addictions, such as your attachment to the illusion that you are his or her one and only true love, the attachment to being sexually desirable; the addiction to winning or being the best.

Frequently, a dating relationship will trigger comparisons and imagined similarities with past lovers or partners. This is a fertile area for getting one's buttons pushed, so let's use it consciously!

Remember I am not suggesting that you fall into sharing such past history unconsciously or for spite. The practice of Deep Dating suggests that you create safe or sacred space for sharing such information, and then that you leave ample time for sharing what this triggered for each of you in a mindful, nonblaming atmosphere. Sharing this kind of information can be scary, and it can cause hurt feelings. That is why it is very important that you approach an exercise like this with love and compassion. When you say something that hurts your partner's feelings, allow your own heart to hurt as well. Such a shared experience can increase the strength of your bond, even as it also hurts. Shared pain can be a bonding experience; but it is a healthy bonding experience only if your intent is to be transparent and to reveal yourself as a way of becoming more conscious. If your intent is to feel powerful by seeing how you can hurt your partner, then this would not be a healthy bonding experience.

Shared Journaling

Many people have discovered the value of keeping a personal journal where they write or draw their feelings, thoughts, plans, and visions. This type of personal self-reflection is an invaluable aid to self-discovery and a wonderful way to deepen your relationship with yourself. There is no one right way to do journaling. Some people write poetry. Some write prose. Some draw or scribble their entries. Others make lists. Often, after I have used journaling to ventilate painful feelings, I notice my feelings changing. I seem to have a stronger witness consciousness after writing things out. I also find I am more peaceful and centered.

> When you say something that hurts your partner's feelings, allow your own heart to hurt as well. Such a shared experience can increase the strength of your bond.

A journal can be an adjunct to Deep Dating when two people agree to let each other read their personal entries. One of you can write and share what you have written, or you both can. Usually it's best if both of you share your journal entries.

After dating for two months, Luanne and Terrence decided to keep journals, which they would share with each other about once a week. They vowed to write their feelings without censoring, even though each knew the other would be reading what he or she wrote. This worked fairly well until they had a misunderstanding that they could not resolve. It had to do with a social situation in which Luanne said something that Terrence took offense at. After this, each of their journal entries took on the appearance of "building a case for my own point of view." In her journal Luanne spent pages explaining and justifying why she had said what she said and how she thought Terrence had misunderstood her. Likewise, Terrence's journal was full of interpretations about Luanne's true motives — how she was "obviously angry at me for wanting to leave the party early." Instead of journaling about their feelings, now they were using the journals to convince, to defend, and to elicit sympathy and understanding. Needless to say, reading each other's entries did little to foster mutual understanding. If they had each stayed on their own side of the net and simply expressed their feelings, as opposed to trying to convince each other, they probably could have reached understanding more quickly.

The example of Luanne and Terrence shows that journaling together can have its pitfalls. However, even in cases like this, where the attempt to control overshadows the intent to relate, at least communication patterns are out in the open where they can be seen by both parties. This can help people own up to their patterns more readily — since it's all there in black and white.

I have used shared journaling successfully in a number of new relationships, and I have never found myself using it to elicit sympathy or to manipulate or control how my partner sees me. Instead, I have welcomed the fact that another pair of eyes will witness what I am saying — which helps me be more aware and present to myself as I write. In one dating relationship, my partner and I used to tape record our feelings about each other and then give each other the tapes to listen to. Our relationship only lasted about five months, but it was a wonderful way to go very deep, very fast. By doing so we uncovered some irreconcilable differences, and we moved on quickly to being just friends. To this day when I see this man at parties, we acknowledge a profound respect and fondness for one another. He says to friends about our relationship, "I got to know Susan more deeply in five months than I knew my former wife in twenty years."

Keeping a Relationship Journal

A variation on the shared journal theme is the option of buying one book that both people write in. This works best if you each make your entries after a significant event has occurred — a fight, a romantic or sexual experience, or some other high or low point. It can also be used to record each of your positions on an issue about which you disagree — and to do so consciously, without trying to prove a point.

Monique and Morey were arguing about the sexual boundaries of their relationship. She wanted to have his undivided attention at parties, and she didn't want him to flirt with other women in her presence. He wanted to feel free to flirt and to express his attractions with other women whenever he felt them — without doing anything beyond talking about these attractions. They used the relationship journal to clarify their feelings about a certain incident that caused pain for Monique. She wrote about how she experienced pain when he spent over an hour talking to one very attractive woman at a recent party. He wrote about how hard it was for him to give himself permission to do this, knowing that Monique would be hurt and angry. When they read each other's entries, they felt a little softer toward one another. This paved the way for a conversation where they were able to start by acknowledging each other's position. They each felt that getting their feelings out in writing helped them develop the ability to accept each other's feelings. Seeing both positions side by side in writing helped them accept their differences.

Giving the Other a Reading

Most people form impressions about their dates that their dates never hear about. A fun, lighthearted way to share these impressions is to offer to give each other a "reading." To do this, agree that you'd like to give and receive such a reading, acknowledging that the reading is based more on intuition or global impressions than on anything concrete. Agree also that you are not trying to be right in your reading but rather are attempting to reveal your secret thoughts — in order to shine a light on these so they do not eventually get blown up into something serious.

To offer such a reading, complete the following sentence over and over until you have run out of things to say: "I see you as someone who . . ." For example: "I see you as someone who loves to be needed. I see you as someone who can't stand conflict. I see you as someone who will be financially wealthy some day. I see you as someone who is very loyal in your relationships."

> Most people form impressions about their dates that their dates never hear about. A fun, lighthearted way to share these impressions is to offer to give each other a "reading."

Agree to listen to your partner's reading without defending yourself. (The reading is as much about her as it is about you.) And there's no need to confirm or deny the impressions, but if you want to, that's okay. In doing a reading for your partner, just say whatever comes into your mind without censoring. After you have each taken a turn, you may discuss your feelings and thoughts about the exercise.

Predicting Your Future

Related to the "reading" exercise is another one that also involves the intuition — predicting your future together. To do this one, take turns making two sorts of predictions: (1) what you see as the highest potential for this relationship; and (2) what you imagine may be your areas of difficulty together.

Agree beforehand to take this information as a possibility but not as reality. Use your intuition, and see what you come up with. Notice and share how you both feel about each prediction. Leave time at the end for discussing what this brings up for each of you.

Having Fun with Your Shadow

One final idea for dredging up shadow material is to play either the Getting Real Card Game, using mostly the Get Present deck and the Get Down deck, or to play the Truth in Dating Card Game, using the Deep Dating deck. Appendix A includes a brief description and ordering information about both games.

The Deep Dating deck is specifically designed to bring up topics for discussion that many people would otherwise avoid. As stated in the game instructions, "These questions are designed to make you uncomfortable." Some of my favorite potentially button-pushing questions from this deck are:

- What have you said to others about me that you have not told me?
- Something I want from you that I'm afraid you cannot give me is_____.
- What lies have you been tempted to tell me?
- Recalling the last time we made love, what did you like best and least?
- If you could change one thing about me, what would it be?

Obviously these questions are for partners who have known each other awhile and who have a real commitment to using their relationship as an awareness practice. Most game questions are applicable for both early and later stages of a relationship.

I recently played the Getting Real game after dinner on a first date with someone I had met a week earlier. After playing for about twenty minutes, I drew a card that said, "What question are you having right now about your relationship to this other person?" My answer was, "Do I want to see you again?" Then he drew a card that said, "What is the inner conversation or self-talk you're having right now?" His answer was,

"I'm wondering if she wants to see me again. I need to know where I stand." At that point, we decided to put aside the game and talk about the question of continuing to see each other. It was an issue that was on both our minds, but without the card game to get us into the topic, we could have avoided it for a while. We felt good about being able to talk about this in a caring way. It was a particularly sensitive topic because he wanted to continue dating, and I did not.

I think we were able to be more transparent and open with each other because of the game. It gave us permission to speak frankly, and it created an atmosphere for compassionate risk-taking. Because we were truthful and present to one another, we both went away from the conversation feeling respect for ourselves and each other and for how we handled the situation. We never dated after that, but we have run into each other at social events, and we always share a big hug and warm feelings. We went through a difficult situation together, and did it consciously. I believe that was a bonding experience for us. Telling the truth does not necessarily lead to getting someone to love you, but I hope you can see that it does help you feel more self-respecting and more open to genuine connection.

> Telling the truth does not necessarily lead to getting someone to love you, but it does help you feel more self-respecting and more open to genuine connection.

Chapter Summary

- If you both feel emotionally strong enough, there are activities you can do together that are designed to speed you along in your personal healing and reveal in advance the difficulties that may lie ahead in your relationship.
- Consciously going into potentially button-pushing situations

allows you to get good at staying present even if a fear reaction is getting triggered.
- Shared journaling, sharing your relationship and sexual histories, and playing the Truth in Dating Card Game are some of the many methods available for playing the edge together.

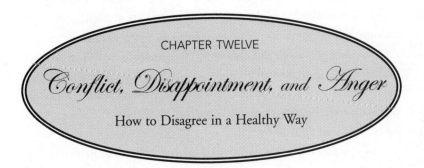

CHAPTER TWELVE

Conflict, Disappointment, and Anger

How to Disagree in a Healthy Way

*If you have no conflicts or disagreements in your life,
you may be playing it too safe.*

In the dating world there are certain norms or expected "rules of engagement." One of these rules is that you are expected to be nice. Being nice is okay except when it's not honest — like when your feelings just got hurt because he was an hour late or when she keeps interrupting you in mid-sentence. Truth in Dating encourages breaking the niceness rule when your date has done something that triggers pain or anger. This does not mean that you should attack or hurt the other person — or blame him for your feelings. It means you should not avoid revealing your feelings — as always, in the interest of transparency.

Perhaps the main reason that anger is against the dating rules is the fear that it will scare the other person off: What if I tell him what I really feel and he judges me for it? What if I let her know I don't like something she's doing and she gets hurt feelings and withdraws or thinks I'm insensitive? Yes, these things do occur sometimes. If you fear that you cannot handle these sorts of consequences, this means you don't trust yourself very much. Your confidence is low and your self-esteem is fragile. Perhaps it's time to give Truth in Dating a chance — as a way to build self-confidence and your ability to handle the challenges of a real relationship.

But even if you do not choose to take on Truth in Dating as your practice, you can still get inwardly stronger and prepare yourself for more honest relating by practicing some of the exercises in this book. Just start with the ones that only scare you a little. Then gradually work up to the more difficult ones.

We avoid conflict because we don't trust ourselves in the face of uncertain, uncontrollable consequences — situations where we might lose something that we imagine we need for our well-being: approval, agreement, sex, affection, or having things go our way. Practicing Truth in Dating will teach you that you do not really need these things for your well-being, but you cannot discover this until you risk losing them and survive.

Three Purposes of Anger

There are three main reasons why people need to know how to express anger: (1) to mark your boundaries — "I told you I need some time to collect myself before I talk to you, and I mean it. I'm angry at you for saying, 'It's never a good time!'" (2) to go after what you want — "I'm angry at you for not looking at me. I request that you put that book down and look at me while I'm talking," and (3) to express and release pain or frustration (to clear the air) — "I'm angry at you for telling me that I have a lousy bedside manner."

Anger is not pretty, and fighting is often scary in new relationships. Yet anger will come up, and you may find it necessary to fight for what you want at times. The reason people fear disagreement is that most people feel cut off emotionally from the other when they are angry or in conflict. This "emotional disconnect" triggers fears of abandonment or punishment. But you can learn how to feel anger and still stay connected to the other person. This is an important aspect of healthy relating — the ability to disagree while keeping your heart open. To learn to stay

open in the face of anger, first you need to believe that this is possible
and to value doing so. Then, you need to be in a situation where you
consciously practice "clearing the air." This will help you learn how to
stay open when you are angry or when someone feels anger toward you.
My book *Getting Real* describes several processes for clearing anger in
detail.

My Story

My life story has been one of a long journey from self-protectiveness
to openness. As a child I feared my dad's anger, so I learned a couple of
really reliable control patterns to keep myself feeling safe and in control.
One was to judge him for being so volatile. The other was to detach
from the adults and create a peer culture based on fun, play, and creative
self-expression. Both of these strategies are examples of how people tend
to disconnect or withdraw in the face of anger. These control patterns
followed me into my adult relationships, so that whenever a man would
get angry at me, I knew how to feel safe and in control. I'd judge him
for it! Over time, I noticed that I kept attracting men who were easily
provoked to anger, just like my dad. (What a surprise!) Being in the business of self-transformation, I had to look at the fact that perhaps there
was something I needed to learn
about anger. Since doing this, I
have transformed my rela-
tionship to anger. I have
learned that it really is possible to receive another's
anger, and perhaps to feel fearful or hurt, without shutting down
my heart.

> The reason people fear
> disagreement is that most people
> feel cut off emotionally from the other
> when they are angry or in conflict. This
> "emotional disconnect" triggers fears
> of abandonment or punishment.

I accomplished this by setting aside time every day for almost a year
where my former boyfriend and I would exchange resentments and
appreciations. He would take a turn naming all the specific things I had
done that day that he had a negative reaction to, followed by all the

things he felt positively about. Then I would take a turn doing this. Then we'd check in to see if we felt complete. If not, we'd repeat the things that seemed to be still bothering us until we felt relaxed and connected. Often, so much energy would get released that we wound up laughing together. As I did this practice during that year, I continued to feel more and more safe in the presence of angry feelings. I learned that anger is just another feeling, and that if you can own your anger and express it responsibly, the energy formerly held in anger may be transformed.

> You can learn how to feel anger and still stay connected to the other person. This is an important aspect of healthy relating — the ability to disagree while keeping your heart open.

How to Fight Right

Given the human tendency to avoid what we're not good at, how do we get good at dealing with conflict, anger, and differences? The answer of course is practice. In the following, we'll look at another process for resolving disagreements and examples of how an actual dating pair used this process to deal with a conflict they were having.

This process requires that both people get an approximately equal time to speak about their own point of view, even if only one partner has a "beef." They take turns expressing (1) their feelings; (2) what the other did that triggered these feelings; and (3) their wants or needs. The other partner listens. Then, once both feel heard, they brainstorm ideas for what they can do to help both people feel more satisfied.

Nora and Todd have been dating for only six weeks, but they are both beginning to notice themselves getting defensive and irritable with each other. Todd finally realizes that he has a "beef," a grievance that needs airing. In *Getting Real* he learned about active listening as a tool for Holding Differences, Truth Skill #8 (see also chapters 3 and 6). Remember, active listening is where you take turns listening to each other, and repeating back what you have heard. Here is how Nora and Todd used active listening to have a healthy fight.

TODD: I want to clear something with you. I think I'd like to try those fair fighting rules in Susan Campbell's book.

NORA: Okay. Now?

TODD: I'd like to do it now... or at least sometime tonight.

NORA: Now's fine.

TODD: Okay, I'll start. My heart is beating fast, and I can feel the heat of anger in my face. But before we get into it, we're supposed to say what buttons might get pushed. I guess I'll have to tell you what it's about first.

NORA: Yeah. But I can already sense some fluttery feelings... like fear. I guess I'm afraid I did something wrong. I guess it's my fear of doing something wrong or of being told how I should do something. That's a button. That's one of them.

TODD: Yeah. Me too. I have that one too. Well, it's about last Saturday on the boat when you said, "Why don't we just drop the sails and relax for a while?"

NORA: What? I don't remember that. What did I say?

TODD: It was when you said, "I'm tired of being up here on deck." Then, I think you said something like, "Why don't we or why don't you drop the sails?"

NORA: Okay, now I know what you're talking about.

TODD: Well, I didn't like it. So let's see... about buttons. I would expect that maybe I have a button about being told what to do.

NORA: So we both have that fear of being controlled or being told there's a better way to do it.

TODD: Yep. Let me take a few breaths here.

NORA: (Silently nods.)

TODD: Okay. Are you ready? I got upset... I got angry when you asked me, "Why don't we drop the sail?" My self-talk was, "What's she after? I want her to tell me what she wants and not couch her wants in 'Why don't we' language. I think that's controlling and it's indirect. If I'm being controlled, I want to know it! Now, can you repeat that back to me?"

NORA: You said you got angry when I said "why don't we?" You thought I was being indirect. You'd prefer to hear what I want, instead of having me ask a question like that. Right? (Here, Nora is using the active listening tool.)

TODD: And I was thinking, "What does she want? Is she indirectly trying to tell me what to do?"

NORA: And you were thinking, "What does she want? And is she trying to tell me what to do indirectly?" (more active listening)

TODD: Yes. And I resent you for saying it that way — for asking a question instead of saying what you want.

NORA: And you resent me for how I said that. (more active listening)

TODD: Exactly. And I want you to respect me enough to simply and directly tell me what you want without couching your wants as questions that start with "why don't we...."

NORA: You want me to respect you enough to simply and directly tell you what I want without asking questions that start with "why don't we...."?

TODD: That's it. I feel heard, I think. Now, do you think you can honor that wish?

NORA: Wait a minute. Aren't I supposed to get a turn too to say my piece?

TODD: Oh yeah, I forgot. Okay, I'm listening.

NORA: I understand why you didn't like my "why don't we" question.

TODD: You understand why I might not like that type of questioning. (Now Todd is taking his turn at actively listening.)

NORA: Thank you. Yes. And I didn't see until now how that comes across to you.

TODD: So now you see how that sounds to me. Is that it?

NORA: Yes, and in the future I will attempt to be more aware of when I ask that question instead of asking for what I want.

TODD: Great. That's all I want.

NORA: Wait, I want to hear you say back to me what I said.

TODD: Oh yeah. In the future you'll attempt to be more aware about asking a question like that.

NORA: Yes. Now I feel finished. Do you?

TODD: Yes. Thanks for listening to me.

NORA: I feel better.

TODD: Me too.

Active listening is a very effective tool for staying centered when you're listening to something that may be uncomfortable for you to hear. Most couples counselors teach this process to their clients. But only a few clients actually take the process home and use it. Those who do use it find themselves more able to resolve their differences, or at least learn to live with them. If partners would use this tool consistently, couples counselors would be out of work! It's one of the best tools I know for keeping your relationship juicy and happy. And you don't have to wait until the Power Struggle Stage to discover its benefits. You can start practicing it with a person you're just getting to know. Even if you and this person discover you're not a match, you'll be better for the practice.

The Six Steps to Forgiveness

Let's look at another important aspect of conflict — what to do when you feel deeply hurt or disappointed by something your partner has done. Some call this betrayal. It's a situation where your deepest fears have been triggered and now your trust bond is damaged.

Forgiveness is an essential survival skill in any relationship — even in dating. No matter how mature and responsible two people are, they will do dumb or hurtful things at times. Forgiveness might occur in an instant, but more often it is a process that takes place over time. Many people want to forgive and forget as quickly as possible, but I caution you to take some time to fully feel and express your feelings. Forgiveness isn't real unless you know what was actually done and what you feel about this, and unless the other knows how you feel. Usually there are several elements or steps in the forgiveness process.

- Describing What Happened
- Identifying What You Feel
- Expressing What You Feel (e.g., anger or hurt or both)
- Listening to Your Partner
- Expressing More Feelings
- Forgiving

Think of a time when you experienced a painful betrayal, disappointment, or breach of trust. To help you see how each step might be applied in your life, refer back to this incident as you read through the six steps below.

Premature Forgiveness

First I want to caution you to beware of premature forgiveness. Many people cannot stand the discomfort of anger or resentment, so they say the words "I forgive you" before they have discovered what really happened or fully felt their feelings about it. To get to true and lasting forgiveness, you need to be willing to go through all the stages — as often as necessary — until you feel within yourself a change of heart regarding the troubling event.

1. Describing What Happened

The first step in any forgiveness process is to identify what the other did that you felt hurt about. You need to think clearly here because people are often hurt by something they imagine or by their interpretation of someone's actions. Ask yourself, "What really happened? What did the other person actually do or say?" Then ask, "What happened after that? What was my reaction? What did I actually feel? What did I say or do about those feelings?"

If, in considering what really happened, you discover that you are more hurt by your interpretation of the events than the events themselves, notice this and admit it to yourself. Soothe yourself for the pain you feel — even though this pain may be self-created.

> If you discover that you are more hurt by your interpretation of the events than the events themselves, notice this and admit it.

2. Identifying What You Feel

After identifying what you felt after it happened, notice what you feel right now. Are you still upset? Are you feeling pain or hurt feelings? Notice the actual feelings and bodily sensations, and do not be confused by your labels and judgments: "I feel betrayed" is actually not a feeling. It is an interpretation about the other's actions. If you are thinking, "I do feel betrayed," see if you can notice the exact feelings in your body that you associate with betrayal. Often the feeling of betrayal means that some old feelings are being triggered — feelings that were never fully felt or released. Now, when a similar feeling occurs, it gets mistaken for that same old wound. You overreact in the present to an experience that appears similar to some unresolved hurt in your past.

By noticing the quality of your present feelings in detail, you will be better able to communicate to the other in a genuine, grounded way. You will be more authentic and more believable (rather than acting hysterically or sounding dramatic).

3. Expressing What You Feel

For most people, expressing feelings is the hardest part. You may fear that the other will be defensive or maybe that you'll create a mess. These things might happen. But if you take that risk now, you won't have to carry the burden of your unexpressed hurt and anger all by yourself. And you probably will get over it once you talk about it with the other person. Remember, the purpose of expressing your feelings is to get over them, to get to forgiveness. Communicate with the intent to reveal yourself rather than with the intent to get agreement or prove your point. Use "I" statements to help you stay in your own experience.

4. Listening to Your Partner

After your partner has listened to you, then listen to his or her feelings and perceptions. Ask clarifying questions to help your partner be more specific, but don't put him or her on the witness stand. "Isn't it true that you...?" questions are not allowed. Such interrogation tactics belong in a courtroom, not in a conversation between people who care about each other.

As the listener, use active listening, as described above. Repeating what the other has just said keeps you grounded in your present felt experience and prevents you from reacting impulsively. It also helps the other person trust that you are present and open, thus increasing the likelihood of resolution.

5. Expressing More Feelings

Now check in and see if you need to express anything more. Sometimes simply stating resentments clearly, specifically, and directly leads to a sense of, "I'm over it now.... I can forgive you.... I just needed to express myself and be heard." Other times, you may still feel almost as upset as you did when you began, so you will need to repeat yourself. Simply restate what you said before, or if you become aware of some new feelings, express these. After each expression, check in with yourself to see if you feel a sense of resolution or closure. When you have finished clearing the air, you will feel more relaxed or peaceful. Keep expressing yourself (even if you think it sounds repetitive) until you feel this sense of inner peace or closure. Sometimes, after you express strong anger, feelings of fear or pain will then surface. Sometimes after expressing hurt or painful feelings, anger will surface. Do not be alarmed if this occurs.

The human psyche is like an onion with many layers. Once you express yourself fully about the current incident, feelings about another event might come into your awareness. Sometimes, you will be reminded by the current situation of something that happened to you long ago, maybe when you were a child. If this happens, be sure to tell the other that old buried childhood feelings are now coming up (so he or she can be a compassionate listener and not get triggered). Then ask him or her to bear with you and just keep expressing yourself.

Often, when you feel you have been carelessly treated, it's a good idea to ask for amends to be made. In one pair I know, after the man planned an expensive vacation trip for himself without inviting her, she asked him to make amends to her by planning an even more exotic trip for the two of them.

6. Forgiving

Once you feel complete in your expression (at least for now), you are probably ready to forgive. Sometimes, to get to a feeling of completion, you may need to repeat the above five steps a few times. If a recent hurtful experience is similar to one that you suffered in childhood, the wound may not heal all at once. Be patient. Accept that emotional wounds, just like physical ones, can take time to heal. It helps if you can take responsibility for the fact that you were triggered by your partner's actions. Your partner is not to blame for that. Your partner is responsible for his or her actions, but no one is to blame for what you are experiencing. Blame is not real. It is a defensive reaction that people use to feel more in control about something that happened. It is more mature to admit that you do not have control over another person's actions. The blaming habit supports an unrealistic view of reality — a view that says, "If I hurt, it's someone's fault." Pain happens. The best way to deal with life's painful moments is to feel the pain, talk about it, forgive, and begin again.

If the hurt was very deep or was intimately connected with a similar hurt in your childhood, you may not get to a feeling of resolution. In this case, you may decide that the wound to your trust is so profound that you must distance yourself from this person. If you decide to end the relationship, that's okay. But before doing so, please be sure to read part IV, which discusses ending relationships consciously.

Affairs Happen: How to Cope

Typically, a dating relationship is an unstable relationship. Agreements about monogamy are often unclear. Even if partners think they have a clear agreement, that agreement is not usually very trustworthy — simply because the relationship has not matured to the place where commitments are reliable.

The discovery of a secret sexual liaison can be one of the most painful things two people ever experience. If this happens, it is important to attend carefully to each of the six steps of forgiveness, starting out by finding out what really happened, and asking any questions you have. Do not protect the other by suppressing questions you fear may be uncomfortable, but don't punish your partner or rub it in. Remember, your goal is to get to forgiveness by airing all the relevant feelings and facts. If you then decide to end the relationship after you have learned what happened and communicated your feelings, your ending will be cleaner than if you end things in a fit of emotion.

> If you decide to end the relationship after you have learned what happened and communicated your feelings, your ending will be cleaner than if you end things in a fit of emotion.

You're in Shock — Now What?

When you find out the person you're dating has been keeping such a secret from you, you may feel so out of control that your natural inclination is to try and get back in control by immediately taking decisive action — such as leaving or threatening to leave. Usually this is a bad idea.

Do not end it until after you have at least expressed all your feelings about the matter and heard all that your partner has to say. If you leave a situation at the height of emotion, you will most certainly carry with you a lot of unfinished business. Such emotional baggage will follow you into your next relationship, or prevent you from engaging in future relationships at all.

A Checklist of Questions

When you're in shock, you may be so numb or so angry that you can't think straight. If this happens, here is a list of questions to consider.

1. What actually happened? (If the other person will not tell you, find out what she is afraid of.)
2. What is going on presently between your partner and this other person?
3. What are your partner's wants and intentions?
4. What does your partner want you to do or want from you? (Often, an affair is a wake-up call, a signal that one or both partners' needs are not being met. Now that this information is out in the open, you can do something to address that situation.)
5. Is this something you can agree to? If not, what would it take before you might agree?

After Forgiveness, Then What?

Each person is unique in what it takes to fully forgive. Yet the six steps give you a general outline of what most people need. Sometimes, forgiveness is only the beginning, however. After this, the two of you may need to come up with a new vision of what you each want in your relationship and a plan of action for how to make your vision a reality.

The forgiving person may request that the partner make some sort of amends (such as spending a day together in bed or at the beach).

If you get stuck in communicating about any of this, seek professional help. Nowadays most people realize that everyone needs third party help at times. View this as a commitment to yourselves and to your relationship, not as a sign of weakness.

And remember that love between two people can become stronger after being damaged and repaired.

Chapter Summary

- We avoid conflict because we don't trust ourselves to be able to deal with uncertain, uncontrollable consequences.
- To deal with conflict in a healthy way, use active listening.
- Forgiveness is essential in any relationship — even in a dating relationship.
- To get to a true and lasting forgiveness, you need to go through a number of steps. It is important not to try to forgive prematurely, before you have fully felt all your feelings about the painful event.

CHAPTER THIRTEEN

Emotional Openness and Sexual Intimacy

Allowing Your Vulnerability to Show

Self-revelation is sexy.

I f you want to have great sex, the willingness to be open about your wants and feelings is a must. To be vulnerable is to allow the other to see how he or she is affecting you — to be transparent about your wants, your feelings, and your response to his or her words or touch. A friend of mine once said, "Loving is receiving." By that he meant that people do not always need to be doing something for their partner. Often the greatest gift you can give is to show how much you want him or her and then to openly receive.

The willingness to be sexually vulnerable brings more love, trust, and relaxation into your sex life.

Control Patterns Are Not Sexy

Sam considered himself to be a very skilled lover. A number of his past lovers had given him feedback that he was "the best." Yet, after less than a year, his lovers always broke up with him, often saying things like, "I can't feel you. I don't feel emotionally connected to you." So while he was quite confident about his ability to offer pleasure to a woman, Sam eventually began to have serious self-doubts. Following his breakup with a woman he had really fallen for, he sought the help of a Getting Real relationship coach. During a coaching session, Sam identified a control pattern that he hadn't seen before: he always focused his attention on giving pleasure to the woman and rarely asked for what he wanted. He thought this was a good way to get women to like him. He had an unconscious fear that if he asked for something the woman was not already giving, she would be insulted or turned off. This had occurred in his former marriage — whenever he asked his wife to do something specific to pleasure him, she would become mechanical in her lovemaking. During the divorce process, his wife confessed that she had always hated it when he asked her to pleasure him in specific ways. She considered it a criticism.

> If you want to have great sex, the willingness to be open about your wants and feelings is a must.

From that time forward, Sam had vowed to "never be demanding in bed," but rather to focus on giving pleasure to the woman. He thought he had become quite good at this until the coaching work made him take another look at this decision. He realized that he was angry at his ex for what she had said and also for not saying it earlier in the marriage. This withheld anger was affecting his current relationships. He thought his nondemanding style would be appreciated, but his actions were coming from the secretly hostile belief that "I know you're too fragile to listen to what I want, so let's just focus on pleasing you.... I know that's all you really care about."

With the coach's help he saw that his eager-to-please façade wasn't working. It was a cover for withholding himself from his partner. He came to realize that his belief about women being fragile and self-centered and his strategy of never asking for anything were ways he used to protect himself from possible pain or disappointment. He learned to admit that he felt vulnerable about asking for anything. This brought a softer, more human element into his lovemaking. He began to risk being more real about his own wants. At those times when he felt afraid to ask, he learned to speak up about his mixed feelings, sharing his fears alongside his wants (Truth Skill #9). He found that his partners pretty consistently appreciated hearing about his feelings.

After completing this coaching work, he had the opportunity to reconcile with the woman who had broken up with him the year before. He was ecstatic when she told him, "I can feel you now. I feel closer to you than I ever did when we were going out before. Now, you're letting me into you."

Sex is supposed to be an area where people get naked with one another, both literally and metaphorically. However, as we saw in Sam's case, your control patterns and unfinished emotional business have a way of creeping into the bedroom and interrupting the free flow of energy and passion. Sometimes, it takes inner work to learn to be transparent.

Saying No Is Vulnerable Too

Sometimes people are afraid to say what they don't want or aren't yet ready for. Perhaps they imagine the other will lose interest if they refuse to go all the way. Have you ever allowed yourself to be pressured into being more sexually involved than you felt like being? Was this an attempt to control the situation — to get the other to like you or not hassle you, for example? How did it work? I have spoken to many people, mostly women, who confessed to allowing themselves to move too fast. What they really wanted was more courting or kissing or fondling. Asking for this would have been an act of genuine vulnerability. But instead of being transparent about their real needs, they conformed to what they thought was expected by their partners. A few of them told me they suspected this was the reason they had difficulty experiencing orgasm with that partner — the fact that they had compromised themselves to please the man. Saying no was seen as too risky.

Safe Sex

Related to saying no is the issue of making sure that a potential sex partner is not carrying a sexually transmitted disease (see fuller discussion of
sexual history disclosure in chapter 8). This conversation also involves
making yourself vulnerable. You must ask questions that could be
difficult for the other to deal with, such as: Whom have you had intercourse with? What is this person's sexual history? Has she ever had an
abnormal pap smear? Do you or any of your former lovers have herpes
or genital warts? Have you and have your former lovers been tested
recently for AIDS? What were the results? Whom are you being sexual
with now? Are you having intercourse? What else are you doing?

You'll need to ask these questions and you'll need to be willing to
answer them truthfully. If you do not trust your partner's answers, that
can make you feel vulnerable, too. Not knowing what to trust is very
scary. If you feel this, admit it as a confession, for example: "This is hard
for me to feel, but I don't fully trust that you will tell me the whole
story." Then wait and listen and notice. Notice what the other says and
does, and notice how you feel in your body as you listen. It's impossible
to know for sure if the other is telling the whole truth. All you can do is
share your own feelings and concerns. There is a spiritual law of relating
that applies to this issue of trustworthiness: if you're not being fully honest with him, it's more likely that he will not be fully honest with you.
You reap what you sow. Don't sow what you'd rather not reap.

Getting Messy

Some people are afraid of "not looking good" when they are in the heat
of passion. Maybe they think they're too intense or needy or out of control. If you fear this sort of thing, talk to your partner about it. Most
people feel honored to be trusted with that level of vulnerability from
someone they love.

As we have already discussed, people tend to protect themselves
around other people. This is especially true in sex because people feel most

vulnerable to being hurt in the sexual arena. When we think the other person might hurt us, we keep a layer of protection around our hearts. What if, instead of doing this, we admitted it when our feelings got hurt? What if we could understand that to allow another person to see us in pain actually brings the two of us closer? It is a bonding experience.

Allowing yourself to be open and potentially vulnerable with your partner is one of the most important things you can do if you want a great sex life. Being vulnerable will also help you learn to trust yourself in dealing with the inevitable emotional pain that intimacy brings up. If pain does get triggered, it's probably old pain that still needs to be felt so you can heal. Hurt feelings, anger, or any emotionally based pain reveal unconscious beliefs you still carry from the past. So pain is not a bad thing. It shows you where you need to focus in your journey toward wholeness. Feel any painful feelings that arise, comfort yourself, and trust that this will pass. What often passes with it is your compulsion to avoid pain. When you learn not to be so afraid of pain, that is a real healing.

Feel any painful feelings that arise, comfort yourself, and trust that this will pass. What often passes with it is your compulsion to avoid pain.

Once you accept that you probably will get your feelings hurt sometimes in a relationship, the pain won't be so devastating when it happens. That's how life works: it gives you the kind of experiences you need to learn to accept and deal with, and once you learn these, it gives you new and different experiences with different lessons. So if you learn to stop defending against being disappointed (for example), then you won't have so many disappointments in your life. Once you stop protecting against "not being heard," your partner will listen better.

Differences Can Be Scary

People have had such unique and varied early learning experiences with respect to their sexuality. This is bound to create misunderstanding at times. Depending upon what years you were in high school, you may have learned anything from "women are not supposed to want it" to "women are supposed to be ready to go at all times"; from "men are supposed to act tough and cool" to "men need to know how to express their feelings." Different regions of the country or the world, different social classes, different religions, different families, as well as differences in age — all these are possible sources of friction between dating partners. They can lead to feelings of emotional vulnerability in that they sometimes cause disharmony in an otherwise wonderful relationship. If Person A has been raised to see sex as something to be saved for one special person, and Person B has been raised in an atmosphere of free love, these differences can lead to misunderstanding and mistrust. Speaking openly about these differences may feel scary. We may see them as a threat to the relationship and thus wish to downplay their significance. If differences exist, however, they will come to the surface eventually. So why not talk about these things earlier rather than later? As we saw in chapter 9, the Romance Stage is actually a good time to raise difficult issues since partners are feeling more open and accommodating toward each other.

> It's not the differences themselves that cause distress between partners. It's the avoidance of addressing these differences.

Talking about your different programming in an open, vulnerable way can leave you each feeling more connected to the other. It's not the differences themselves that cause distress between partners. It's the avoidance of addressing these differences. So if you and someone you love grew up with different sexual programming, invite this person to have a long conversation about the different "rules" that you learned in your family of origin, your religious training, or your peer group. Talk about how you feel as you become aware of how differently the two of you were conditioned. Talk about your fears that these differences could destroy what you have, but focus also on your excitement for what you can learn from these differences.

Control Patterns in the Bedroom

Everyone has at least one or two favorite fears. For some people rejection may be an issue. For others, it might be abandonment, betrayal, being judged, being embarrassed or ashamed, being ignored, being misunderstood or not heard, being smothered, and of course the old standby, being controlled. These fears originate in childhood, but even when we become adults, fears have a way of finding their way into the bedroom.

We have already addressed the most common control pattern in sex — trying to push aside your impulse to ask for what you want or don't want in the interest of being pleasing to your partner. Another pattern is that of behaving in an overly pushy way. You assume that your lover needs detailed instructions before even giving him a chance to do it without your guidance. This pattern may originate in a childhood where your adult caregivers were insensitive to your needs.

To heal this pattern, tell your partner about your past, and ask him or her for feedback from time to time about whether you are giving too many instructions. This kind of request is an act of making yourself vulnerable. You are revealing things about yourself that you feel shaky and unsure about. You are allowing your partner to see you and help you. This is a turn-on for most people. Remember, what bonds two people is feeling significant or needed by the other.

Dealing with Fears of Intimacy

An intimate sexual relationship can provide a safe place to uncover and own up to your fears. While this might not sound like much fun, it is a very valuable thing to do. As we saw in Sam's story at the start of this chapter, disclosing fears can deepen your intimacy and strengthen your sexual bond. Besides this, when you can speak about your fears to your partner, this is a big first step toward healing whatever early wounding led to the fear in the first place. Here is an example: When Lila was a little girl, her mother ignored her when she cried loudly for what she wanted. So Lila came to the unfortunate conclusion that "it's not safe to ask for what I want."

Now, in bed with Steve, she is hoping he'll stroke her head as part of their foreplay. But based on her early experiences with asking and not getting, she is afraid he will just ignore her, so she doesn't ask. Instead she attempts to override her desire and focus on enjoying the feeling of Steve's hands on other parts of her body. The only trouble is that she isn't able to push her real desire out of her thoughts. So she cannot be fully present to enjoy Steve's touch. She's in her head worrying about what to do, rather than in her body enjoying this present moment with her lover. When you try to push a feeling out of your awareness, it usually doesn't go away. It keeps demanding your attention. This is especially true if the feeling is related to an old conditioned fear that needs to be addressed and healed.

How Healing Works

If you find yourself in a situation similar to Lila's, first gently remind yourself that the beliefs about what is and isn't safe that you learned in childhood are not true. That was then, and this is now. When you were little and dependent, it was indeed scary if you asked for something and were ignored. As a little person you were totally dependent on the big people for your survival. But now you are big and self-supporting, not little and dependent. If Lila asks Steve to stroke her head and he ignores her, or if he does it but not the way she really likes, she will survive just fine. So the idea that it's not safe to ask for what you want is an outdated belief that she now has the opportunity to outgrow. If she asks and doesn't get what she wants, at least her asking gets her back into present time with herself and her lover. The healing comes not so much from asking and getting, but from asking and finding out that just the act of asking is an act of supporting or affirming yourself. Becoming self-validating and self-supporting is what

> When we think the other person might hurt us, we keep a layer of protection around our hearts. What if, instead of doing this, we admitted it when our feelings got hurt?

adults do. Waiting for someone else to make you happy is what children do. Let me be very clear that asking for what you want is not the same as "waiting for someone else to make you happy." Everyone has needs for help and for intimate contact. Revealing these needs, being vulnerable in this area, takes inner strength. Openly and directly asking for what you want is taking responsibility for what you want.

If you share your fear alongside asking for what you want, it's good to mention that this fear is probably associated with some old programming; it's not about your partner. Telling someone that your fears are about you and not her can help a lot. This helps your partner not take your feelings personally. Mentioning your fear out loud also helps you accept yourself just as you are. And it helps you take your fear less seriously and get over it. As we have seen, after we express a feeling, the feeling usually changes.

Here is how an intimate request like this might go: "Darling, I'm feeling very close to you, and I'm also feeling that I want to ask you to touch me in a particular way... but I'm afraid to ask. I think this fear is something very old... something I've always had... long before you and I met. What I want to ask is that you stroke my head as you were doing last night while we were watching TV. That always feels so special when you do that for me."

Here is a summary of the steps you can take to ask for what you want if you're feeling fearful about doing so:

1. Feel both the want and the fear.
2. Express the fear to clear it out of your "foreground."
3. Appreciate something about what is going on right now.
4. Express the want in specific terms. (Say what you want, not what you don't want.)
5. Be open (to receiving it or to not receiving it).
6. Remember that it is a good thing to ask, even if you don't get what you ask for.
7. Appreciate yourself for taking a risk.

If You Want More Practice

Other ways to practice being open and vulnerable are:

1. Looking into each other's eyes while in the heat of passion.
2. Telling your partner exactly how his/her touch or body feels to you.
3. Letting your partner know when you are feeling unsatisfied or when you are longing for more closeness (without blaming your partner for what you are feeling).
4. Asking your partner for feedback about what you are doing to pleasure him or her (with an attitude of sincerely wanting to please).
5. If you can't easily tell your partner what you want in the moment, then having a discussion with him or her on this topic outside of the bedroom.

Sex as Therapy

Anything that you carry inside you that is still unconscious will come to the forefront in your sexual relationships. Any difficulties you have accepting or loving yourself, for example, will become externalized and show up in how you give to or receive from your partner. If Shelly feels that she is basically unloveable, she will have trouble loving and accepting love from a man who purely and uncritically loves her. She'll find herself more turned on by men who criticize her or give her a hard time.

Being sexual with someone, because of the physical closeness, reminds us of our infancy. For this reason, we tend to regress back to some of our infant feelings and behaviors when we get close in this way. This is more than most lovers bargained for, and they can be shocked when they see how much stuff there is below the tip of the iceberg. If you're not prepared for this, you may want to run away. But if you stay, there is an opportunity for real mutual healing — sort of a do-it-yourself therapy program.

It is important to make room for each person's deep hunger for physical merging with another. This urge to merge is expressed in the need for skin-to-skin contact. Touch is a very basic human need. If you are not touched in infancy, you will not develop normally. As adults the hunger for touch and nurturance is alive and well, but it often gets masked as a need for sex. Sometimes a person's touch needs were so frustrated during infancy that they become quite frightened when these unfulfilled longings resurface in an adult sexual relationship.

If your touch needs were deprived as an infant, you may feel pretty ambivalent about sex. You crave it, and yet it scares you because of the pain associated with that early unmet longing. You may have learned how to do without touch or closeness — by becoming overly busy or burdened by responsibilities, for example — so in sex you give double messages. You need it, but you don't make time for it. Or you want it, but you never seem to get it. Or you get it, but it's never quite right.

> Anything that you carry inside you that is still unconscious will come to the forefront in your sexual relationships.

A way to unravel and move through this confusion is to acknowledge your unmet childhood longings and your unmet needs for touching, caring, and closeness. Here is an exercise you can do with a partner. Take turns being the giver and the receiver. Gently and softly caress your partner's skin — all over the body, front and back. You may cup the genitals lovingly, but leave the eroticism for another time. You may follow this by spooning or lying face-to-face, breathing slowly and deeply. After a while begin sharing feelings and thoughts in a free association style, just saying whatever bubbles up from the depths of your subconscious without trying to have a normal conversation.

This exercise can help satisfy your needs for loving touch so you won't be using sex as an indirect way to service this need.

A sexual relationship is a many-layered thing. As you both become more conscious and transparent, your sexuality will involve parts of your whole being that you didn't even know were there. For that reason, if you decide to be sexual with someone, be sure you're ready to get real.

Sexual Lifestyle Differences

What if two people appear to want very different things in terms of their sexual lifestyle? What if Person A is monogamous and Person B is not? Communicating openly about these differences can feel scary. That's normal. But I have found that open communication often leads to a change of heart in one or both people. It often creates an expansion of each individual's capacity for love, resulting in an even deeper sense of unity. To illustrate how this happens, here is a story about two people in conflict about the issue of monogamy versus "open lifestyle."

Carla is fifty. Saul is forty-six. They have been dating for a year. When they first got together, they agreed to be monogamous, but now things have changed. Saul's sexual self-esteem has risen considerably as a result of being with Carla. Now that he's feeling more confident and capable in this area, he wants to try having other sex partners. As a young man, due to low self-esteem and other factors, he never had the chance to fully express his sexuality. He has only had four sexual partners in his life; he imagines he has "only a few good years left"; and he has the idea that being monogamous is killing his passion and his sense of vitality as a man. He sincerely believes that it is dishonest for him to pretend to be satisfied with just one sex partner. He loves Carla and enjoys the sex life they have together, but he can't help feeling that his life is missing something important.

Carla is beside herself with pain and anger. She wants to stay monogamous. She believes that sex is a sacred act, and she has no desire to be with other sex partners. She imagines that if Saul does start sleeping with other

> Can you imagine feeling two contradictory things at once: the wish to have what you want alongside the wish for your partner to have what he or she wants?

women, her trust and openness with him will suffer. They have arrived at a true impasse. Saul feels strongly that he cannot be true to himself and stay monogamous. He also feels genuine empathy for Carla. It hurts him to see her in pain. And of course, Saul wants Carla to feel safe and open with him.

Carla trusts what Saul says about himself — that he feels he's violating his integrity by being monogamous. She wants Saul to have what he wants, and at the same time, she thinks she'd be untrue to herself if she stayed in a nonmonogamous relationship. And she's pretty sure that if Saul has sex with other women, she'll resent it and resort to protecting herself instead of staying open and vulnerable.

If you were Saul or Carla, can you imagine how you might experience such a predicament? Can you imagine feeling two contradictory things at once: the wish to have what you want alongside the wish for your partner to have what he or she wants? This is what it feels like to be Holding Differences (Truth Skill #8). It's like hanging out in an unresolved predicament without knowing if there will ever be a resolution. Some people can't stand the tension, so they jump to a premature conclusion like "I'm out of here" or "I know I'm not being fair to you, so I'll just leave." Yet sometimes, when you are able to stay with the experience of inner and outer conflict, you get to a deeper level of what the conflict is really about. This can be painful, but if partners can stay with their pain consciously, a breakthrough may occur. If you stay in an impasse for enough time, allowing the difference to exist rather than rushing prematurely to a resolution, you will be changed by the experience. This change is not predictable. It doesn't take the form of giving in or compromising but rather of expanding yourself.

In Saul and Carla's case, with the help of a relationship coach, they managed to stay with their pain and uncertainty for about six months. After this amount of time, they each disclosed that their sense of personal identity had undergone a change. Saul discovered that his need for other lovers was connected to some unresolved anger both at Carla and at his mother. After he was able to express his anger to both of these

women, he noticed that his fear of their reaction was no longer controlling him. He then realized, "What I thought I needed for my survival doesn't seem so crucial now. I feel like I have myself back . . . like
I'm not always having to accommodate to a woman's wishes." Carla
also got a deeper look at herself after staying with her pain for what
seemed like an eternity. She remembered a time early in their relationship when Saul broke one of his agreements with her — an
agreement that had to do with money, not sex. The coach helped her
clear this up with Saul by expressing
her anger "in the interest of
transparency." She then
saw that "breaking agree-
ments" had been a trigger
for her all her life. She did some
crying and grieving for some of the disappointments she had felt
throughout her life. After a few weeks punctuated by occasional
episodes of sadness, she was finally free enough of old baggage to say
truthfully, "I feel a lot safer, like my security doesn't depend on other
people; I know I'll be okay if the relationship ends, even though I still
really want things to work with Saul."

> By speaking the truth of your experience, you become a bigger person.

The outcome of staying with the impasse rather than rushing
quickly to a resolution was that both Saul and Carla let go of their rigidly
held positions and saw the situation from a bigger perspective. Each realized that what was fueling their individual positions was a defensive pattern adopted in childhood as a strategy to prevent the recurrence of
certain painful events, and carried over into adulthood to prevent their
buttons from getting pushed.

Outcomes like this often feel magical or unbelievable to the people
involved when they consider where they were before they got unstuck.
If you find yourself in such a conflict situation, whether it's about sex or
something else, try staying with your differences for a while, holding
both sides of the difference and communicating your feelings as they
come up. Do this for a period of time — at least a few months. See

if you can feel both your own wants (your commitment to having what you want) and your partner's wants (your wish for him or her to be satisfied also). Holding differences can produce an inner expansion or transformation that enables you to experience a deeper level of what's real for each of you. It will also expand your capacity for love, both in the relationship and in the rest of your life.

By speaking the truth of your experience, instead of trying to run away from a painful or potentially painful experience, you become a bigger person. You own parts of yourself that had been repressed or denied. In doing so, you are loving yourself more and expanding your capacity for loving.

Tools for Enhancing Emotional Intimacy

The practices offered so far in this chapter are designed to help you discover a deep sense of trust in yourself and in life — a sense that whatever life deals to you, you can deal with it. They are designed to help you own your bigness and do what you need to do to heal the little wounded child that hides inside of you, so that you can fulfill your innate potential for pleasure and aliveness. This last section contains some other practices for enhancing intimacy and self-knowledge: creating safe space, word fasting, free association, gazing, and meditation.

Creating Safe, Sacred Space

Whenever you and your partner have something important or difficult to discuss — something that requires Holding Differences — it's a good idea to have a special place in one of your homes or in nature that you set aside as a safe or sacred space. This is where you go to talk about matters of importance. To sanctify this space, you might light a candle, burn some incense, or "smudge" by burning herbs. Whenever you enter this space, even if there is disharmony in the air, you enter it with an attitude of openness to what is — willing to speak about and to hear whatever is ready to be revealed.

Start the dialogue by taking turns stating your intentions: What do you want to come out of this conversation — for yourself, for your partner, and for the relationship?

Word Fasting

If you and your date are planning to spend the day together, and you want to do something that will deepen your sense of connection, try agreeing to be totally silent the whole time. Some people like to do their word fast while taking a long hike in a beautiful natural setting. Looking at each other, touching, pointing, laughing, and any form of nonverbal contact is permitted; but no talking, no writing notes in the sand, no sign language. Shared silence can be a wonderful thing to experience with someone you're getting to know. After the day is over you can have a conversation about how it felt.

Shared silence can be a wonderful thing to experience with someone you're getting to know.

Free Association

This practice is modeled after the free-association technique used by Freud and other psychoanalysts since Freud. The two of you lie on a bed or on the floor in a comfortable nest of pillows and blankets that you have created for the occasion. Just lie there, maybe looking at one another, though you needn't necessarily do so. Agree to start with a few minutes of silence. Then if either person feels like speaking, go ahead. Then fall silent again until another thought or feeling bubbles up from either person's subconscious. The idea is to share anything and everything that enters your consciousness, uncensored. It could be something related to the present situation, or it could be a memory, a feeling, a thought, a wish, a dream fragment, or an idea. Allow plenty of spaces between the sharings. And do not try to have a regular conversation — although if conversation happens for a little while, that's okay too. This practice creates a safe place to reveal subconscious thoughts and feelings — something you don't usually get in a normal conversation.

Gazing

Sitting together facing each other and gazing into each other's eyes can be a profound experience. Be sure you are both physically comfortable and that your breathing is unconstricted. Some traditions recommend looking into the left eye since this is connected to the nonlinear hemisphere of the brain, but I'd recommend experimenting to see what feels most vital and real for you. As you gaze, it's okay to blink. And if you need to rest, to withdraw for a moment with eyes closed, that's okay too. Do not make this practice into a contest about who can do it the best. Look with soft eyes. Imagine you are looking deeply into the other, beyond the personality. And allow yourself to be seen.

Do it for at least ten minutes at a sitting. Then discuss how it felt and how you feel now.

Meditation

Meditation is usually practiced alone, but you can also do it with a partner, side-by-side or face-to-face. There are many traditions of meditation, such as Zen, Vipassana, and Transcendental™. There are also a number of acceptable postures, including sitting or standing. Basically, the practice involves being aware of the other's presence and at the same time being totally present to yourself. Paying attention to your breathing, to your physical sensations, or to a word or phrase that you repeat silently to yourself can help you stay present. Some partners attempt to synchronize their breathing, but this is not a requirement. Some like to practice mutual meditation at the same time every day.

Sitting together facing each other and gazing into each other's eyes can be a profound experience. Look with soft eyes. Imagine you are looking deeply into the other, beyond the personality. And allow yourself to be seen.

Others like to do it right before or after making love. They say that this brings an expanded spiritual dimension to their loving — even a sense of harmony or unity with all of life.

These practices, while perhaps unconventional in the dating world, can help to create a deep and satisfying emotional bond between two people. Sex is only one of the many wonderful forms of intimacy. Spicing up your sex life with these other forms of intimate contact will enrich it.

Chapter Summary

- Being transparent about your needs, your feelings, and your responses to your partner makes you more sexually alive and attractive.

- Saying no can be an act of vulnerability, too. If you accept unwanted sexual advances, this will affect your ability to be present and responsive.

- Speaking openly about differences can also make you feel vulnerable. Remember to share your vulnerable feelings when talking about differences that seem threatening to the relationship.

- Being sexual reminds us of our infancy, so it can trigger regressive feelings like dependency or fear of being alone. If this happens, we can use it to become more conscious of old wounds in need of healing.

- We can help each other heal with gentle caresses and non-sexual touching.

CHAPTER FOURTEEN

Ten Common Myths about Sex and Intimacy

Each person's and each couple's path is completely unique. Beware of your mind's tendency to define, categorize, and compare.

While dating may or may not lead to overt sexual activity, sex is usually on people's minds: Am I sexually attracted to this person? Is this person attracted to me? How should I behave in order to be most attractive? How well should we know each other before we do it? Will she be hot at first and then grow indifferent? Will his ardor cool once he is sure of my love? These are some of the questions that come up as the dating process unfolds. In this chapter, I will deal with these questions as we consider ten common myths or untruths about sex in dating and new relationships.

Myth #1
You Shouldn't Make Him Wait Too Long Before Having Sex

There is a belief out there in the dating world that men are a lot more focused on getting sex than women are. And there's some truth to this in a general sense, especially among younger men. Statistically, at every age, there are more men than women who are ready to "do it" sooner.

If you are a woman, you could feel pressure (either real or imagined) to adapt to fit the man's timetable. But remember how important it is to be true to yourself. Your sexual responsiveness depends on how real you are. If you rush yourself and blame the other for it, this cannot be good for a relationship.

If you are a heterosexual man, and a woman you're dating seems to be moving faster than you are, you too might feel pressure to adapt. If you do, notice this and talk about it with your partner. You may be projecting onto the woman some expectation you have in your own mind about how a man should be. See if you can own this as your belief instead of automatically attributing it to her (Taking Back Projections, Truth Skill #6). Then initiate a conversation about what her expectations actually are; for example, "I'm feeling some internal pressure to move toward being more sexual with you than I'm actually ready for. I think this is some 'should' I have in my own head, but I'm also wondering about your expectations of me. Are you getting impatient or anything like that?" She'll probably tell you she's not impatient. But you'll get to hear how she really does feel, and that's the point of asking.

> Your sexual responsiveness depends on how real you are.

But what if you have already had sex before you were ready? Then it's time for Truth Skill #7, Revising an Earlier Statement. This could be difficult for the other person to hear. You may need to go back to the beginning and share what you were really feeling at various steps along the way, and how you compromised yourself due to a fear of disappointing her (or whatever fear was motivating you). Simply tell the story of what was really going on inside you and pause often to inquire about her response. This new information may hit her pretty hard. Listen to her feelings. If she goes into accusations or imaginings instead of being transparent, ask her how she is feeling. Then tell her how you feel hearing this — for example, "Hearing you say that, I feel sad" (or "I feel sorry I did things the way I did," or "I feel empathy with you").

Just because you have begun to be sexual with someone doesn't mean you have to continue if you discover later that this is no longer what you want. It's awkward to backpedal, but sometimes it must be done.

Myth #2
Men Are from Mars, Women Are from Venus

Where sexuality is concerned, each person is unique. While there are some generalizations that apply to most women or most men or most people in their twenties or their fifties, I think people give far too much attention to the search for reliable generalizations and far too little attention to learning about each other's uniqueness. It's useful to inform yourself about typical gender differences, but then I advise you to throw away the rule book. There is no substitute for open curiosity and honest communication. So if you wonder how someone likes to be treated, ask.

Philip had not been sexual with anyone for seven years. He had only had a few dates during this time, so he was really ripe for a quick fix to his low sexual self-esteem. He was excited when he stumbled across a book and audiocassette program purporting to explain how men and women should behave in the bedroom. He bought it and devoured the author's advice in one evening. After that, he couldn't wait to try out what he had learned. The book said that women tend to identify with their emotions, so they need a man who is not driven by his emotions. They need their man to stay calm and present and not interrupt as they express their feelings. Armed with this new knowledge about women, Philip met and became attracted to Lilly. And after a few months, they began sharing sexual intimacy.

Lilly was a woman who expressed her emotions easily, quickly, and forcefully — especially her upset and angry feelings. ("Just like the book said," Philip thought.) One afternoon as they were making love, Lilly sat up abruptly, pushed Philip away from her, and began telling him in a strident voice how insensitive he was as a lover. In an attempt to "stay present" Philip tried to appear unperturbed. He looked at her without commenting. In truth, he was feeling hurt and afraid, but from the reading he had done, he knew that expressing his own upset at a time like this would not be a good thing. Eventually Lilly's voice got softer, and Philip felt his whole body relax. Unfortunately, he had not heard anything she had said. He had been working so hard to act calm and present that he entirely missed her main criticism of him, which was, "I hate it when you just sit there and don't tell me what *you* are feeling. You look like a zombie!"

In spite of their conflicts, the relationship between Philip and Lilly endured for over a year. But things kept getting worse. Eventually, at Lilly's insistence they enlisted the help of a relationship counselor. During the counseling sessions the counselor helped Philip become aware of how hurt and afraid he was every time Lilly yelled at him. He had been denying his feelings because he thought that he was supposed to stay calm, no matter what he felt inside. One day, during a heated argument in the counselor's office, the counselor urged Philip to express his own hurt and fear in the face of Lilly's anger, and a very surprising thing happened: Lilly's body relaxed, she smiled broadly, and told Philip, "This is the most alive I've ever seen you be. Now you're sounding like a real human being instead of a robot."

After a few more couples counseling sessions, Philip learned to express his own emotions to Lilly — even in the bedroom. He threw away his rule book, and instead of trying to appear calm, he told her what he was feeling. Their relationship improved, their sex got hotter, and Philip learned what it really means to be present to another person.

Perhaps it was not the book's advice that led Philip astray but rather the book's implicit message that if you can learn "how women are" (the rules), then you'll know how to manage them so you can stay out of trouble. When your intent is to stay out of trouble, you are not being real. And when you're not real, you're less juicy, less alive, and therefore, less sexy.

Myth #3
Regular, Satisfying Sex Is Good for You

Sometimes regular, satisfying sex is good for you, and sometimes it's not. When would it not be? It's not good for you if: (1) you or your partner are doing it with an ulterior motive, e.g., to get something from the other rather than simply because you want to be intimate with this person; or (2) you're addicted to it, and the fact that you're having satisfying sex makes it hard for you to break off a dysfunctional relationship.

Many people use sex in trade for something else, and they are good at it! Usually the "something else" is some kind of financial help, but it could be other tangible help (such as handyman services or help with the kids). Less often, sex is traded for access to an exciting or high-status lifestyle. Such people are often very skilled lovers because, unconsciously, they have learned that to bind someone to them sexually ensures their survival.

In my interviews with wealthy or well-known singles, I have heard numerous stories about how great the sex was with someone who eventually wound up taking advantage of them. Most of these wealthier interviewees had felt uncomfortable early in the dating process. They sensed that something wasn't right, but they did not communicate these feelings to their partner. In reporting this finding, it is not my intent to make you paranoid. Rather, I am urging you to speak up if something doesn't feel right between yourself and the other. If sex is really good, it's often difficult to let it go — even if you are paying too high a price for it.

> When your intent is to stay out of trouble, you are not being real. And when you're not real, you're less juicy, less alive, and therefore, less sexy.

The difficulty of letting go of good sex in a bad relationship brings us back to the issue of sexual addiction. Passionate sex can be quite addictive. The need (or sometimes the addiction) for sex can cause people to go into denial rather than face a truth that could lead to losing the thing they are addicted to.

When addicted lovers do finally break up, they frequently report withdrawal symptoms such as depression, the inability to eat, insomnia, and bodily weakness or pain. Some people may prefer to stay in a self-destructive situation rather than suffer the consequences of calling it quits.

Mark met Leona through an internet matchmaking service. After corresponding for a few weeks, they met and felt an immediate sexual chemistry between them. They were delighted, since they had both met and rejected many potential matches before getting lucky with each other. After meeting for coffee a few times, they became lovers on their first "real date." Sex was easy and intensely satisfying right from the start. Unfortunately, they had difficulty communicating about the areas of their relationship that were not so easy — Leona's jealousy and possessiveness, her criticisms of several of Mark's friends, and her criticisms of how he spent his time. As their relationship progressed, Mark found himself limiting his contact with the outside world so as not to cause pain for Leona. He felt compassion for her pain, so it did not feel like a big sacrifice to make. This pattern continued for about a year. Then, after reading my book *The Couple's Journey,* Mark began to take stock of how much of himself he had given up in order to maintain relationship harmony. In the book, there is an exercise that asks partners to list all the things that they used to do before becoming paired that they no longer do now. His list was so long that it stunned him. He realized how many of his favorite pastimes he was no longer pursuing and

> The need (or sometimes the addiction) for sex can cause people to go into denial rather than face a truth that could lead to losing the thing they are addicted to.

how many of his favorite people he was no longer seeing. For a day or two after doing the exercise, he thought about showing the book to Leona, asking her to do the exercise too, and then discussing their answers. But he chickened out. He still harbored the wish to bring up this topic with her, but he feared she would get upset and withdraw from him sexually — something she often did when she became angry or threatened. The relationship continued for seven years before Mark ever got up his courage to speak about this source of frustration. By that time, he had built up so much suppressed anger that his delivery was cold and harsh — which, of course, triggered Leona's fear of abandonment even more. In an effort to maintain her sense of control, she blamed him for his tone of voice and attacked him for his timing. He felt powerless, ineffectual, and ashamed of himself and withdrew from the conversation. Mark went back into denial about the whole situation, and they kept having great sex and terrible communication for another seven years. After fourteen years with Leona, he had an affair, which helped give him the "courage" to break off the relationship with Leona. Having another reliable source of sex, he was able to break his addiction to her.

The story of Mark and Leona illustrates not only the power of sexual addiction, but also the power of denial about it. Addiction and denial are forces to be reckoned with in dating and relationships. Just because the sex is great doesn't mean it's good for you. Learn to look at sex in the context of who you really are, your life's purpose and vision, and the other values that are important to you. If the sexual part of the relationship enhances the rest of your life, go for it. If it causes you to compromise yourself, wean yourself from it as quickly as possible.

Myth #4
You Shouldn't Keep Initiating Sex If the Other Never Initiates It

Alan had the reputation of being a real catch. Where relationships with women were concerned, he had always enjoyed the role of being pursued rather than the role of the pursuer. But now, after dating Terese for a few months and recently becoming sexual with her, he found that she was not comfortable initiating sex or affectionate contact. If it was going to happen, he was going to have to initiate it. He really loved Terese, but after the first few months of actively romancing her, he fell back into his old, habitual pattern of waiting for the woman to initiate.

Somewhere in his childhood or adolescence, he had acquired the notion that if you pursued someone who wasn't giving you clear signals that the answer was going to be a resounding yes, then it was not safe to ask. He camouflaged his fear of asking by holding to the position: "If I have to ask for it, it's not worth having. Asking for what I want is demeaning. . . . It's like begging." Such self-talk is a control pattern. I call this pattern "too proud to beg." Have you ever found yourself in such a predicament — wanting sex or affection but too proud to beg? Many people find it risky and uncomfortable to ask for sexual contact, especially if the other person seems indifferent. If you have tendencies in this direction, consider this: When you ask for what you want, you are supporting your right to have wants. This helps you heal or let go of the notion that asking puts you in a one-down position. You are affirming yourself as a person who has the right to want things for himself. You are also supporting the reality that you'll be okay whether the other says yes or no. When you withhold expressing wants because you fear hearing "no," you are affirming that you are only okay if you get a positive response.

> Truth in Dating is about having fewer conditions on your happiness. It's about developing yourself into the most real, self-trusting, and loving person you can be.

As you get more real, and less addicted to having things go your way all the time, you learn that it's not so important to always get what you want. The important thing is that you express your wants and allow yourself to experience stepping into the unknown. This is what builds inner strength and confidence, the confidence that however things go,

you'll be okay. Remember, Truth in Dating is about having fewer conditions on your happiness. It's about developing yourself into the most
real, self-trusting, and loving person you can be. These are the qualities
that lead to happiness.

The additional benefit of asking for what you want without knowing the outcome is that taking a risk on behalf of greater closeness is an
act of transparency and vulnerability. When you become more transparent and allow yourself to be affected by the other's actions, you
become more real. Being real is more attractive than playing it cool, so
you are more likely get what you want.

To look at this from another perspective, if you are usually the initiator of sex or affection, it is also important to let your partner know
that you long for him or her to be more active in approaching you (if
this is true). So, while you may accept the role of initiator most of the
time, it is still important to stay in touch with the reality of your deeper
wishes.

Some of my interviewees told me how they dealt with this situation
where one person seemed to be stuck in the role of initiator. They had
an honest conversation about both people's feelings and worked out an
agreement whereby the initiator would consciously refrain from initiating for an agreed-upon period of time — maybe a week. This would give
the less active member of the pair time to build up her desire or need for
intimate contact. The people who described this idea said that it worked
well as an awareness practice for both parties. It gave both of them a
chance to break out of their habitual pattern.

Myth #5
If You're Not Attracted at First, You Never Will Be

I have known many people who were not at all attracted to someone on
the first few meetings but who later developed a strong attraction and a
lasting bond with that same individual. The idea that "if she's not
attracted to me right away, I should just forget it" is not true. You can't

know certain things in advance. If you have a tendency to quit at the first sign of rejection, perhaps this is a control pattern, a way you protect yourself from discomfort or anxiety about not knowing the outcome.

When I was in my twenties, I worked in an office with a man for a year and never felt anything for him. In fact I had made some fairly harsh judgments about him. I thought he was a big show-off and too loud. But over time, as we came to know each other, he became more and more attractive to me. We eventually became lovers for two years, and the sexual part was truly memorable. The only reason we broke up is that I heard that his ex-wife wanted him back, and they had three kids together, so I bowed out of the picture. I have had quite a few experiences of having the attraction "creep up on me," and so has almost everyone I interviewed. Sometimes you just know that it won't ever work, and you're right. Other times, you just know it won't work, and you're wrong. I haven't found any reliable method for predicting the future in these things. So much about a relationship is revealed over time. Practicing Truth in Dating will help you learn to trust the dynamic unfolding and the mystery of life by expressing whatever you feel innocently, without the intent to control the outcome. What you will learn from this is that you are not in control of the outcome. You just thought you were!

> For most partners, their first sexual intercourse together has some bugs in it.

Myth #6
If Sex Isn't Great at First, It Never Will Be

For most partners, their first sexual intercourse together has some bugs in it. It generally takes some time and practice before things reach their full potential. Usually, if people take the time to really get to know one another's preferences, their sex will get better and better over the first few months — assuming that they have a mutual attraction and that they have learned to communicate openly with each other before becoming sexual.

Paul has a pattern of becoming sexual with his dates as soon as possible. He tells himself that this insures that he won't waste his time with a woman who isn't totally open and turned on to him. Typically, he gives a new woman about a month, and if their sex isn't pretty hot by then, he breaks things off. I have known Paul for quite some time and have also met many of his lovers and would-be mates. From talking to the women he's dating, I conclude that they often consent to be sexual with him before they feel emotionally safe and connected with him. They get the impression that if they don't hurry up and start showing their stuff sexually, they're going to be history! So, instead of risking losing him, they get with his program and leap prematurely into sex. He then finds them less than 100 percent enthusiastic, and soon he's on to the next.

As I ponder Paul's situation more deeply, I think he has a fear of failure that he avoids via his "let's get it on" pattern. You see, he is trying to avoid the awkward trial and error stage that many lovers must go through in order to have satisfying sex. His sexual self-esteem is so fragile that he cannot tolerate it if things don't work great right from the start.

I know many singles like Paul who would rather keep searching for something easy rather than allowing things to develop over time as feelings of love, trust, and bonding occur. Ours is a quick fix culture. We don't like to invest too much in something if the outcome is unclear. The only problem with this philosophy is that you cannot know how something will feel in the future until after you have put some effort into it. Things may get better due to your efforts, and they may not. But it's certainly not true that "if sex doesn't work so well at first, it never will." Truth in Dating is a practice that steers us in the direction of letting go of controlling the outcome. More and more people are finding that when they insist on trying to maintain such control, they rarely get the results they were hoping for. Perhaps life is trying to teach Paul (and people like him) something about being willing to participate fully in a relationship without knowing for sure where it's going. The benefit of this attitude is that it teaches you to accept life as it is, with all its uncertainty, ambiguity, and unpredictability. Life on your own terms is an illusion.

Myth #7
If Sex Is Great at the Start, It'll Stay Great

People who put a great deal of importance on immediate sexual chemistry are often disappointed to find that, even when this is present right away, it may not last. If you are such a person, what might you be avoiding? Perhaps you are not willing to go through the sometimes difficult communication work of really becoming intimate with someone. Sex can be used as a shortcut to intimacy. But if you use sex this way, it may backfire on you. The key to a successful long-term relationship is the ability to adapt to change. Before you make a long-term commitment, ask yourself, "Am I really willing to work through whatever difficulties may come up between us? Do I even have the capacity to make such a commitment?" If you demand that your partner "stay as sweet as he or she is," you're probably setting yourself up for some painful lessons about how things change and how little control you have over these changes.

When choosing someone for the long haul, be sure you have known this person long enough to understand how resilient and adaptable they are in the face of change and crisis. My own rule of thumb is that I need to know someone for at least a year before I can trust my sense of how they react to the slings and arrows of life: Can we deal with difficulties and disappointments in our relationship? Can we speak about things that might be hurtful? Will he stay with me if our sex life goes through a dry spell? Do we have enough going for us besides the sex to carry us through our sexual ups and downs?

Myth #8
You Can Predict How It Will Go by How It Begins

We have all heard stories about women who are very hot before marriage, and then, once the honeymoon stage is over, things change. A number of these women have told me that they feel they can relax and just be themselves once they feel securely married. On a deeper level, I think they are now feeling safe enough to admit that all is not right with their own sexuality. They may need some sexual healing — though few are self-aware enough to admit this.

The same change can happen in men after the honeymoon, too, although a man's sexuality may be covered over with more layers of defensiveness if his identity is strongly tied to his sexual performance. If you and a partner find that things have changed in this way, it's time to get third-party help from a relationship counselor specializing in sexual healing.

Another change that occurs, more often with men than women, is the change from being monogamous at first to later realizing he or she is not well suited to monogamy. This change often occurs after partners make the transition from unmarried to married. Men who have switched from being monogamous to nonmonogamous report that when they were not married they still felt autonomous and free, but with marriage came a sense of being confined, which seemed to trigger a need to expand their field of potential sex partners.

Given this situation — the fact that you cannot predict how a person will be in the future — how do you make an informed mate selection? I think that

> Truth in Dating gives you a program for uncovering and owning your fears so you can see them for what they are — thoughts about an uncertain future over which you have no control.

if you put too much importance on having things remain as they are, that attitude will backfire on you. The very thing you fear most is the thing that seeks you out and bites you in the backside. Fears are powerful thought forms, even more powerful than wishes. Truth in Dating gives you a program for uncovering and owning your fears so you can see them for what they are — thoughts about an uncertain future over which you have no control. That's a sobering fact: You cannot predict whether your partner will continue to love you in the same way. Odds are he won't. Getting Real is akin to "getting sober" in the most profound sense of that word. Most of us are addicted to controlling the future. But reality keeps telling us to "give it up." Control of that sort is, and always has been, an illusion.

Myth #9
Being Truthful about Former Lovers Will Ruin the Romantic Feelings

There is no one-size-fits-all rule about how much to speak about former lovers. People are different in this regard, so it's best to ask rather than make assumptions. If you are committed to Truth in Dating, chances are you will seek a partner who is as well. If you find such a match, this does not mean that you will now proceed to share all the details of how it was with your other lovers. What it does mean, however, is that you do not keep secrets or withhold anything. If you have a fond thought about a past lover, notice this, and be willing to share it in the interest of transparency. This does not mean that you must share it. In other words, you are free. You have the choice to do so or not. You are not compelled either way.

> If you find yourself talking a lot about a past relationship with your current partner, ask yourself if this is a way of "safely" (and indirectly) expressing something that might otherwise be too risky to say.

Once in a while a person will tell lots of stories about a particular past lover as a way of sending the covert message, "I wish you were more like him," or "I'm angry at you for not being more like him." Other times the hidden message might simply be, "I want you to know that I'm still hung up on her, so don't expect me to be fully present with you." If you find yourself talking a lot about a past relationship with your current partner, ask yourself if this is perhaps a control pattern, a way of "safely" (and indirectly) expressing something that might otherwise be too risky to say.

If you find yourself with someone who indulges in a lot of past-centered conversation, tell this person what you feel when he does this. Does it push your button? Do not get caught in your own control pattern of trying to privately figure out his motives. Express yourself and inquire about his reaction to your feelings. Then stay present and listen. Try relating instead of controlling. It'll bring you both into the present, which is what needs to happen.

Myth #10
Having Sex Means Having Intercourse

Sexual intercourse can be a profoundly sacred act. But sex researchers have found that the penis is not necessarily the best instrument for bringing about a female orgasm. And many men admit to getting off better with oral sex.

There is more to sex than intercourse. There's outercourse. Outercourse may involve stroking, nibbling, licking, sucking, gazing, breathing together, rubbing bodies together, and anything else that excites or delights partners without penetration. It may involve one-way sex where one partner is active while the other passively receives.

Outercourse is viewed as foreplay by most, but more and more people are discovering that it can be a fully satisfying end in itself.

Many of the singles I interviewed told me they preferred outercourse to intercourse, particularly in the precommitment stage, for a number of reasons (different people gave different reasons):

- It offers more opportunities for really getting to know each other's pleasure zones;
- There are more options for being creative;
- It allows each person to take turns receiving, which can be an act of deep surrender and vulnerability;
- It's easier to talk to your partner when you're doing "one-way sex," so you're more likely to communicate clearly about what feels most pleasurable;

- There is less chance of contracting an STD;
- The orgasms are often more intense;
- The orgasms are often more reliable;
- "If I'm dating and being sexual with more than one person, the others that I'm dating don't get as upset about this if I'm not having intercourse with anyone. This can make it easier to be truthful."

The man who made this last statement said he was committed to truth-telling above all things. He told me that his three lovers were all okay with the fact that he was having outercourse with all of them, but each woman said that if he had intercourse with someone else, then they would not want to have a sexual relationship with him anymore. None of these relationships endured, so he never had intercourse with any of them. He said it was easier to separate from them, too, because they had never shared intercourse.

Outercourse is viewed as foreplay by most, but more and more people are discovering that it can be a fully satisfying end in itself.

Apparently, for most people, intercourse is seen as more serious or more sacred than outercourse. Notice your own feelings about this. Whatever your feelings, it is important to know your preferences and be able to communicate these. There's nothing wrong with you if you like outercourse better, for example.

The purpose of this chapter has been to help you get over any stereotyped thinking that you may be stuck in. If people talked more openly and honestly about sexual preferences, they would find that there is more diversity than the popular images of the media would have us believe. See if you can question the beliefs you were raised with and create a way of being intimate that is real for you.

Chapter Summary

- If you start being sexual before you're really ready, it's okay to shift gears and start over.
- If you find yourself searching for reliable generalizations (rules) about how women or men like to be treated, ask yourself, "What is it that I really want to know about this particular woman or man right here in front of me?"
- If you're having great sex but not much else, you may be in an addictive relationship.
- Sometimes one of you will be more active in initiating sex than the other. This does not necessarily mean anything about the mutuality of your love. Don't be too proud to beg; but if you do wish your partner would take a more active role, express this as well.
- Sometimes a person will not be attracted to you at first and then things change. Of course, the reverse is also true — sometimes they'll start out being attracted, and that will change. A relationship is a living, growing, ever-changing thing. The future is always uncertain.
- To discover your full sexual potential as lovers, you and your partner may need to "practice" for a while.
- If you put a lot of importance on having things stay as they are, this attitude will backfire on you. When you relax and let change happen, you might lose what you had, but you will gain something else.
- If your date talks a lot about former lovers, don't jump to conclusions about what this means. Express your feelings each time it happens. Ask questions if you have them. And ask for what you want.
- Outercourse is often an excellent alternative to intercourse, especially during the precommitted stage.

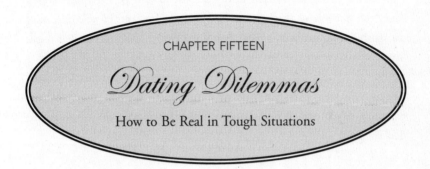

CHAPTER FIFTEEN

Dating Dilemmas

How to Be Real in Tough Situations

Honesty hurts sometimes, but it's worth it.

When the going gets tough, it's an especially good time to use dating as your awareness practice. If you can be honest in situations where many people would not do so, you will gain self-respect and confidence. You'll also grow in your ability to deal creatively with the unexpected, so you'll be less apt to get flustered by tough situations.

Mary is dating three men at once, and doesn't want to ruin her chances with any of them. How much should she tell each of these men?

Leslie is a single parent with two preteens. She's still in the divorcing process with her ex but is also having sex with her new boyfriend. What should she tell her kids?

Faye has been in a noncommitted sexual relationship with Leon for six months. Recently she has begun to see him as someone she might want to marry. When it was a casual relationship, she felt okay about faking orgasms, but now she wants to tell him the truth — that she has never in her life had an orgasm during intercourse. How does she disclose this without losing his trust?

When you find yourself facing a difficult and perhaps high-stakes situation like one of these, it can be a real test for you. How committed to truth-telling are you, really? For some people, the more they think they have to lose, the less likely they are to speak truthfully. Lying is always about control. If you can be honest in the most difficult of situations, you have a chance to grow significantly in your ability to trust yourself — to trust that you do not need to control things in order to feel okay.

Dating More Than One Person

In the opening paragraph I mentioned Mary's fear of being truthful with the three men she is dating. What would you do in Mary's situation? And if you were one of these three men, would you want to know the truth? Most of the people in my research study said they'd rather know the whole story, even if it were difficult to hear. But they also said that if they were in Mary's shoes, they might not tell all. Most people believe that if Person A is dating more than one person, then Person B will feel freer to date others also. This may be why they don't want to reveal their other dating activities. They are trying to stay in control.

Telling the whole truth about the number of people you're dating tends to influence how committed the other person feels toward you. Still, if you do not disclose this, you are being manipulative — perhaps simply wanting to avoid conflict, or perhaps trying to get the others to feel more committed to you by allowing them to think they're "the only one." How do you feel about yourself when you do things like this? Can you admit to yourself that you are manipulating the situation for your own self-interest?

Let's consider how Mary might handle her situation if she were practicing Truth in Dating. I'd coach her to start by noticing her feelings about telling each of these men the truth: Are you afraid about how they might react? What specifically are you afraid of? And what if this did happen? What would be wrong with that? Now imagine yourself telling each of the people you're dating about your fears. Just imagine this, and notice how you feel. If you fear their judgments or anger, do you have judgments of your own about anyone who would date more than one person? Do you have judgments about yourself? Are you projecting these judgments onto the other person?

Often our fear of judgment is a projection onto others of our own self-judgment. If I judge myself as "a player," for example, then I'm more apt to fear that others may see me this way. That's projection. Understanding this mental mechanism is what Truth Skill #6, Taking Back Projections, is about.

The last time I was single, I was dating three men and being sexual with only one of them. I told each of these men that I was committed to Truth in Dating. I felt I needed to be honest about anything that affected our relationship. So when Gerard (whom I had not been sexual with) asked if I was being sexual with either of the others, I told him that I was being sexual with Jay. Then I asked, "How is it for you to hear this?" Gerard was hurt, but he was also glad I had told him the truth. Of course he then wanted to know "why not me?" That was tough for me to explain. I told him that while I liked him a lot, I just didn't feel moved to be sexual with him. He still didn't understand "why not me?" but he said that our conversation actually made him feel closer, not more distant. This talk with Gerard was

> I think the fact that he and I had such a satisfying conversation about something so difficult helped me feel closer to him.

very moving. I think it had the effect of deepening our bond. A week later I stopped dating both Jay and Larry and became lovers with Gerard. Why? I'm not sure, but I think the fact that he and I had such a satisfying conversation about something so difficult helped me feel closer to him.

The point I want to convey with this story is that saying something that hurts does not necessarily create distance. I know I have said this before in these pages, but since most people find this hard to believe, I want to keep stressing it. What seems to occur when you are honest with someone is that you begin to feel closer to that person. But don't just take my word for it. Try it for yourself, and see how it is for you.

Sex and the Single Parent

Most single parents I surveyed felt a lot of confusion about what to tell their kids about their dating life. To start off this important discussion, ask yourself (if you have kids), "What am I doing that I'm reluctant to tell my kids?" Or (if you do not have kids), "What would I be reluctant to talk about if I did have kids? Is this something I feel some guilt or shame about? Or do I view my behavior as completely respectable?" If you're afraid to tell your kids about it, maybe you're doing something that goes against your own sense of integrity. If so, this will be damaging to your self-esteem. Are you the type of person you want your kids to grow up to be like? Or are you hoping they'll be different? If the latter is true, I suggest you have an honest conversation with them about the ways you hope they will choose differently than you. Children can learn best from their parents' mistakes if the parents are open about those mistakes. The secrets you keep from them are what will damage your children most. These same secrets will one day become your children's unconscious impulses. So, even if your dating behavior is less than impeccable, I advise telling your kids whatever they want to know. Tell them you're willing to answer any questions they may have about your life; but don't use them as confidants until they are adults.

> If you want your kids to be honest with you, start by being honest with them.

Leslie, in the above example, was allowing her boyfriend Perry to sleep overnight at her home when her kids were with their dad. But she didn't want her two girls to know that she was having sex, or even that she had a serious relationship. What Leslie didn't realize was that they could tell something had changed in their mom's behavior after she met Perry. And they often heard her talking about him on the phone with her friends. So they actually knew much more than she was telling them. What was Leslie's behavior teaching her kids? For one thing, they were learning that it's okay to have secrets from the people closest to you. Their mom's secretive behavior was a cue to them to keep their eavesdropping a secret.

If you want your kids to be honest with you, start by being honest with them. Sure, sometimes they will feel things that you wish they didn't feel — like feeling fearful or uncertain about their future, or judging you for your behavior. That's going to happen anyway, and not just because of your dating behavior. I'm advising you to get over trying to control how they see you, and instead be curious and open about how they see you. Learn to ask for feedback (Truth Skill #4). If you're afraid of their reaction, the way to help yourself and them get over this fear is to ask them how they feel after hearing your "secret." If you give your kids the chance to express themselves without the threat of punishment, they'll learn to express feelings and then let them go. Then they won't be carrying unfinished business about you into their adulthood and into their adult relationships. If you try to control what they feel about you, you'll always be a little defensive around them because your behavior is coming from a fearful, protective place. And it's a pretty sure bet that they'll be burdened with unfinished business.

When I advise single parents to be honest, I do not mean to suggest that you blurt out the details of your personal life without first connecting with your child heart-to-heart. If you are disclosing your dating activities within a year or two after a divorce, remember that your child may not be reconciled to the fact that you and your ex are never going to get back together. When children ask questions of their parents about their dating activities, what they may really want is some reassuring but realistic information about the possibility of a reconciliation. The following story illustrates how one parent dealt with this concern.

After working with a Getting Real coach, Leslie decided to tell her

girls about Perry. She prefaced what she had to say by telling them that
she was feeling a mixture of feelings about talking to them about her personal dating life (Truth Skill #9, Sharing Mixed Emotions). She said she
didn't want to burden them with too much detail, but now she was
afraid that she was being dishonest. She was also afraid they would feel
upset if they knew that she and their dad were never getting back
together. The only specific detail she actually told them was that she was
dating Perry. She said she'd answer any question they asked about the situation. As it turned out, they only asked one question, which was one
she could not yet answer: "Are you going to marry
him?" When your kids ask some-
thing like this, a question that
is often on a child's mind, I
think it's best to find out,
"Why do you ask?" before
answering. Asking this question will give them a chance to say
what they are really feeling instead of hid-
ing their feelings behind a question. What Leslie's kids revealed was that
they were longing for the kind of stable family life they had had in the
past. They liked it when they were all "married and faithful forever." So
the girls' biggest concern was, "When can we get back to a more stable,
predictable lifestyle?"

Kids need to hear apologies from parents far more often than they ever do. It is one of the most healing things you can do for your children.

With kids, this is often a big concern, even if they are not able to
voice it. A divorce often disrupts a child's sense of stability. But life will
do this sooner or later anyway, so try not to take on guilt about this. Talk
to your kids openly about the topic, ask them about how the change has
affected them, listen attentively without defensiveness (watch out for
your control patterns!), and then respond with whatever feelings you
have. If you feel apologetic, go ahead and apologize. In most families,
kids need to hear apologies from parents far more often than they ever
do. It is one of the most healing things you can do for your children.

Coming Clean about Coming

Faye was ashamed of herself for faking orgasms these past few months with Leon. She had rationalized her behavior by telling herself that she was doing it so he would enjoy sex more but now that the relationship seemed to have long-term potential, she wanted to come clean about the whole thing. She wanted to, but she was also very fearful that Leon would be upset, that he would judge her, and that he might even break up with her. She wondered if there was any safe way to do what she had to do.

She thought of fabricating a story that all of a sudden her orgasms weren't happening anymore. But then she realized that could backfire on her and upset Leon even more than telling him the truth. She lived with this dilemma for several weeks.

With the help of a relationship coach, she decided to start by telling him that there was something important that she had withheld from him, and she wanted to create a safe space for sharing her disclosure. They agreed together upon an appropriate time and place. This got him involved in setting the stage and made it unlikely that she would chicken out. When the meeting time arrived, she asked him to hold her because this was a very emotional moment for her. Then she told him she had never in her life had an orgasm during intercourse, but had been afraid to tell him since she imagined most of his former lovers had been very hot. She said she had been afraid he would reject her if he knew her true sexual history. She was careful to speak only about her own feelings and not to blame him or hold him responsible. She did not say, for example, "I know you like hot women," or "I know you put a lot of importance on pleasing a woman." These statements would not be real because you can only be real or honest about yourself. She was careful to talk only about her own feelings and actions.

Leon was very upset. He thanked her for telling him, but he was cold and distant in his tone. He expressed how disappointed he was to learn that all this time he had been experiencing one thing and her experience had been quite different. He said he'd need some time to let this new information sink in. In the meantime, he thought it would be best if they did not have sex.

Faye was stunned. She knew he might be angry with her, but she was not prepared for this reaction. She thought he was punishing her. Her coach helped her refrain from jumping to any conclusions. Yes, Leon was upset; but maybe he just needed some time to assimilate this. Faye did not withdraw. She affirmed that she was telling him this now because she was feeling so close to him that she could no longer engage in any behavior that might contribute to separation. She said she wanted to have a relationship with him that was completely transparent from now on, with no secrets. She was tempted to justify her actions by noting that most people keep secrets from their partners, but she was able to curb this impulse to defend herself.

After a few days, Leon recovered and told her he was ready to go forward with her, this time with an expectation that there would be no more deceit. She was relieved and was tempted to just put the whole episode behind her as quickly as possible. But her coach encouraged her to ask Leon to tell her more about his experience: How had these past few days been for him? What were his feelings and thoughts about her and about the relationship? They talked about these things, which seemed to help him get over the anger and disappointment he was feeling.

Their relationship survived. And Faye was now able to relax during sex more than she ever had before, trusting that she did not need to perform for him anymore. From this point onward, they found themselves communicating more during sex. She began telling him what she wanted and what he was doing that felt especially good. They put more time and attention into their lovemaking instead of expecting things to magically work out. And although their sex life seemed to take more work, it also became more real and satisfying.

> She was tempted to justify her actions by noting that most people keep secrets from their partners, but she was able to curb this impulse to defend herself.

Stalking

There are a lot of lonely people out there. Some of them can be quite fascinating at first. But then, when you get to know them enough to know that you do not want to continue seeing them, you may be shocked to discover that they will not take no for an answer. Stalking can take a number of different forms — a former date coming to your door or driving by your house, calling on the phone, showing up at your workplace, or barraging you with emails. The type of stalking I'll be considering in this section is not the life-threatening kind, but even so, it's still a serious matter. I personally have been stalked, and I have coached many people with this problem.

If this should happen to you, see if you can make it a positive learning experience for yourself. It's an opportunity to learn how to mark your boundaries, which is an application of Truth Skill #5, Asserting What You Want and Don't Want. If stalking happens to you, perhaps you have not been as clear as you could have been about your real feelings for this person. Perhaps you had an intuition that they would not be able to handle "bad news," so you protected their feelings by avoiding full disclosure. And now you regret it.

The first step in handling a stalker is to tell the person firmly that you do not want any future contact whatsoever. You ask if they understand this. And you listen. If they seem to get it, you close the conversation immediately, wishing them well with their life. If they do not seem to get it, if they become defensive or aggressive, end the conversation right there by telling them, "I refuse to interact with you any further." Period. Then, do not explain or justify. That would be a control pattern designed to manage your own anxiety about the situation. Leave the situation, hang up, or whatever. If they ever contact you again, do not engage with them in any way. Don't answer their calls (You may have to screen your calls for a while.) Delete their emails. Don't open the door to them.

To get rid of a stalker, you have to mean what you say and demonstrate this by your behavior. Many people who have dealt with stalkers admit that they are not too good at clearly and firmly marking their boundaries, so the experience has ultimately turned out to be an important lesson for them.

Stalking behavior can range from mildly annoying to seriously threatening, so trust your instincts and get legal, professional, or law enforcement help if the problem seems more serious than you can handle.

In most of this book, I have stressed the importance of saying what you want without attachment to controlling the outcome. In the case of a stalker, of course you want this behavior to stop. To be true to yourself, you may need to get over your control pattern of being too nice or too passive. Don't confuse marking your boundaries with being "controlling." There are times when you need to be very firm in order to protect yourself.

My Date Is Not Complete with His Ex

Sheila has had three dates with Armand, and she's beginning to feel worried about the fact that Armand still calls his ex-girlfriend at least weekly. He seems very attentive to Sheila when he's with her, but she wonders if he's really ready for a new relationship. When they talk about the issue, Armand tries to be reassuring, but his reassurance doesn't dissolve her fears. Should she trust her intuition that he's really still in love with the other woman? And if this is actually true, should she stop seeing him? Or would it be best to continue to build the relationship in hopes that if things go well, he'll just naturally drift away from his ex?

If you find yourself in this situation, it's important not to censor your self-expression in the interest of protecting your date and yourself from discomfort. If you have questions, ask them. And notice how you feel as you hear the answers. Perhaps the most important question to answer is, "Do you trust Armand to be truthful with you about his real feelings?" If you do not, why is that? Do you perhaps have a pattern of not trusting people? Or is yours a pattern of attracting untrustworthy people?

There is no rule that says you should not become involved with someone who has unfinished business from a prior relationship. Most people do have some unfinished business with an ex. The real question is this: Can you allow yourself to talk about the things that bother you? Do not censor yourself. If you don't trust his answer, tell him so. It's your life at stake here, so don't give yourself cheaply to someone you cannot trust or to a relationship where you don't dare to be honest about your concerns.

If you tend to have a pattern of feeling jealous and insecure, maybe there are things about yourself that you don't trust — because if jealousy is your pattern, your ability to process information is probably not trustworthy. Jealous people often make up problems that do not exist. The difficulty will be in discerning, "Is this one of those times when I should mistrust my fears? Or is my intuition working well this time?" The only way you

> Most people do have some unfinished business with an ex. The real question is this: Can you allow yourself to talk about the things that bother you?

can find out is to: (1) communicate what you feel from a place of humility, admitting that your fears are sometimes unfounded; (2) listen to his responses and tune in to how you feel in your body as he responds to you; and (3) repeat this process over and over as long as you need to, until you learn to let go of your fears or until you decide on a course of action that feels right to you.

I'm Ready to Commit and He's Not

Eileen and Gene have been dating each other exclusively for over a year. She is sure that he is the man for her, the one she'd like to spend the rest of her life with. Gene, having been divorced twice, is not so sure of his ability to make a lasting commitment. Besides, he just doesn't feel toward Eileen the same way she seems to feel toward him. She really wants to get married. He isn't sure he can ever do that again, and he has told her this. Several of Eileen's women friends are telling her to "get out

now, before you get really hurt." Others advise her to give him an ulti-
matum: Either marry me now or lose me. If you were in Eileen's place,
what would you be feeling and thinking? And what would you do?

I have coached many precommitted couples in this situation.
Sometimes it is the woman who is quicker to commit, and sometimes
it's the man. In all these cases, the quicker-to-commit of the pair has had
trouble keeping their hearts open when they were not getting what they
wanted. My job as coach is to help my clients discover and act on what
is most real for them, not to help them avoid being hurt. I help them
learn not to turn off their feelings just because these feelings are uncomfortable.

In almost every situation I've dealt with, eventually the person who
was slower to commit did become committed. Sometimes it took years.
It always took a lot longer than the quicker-to-commit person would
have wanted. It seems to me that some people are just slower to make up
their minds. This is more a function of personality style than of how
much they love their partner. It's tough when you're in the position of
waiting for your partner to commit, but pushing the other to hurry up
and decide is controlling and will likely backfire on you. Even relating
your honest feelings whenever they come up probably isn't too attractive
either. Yet I think relating is the way to go. See if you can feel your fear,
anger, or frustration and at the same time not lose touch with your loving feelings. This is an application of Truth Skill #8, Holding Differences.
Talk about your feelings with your partner in the interest of transparency,
not as a manipulation. And ask for feedback (Truth Skill #4). Find out
how the other person is experiencing the discrepancy in commitment
readiness between the two of you. Perhaps it is painful for him, too. Don't
assume you're the only one in distress, and never blame your partner for
causing you distress. You have chosen to stay in the relationship knowing
the outcome is uncertain.

Is Your Eagerness a Control Pattern?

See what you can learn about yourself in this situation. Try on the
theory that perhaps your eagerness to get into a committed relationship

is a control pattern — perhaps you can't stand the uncertainty. And notice which of your buttons are getting pushed. You can use the situation to become more aware and self-accepting. What fears are coming up for you — your fear of abandonment? Your fear that you won't get what you want? Your fear that you're not good enough and if you don't hook him now, he'll find someone better? These fears need to be noticed, felt, and aired. Remember such fears are not real. They are about something that could happen in the future. Shining the light of conscious attention on them will help shrink them down to size. But they may come up again and again. All you can do is notice them, confess them, and try not to confuse them with reality.

Growing While Waiting

When you're not getting what you want, you may tend to regress into believing your fears. Remember that the main value of Truth Skill #5, Asserting What You Want and Don't Want, is to help you learn that you'll be okay even if you don't get what you want. The important thing is to feel and express your wants without attachment to the outcome. You will learn how to do this as you practice feeling them, expressing them, and then being okay with whatever happens.

In the case of Eileen and Gene, as she hung in there, she learned that she had a very high need to control the outcome. This was a valuable insight. She had never seen herself as a controller before because her controlling mainly took the form of feeling and acting insecure. Her ability to see this about herself helped Gene to trust her more.

> My job as coach is to help my clients learn not to turn off their feelings just because these feelings are uncomfortable.

During the years she was doing coaching with me and waiting for Gene, she was developing the ability to be with her uncomfortable, not-knowing-what-will-happen feelings, instead of acting them out in fits of anger or judgment. One of her control patterns had been to criticize him for his fear of commitment. This, of course, only made him doubt the relationship more. But in the end, after Eileen learned to take responsibility for her own insecurities, instead of expecting Gene to rescue her from herself, Gene realized he really did love her deeply. He just didn't want to get into another situation where he might let himself be controlled. They got married five years after their first meeting. To some that may seem like an eternity. But that was fourteen years ago, and they are still very happy together.

Chapter Summary

- If you do not disclose to your date the fact that you are dating others, you are being manipulative.
- If your kids ask you details about how serious a particular relationship is, find out what's behind the question before answering it.
- If you confess that you've lied to your partner, don't be shocked if he or she takes some time to let this new information sink in.
- If you're being stalked, you're being called to learn to mark your boundaries clearly and forcefully.
- If your date is still relating with his ex, express your feelings and questions, and keep expressing these until you feel satisfied.
- If you're ready to commit and the other person is not, focus on feeling and expressing your own feelings, not on trying to get the other to feel differently.

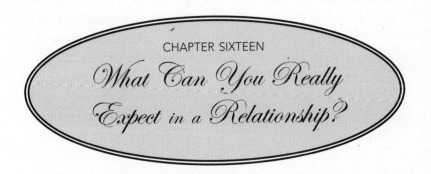

CHAPTER SIXTEEN

What Can You Really Expect in a Relationship?

*A relationship always takes more work
than you think it should.*

Have you ever found yourself in the predicament of loving almost everything about a person, but finding that there is one important thing missing, one fly in the ointment?

Mary has been dating Ted for almost a year. In many ways he is her ideal man, but he is not as interested in lovemaking and cuddling as she is. She resents the amount of time Ted spends at work, and while they have talked about this issue a lot, nothing seems to be changing. Should she stay or call it quits?

Art is in love with Trang, but he has one major frustration. After six months together, they have never, in his opinion, had a deep, soulful conversation. This is something he has had with lovers in the past, and he really misses this aspect of relating. Should he leave now or stay and try to work it out?

The quandary that Art and Mary find themselves in is a common one in dating and new relationships. Of course, a book like this cannot tell you what to do in any particular case, but I can offer you some things to consider as you address this important decision. In this chapter, we will look at what you can realistically expect in a relationship and how to take stock of your wants and needs in a way that supports long-term happiness and personal evolution.

> The more interdependence you have with each other, the greater is the opportunity for conflict.

It's important to remember that in a dating relationship, anyone is free to leave at any time. Some people are so afraid of hurting the other's feelings that they stay with someone as a way of avoiding making a mess. If this is true of you, the next two chapters on how to end things consciously will be useful to you.

What Can We Realistically Expect?

Most people enter a relationship with expectations, but often these expectations are based more on wishes and fears than on realism. When I talk about what you can expect, I am not going to give you a list of what is reasonable for partners to get from one another. My list is more about understanding the things that typically occur as two people grow more intimate, things like change and conflict and uncovering your shadow sides. Some of these things have been mentioned in previous chapters. In this chapter I'll discuss five developments you can expect. As I consider each topic in detail, I'll give you some questions to ask yourself to help you decide whether to leave or to hang in there. The six developments we'll consider are:

- It will change your life.
- It will not change your life.
- You will be disappointed.
- Your feelings will change.
- You won't meet each other's every need.
- You will get your buttons pushed.

It Will Change Your Life

When you decide to share your life with another person, you become interdependent with that person. That's both good news and bad news. His or her family and friends become your family and friends, at least to some degree, whether you like them or not. His money karma becomes your money karma. And if you are sexually monogamous, your sexual needs cannot be fully met without this other person's participation. If you want to spend time together, you will at times compromise what you would normally choose to do so you can share more time with your partner.

People's differences surface most often in the realm of money. Research has shown time and again that this is the topic partners fight most about. If you decide to have a joint bank account or other joint assets, this will really increase the opportunities for conflict. This isn't necessarily a bad thing because you will learn more about yourself this way. But you do have choice in how interdependent you become. Just remember, the more interdependence you have with each other, the greater is the opportunity for conflict. The only way to avoid conflict in this area is to keep your finances separated. Be aware, however, that if you decide to get legally married, you are automatically seen as a legal unit, and this other person's financial obligations will become your financial obligations.

Even if you choose not to marry, if you are a committed couple, your good fortune or bad fortune and hers become intertwined. If she loses her job or gets sick and can't earn a living, for example, this will affect your finances.

The most significant area of interdependence will be your sex life. For instance, if you decide to be monogamous, and you have differences in sexual appetite, this is a huge area of potential conflict. Again, her karma becomes your karma. If you like sex once a week, and she likes it once a day, that's not going to be fun for either of you. If she loses her interest in sex, which often happens when there is an accumulation of withheld communication, that's your problem as well as hers.

I hear many stories from my couples coaching clients about how painful it is when you love someone, but they just won't (or can't) give you what you want. I recall one couple, Jonathan and Hanna, whose sexual problem was that he loved oral sex and she just could not get herself to enjoy this. Even when she tried, it didn't satisfy him because he sensed her resistance. This had been a problem from the start of their relationship, but their lovemaking was pretty passionate at first, so he thought he could learn to live with things as they were. Later on, after the romantic bubble burst, he realized he could not. Such a change of heart is predictable, as we learned in chapter 9, "The Couple's Journey." Something that seems like a small issue may get much larger after the pair moves from Romance into Power Struggle, that is, after they feel bonded and safe enough to let it all hang out.

The point of this story is this: When you commit to sexual monogamy, you become dependent on one another for better or for worse. Moving from relative independence to relative interdependence has its joys and its heartaches. If you like the freedom of the single lifestyle, if you like deciding things by yourself without taking another's wishes into account, be honest with yourself about this. Getting hitched will require you to adapt and change. If you prefer doing things your own way, maybe commitment is not for you.

It Will Not Change Your Life

We have just considered how commitment to one person will change your life. From another perspective, it will not change your life. You will not be any happier. You will not feel any more secure. You will bring into the relationship the same state of mind that you had before it began. In most cases, just as before, when things go your way, you'll be happy and when they don't, you'll be unhappy.

Wendy had been single for three years since her last breakup. She considered herself to be a pairing type of person, one who is much happier when she is in a relationship. Three years without a significant other was a very long time to her. She felt lonely most of the time, and longed for someone special to just hang out with every night. She met Rich at her church, and after a year of dating each other exclusively, they decided to be married. After only a few months of marriage, she noticed that she was feeling lonely once again. Rich was an avid golfer, who often left the house before she awoke in the morning to hit the links. Then, because he started his days so early, he would be tired after he got home from work — too tired to do anything but eat and plop himself in front of the television where he would promptly fall asleep.

Wendy would joke to her friends, "At least I know where he is every night." But inside she was very unhappy. Nothing had really changed in her internal sense of herself or her life. Her basic experience was still one of "waiting for him to show up." Before she met Rich, she was waiting for him to show up, and now that she had found him, she was still waiting for him to show up.

> In most cases, just as before, when things go your way, you'll be happy and when they don't, you'll be unhappy.

Each person's life contains certain lessons and themes. One of Wendy's recurring themes was "waiting for someone to pay attention to her." As a child she had waited for her parents to get home from work. As a teen, she had waited for them to finish remodeling their home so she could have friends over. As a graduate student, she had waited to have a life until she got her doctorate; and so it went. One of Rich's themes was "being a disappointment to others." He had been a disappointment to his parents, to his former wife, to his children, and now to Wendy. Wendy and Rich each brought their "core issues" into married life. These issues didn't get magically healed after they said their marriage vows. As the wise saying goes, "wherever you go, there you are."

You Will Be Disappointed

Sooner or later another person is going to do something that hurts or disappoints you. Perhaps it is a carelessly spoken word. Or maybe he'll do something that you find inconsiderate of your feelings. Or it could be a broken agreement or a betrayal of confidence or trust. A few years ago, I did a major research study for a book that never got published on "Why Relationships End." What I discovered, after interviewing about fifty people, was that almost everyone I spoke with recalled one major disappointment that seemed to mark "the beginning of the end" — usually during the first year of the relationship. In reflecting upon why the relationship ended, they all told me that the fact of that first big disappointment coupled with the fact that they never spoke openly about this with their partner seemed to damage their bond irreparably. The conclusion I came to after exploring this issue more deeply with them was that if they had talked openly about their feelings with the other person, the relationship probably could have been repaired in most instances.

Barry and Deidre had been dating exclusively for about three months when he injured himself with a skill saw at his carpentry job. He immediately called her from the hospital emergency room before going into surgery to have about one hundred stitches in his leg. The hospital nearest the site of the accident was in a nearby city about two hours' drive from where Deidre lived. The injury was not life-threatening, but Barry was a big, burly man not used to feeling so helpless. Calling his new girlfriend to come and be at his bedside was a major act of vulnerability for him. He had not yet told her he felt committed to her and to the relationship; if he had, she would have told him that her feelings were not quite that strong yet. She adored him, but wasn't sure he was the one. Still, she consented to come and be with him, to stay at the hospital overnight with him, and to be there as long as he needed her.

> Almost everyone I spoke with recalled one major disappointment that seemed to mark "the beginning of the end" — usually during the first year of the relationship.

He told her on the phone that he was about to go into surgery and hoped to see her at his bedside when he came out. Since the trip was going to involve at least one or two nights away from home, Deidre had to pack her bags and make a few phone calls. Then she had a two-hour drive ahead of her, so her arrival at his bedside was two hours later than Barry expected. He thought she would just get in her car and drive to the hospital. (After all, he was her man, and he needed her there with him.)

She wasn't aware of this expectation. She took the time she needed to get ready for the trip, got lost once on the way, but still managed to get there before Barry's bedtime. She felt good about being able to take the time to be with him and thought he would be grateful and happy to see her.

When she entered his hospital room, he was sitting up just staring out the window. As she approached him for a kiss, he scolded, "What happened? Where were you?" She explained that she had to pack and that she'd gotten lost once, since this was not a city she had been to before. He seemed to accept her explanation, so as far as she was concerned the matter was settled.

Four years later, as they were in the process of divorcing, they had a few sessions with a couples counselor. In these sessions, Barry confessed that he had never trusted her and never really "let her in." He said this feeling started that day at the hospital when he was lying there alone, feeling weak and vulnerable, wondering what was taking her so long. He had decided then and there that he could not trust her (just like he was never able to trust anyone, his recurring theme). Deidre was shocked and sad, but it was too late to change his mind. That big disappointment had created a deeper wound than the skill saw had. And no amount of stitching was going to repair it at this point.

What Makes You Feel Loved? An Exercise

Most people have unspoken expectations of their date or their partner. We all have our favorite ways of being treated that are unique to us. To help bring these into awareness, I suggest you have a conversation with your date or partner about the secret expectations you both have. You can start such a conversation by doing the "How Do You Know That You're Loved?" exercise. The exercise asks that each of you take turns asking and answering the question, "How Do You Know That You're Loved?" For example:

HARVEY: How do you know that you're loved?

ANITA: When someone listens to me attentively… looks at me and acknowledges what I have said.

ANITA: How do you know that you're loved?

HARVEY: When someone appreciates something I have done and tells me I've done a good job.

HARVEY: How do you know that you're loved?

ANITA: When someone I care about gives me a foot rub.

ANITA: How do you know that you're loved?

HARVEY: When someone I love says she doesn't want me to go home after we've made love.

Continue this question and answer process back and forth for a few minutes until you both feel complete.

In a slightly more mature relationship, you might also try the "If You Really Loved Me…" exercise. Even if you have never uttered the words "if you really loved me," you may secretly harbor some ideas about what love means that your partner does not know about. This is another way to find out who expects what and who will be disappointed by what. Each of you writes the words "If you really loved me…" at the top of a sheet of paper. Then list all the things you can think of, as in: "If you really loved me…

- You would help with the dishes without my having to ask.
- You would buy me gifts when you go on business trips.
- You would hold my hand when we're walking down the street.
- You would touch me the way I've told you I like it without my having to repeat myself.
- You would tell me about the things I do that you like during lovemaking.
- You would tell me you love me at least once a day.
- You would tell me you're proud to be with me."

This is just a sampling of the kinds of wants and longings partners keep secret from one another — until their sack of grievances gets too full, and then everything comes tumbling out.

Once you have both made your lists, read your partner's list, and discuss the differences, similarities, and surprises. Doing this exercise together can help you prevent needless disappointments. It can also raise awareness of your own beliefs about love and the origins of these beliefs. The statement "If you really loved me, you would get here on time for our dates" can now be seen as nothing more than an expectation. An expectation indicates a belief. It is one person's story about how life should be. It is not necessarily how life is. The exercise is designed to help you get a healthy distance or detachment from your expectations and beliefs. Maybe, after reading your list, you'll even be able to laugh at yourself a bit. That would be a good first step toward creating a relationship where disappointments (i.e., disappointed expectations) are not taken personally.

> An expectation indicates a belief. It is one person's story about how life should be. It is not necessarily how life is.

Collecting Grievances

In his classic *The Intimate Enemy*, famous fair-fighting guru George Bach cautions partners to beware of saving up their disappointments and angers and then dumping them onto their partners all at once. He found that many people collect grievances in a big imaginary gunnysack. When you have held on to as much as you can, the sack finally gets so full it won't hold any more. Then if your partner does "one more thing," you dump your collected grievances all over him or her. The present gripe is just a trigger and may be followed by a barrage of other resentments: "You turned over and started snoring after we made love last New Year's... and you cut me off in mid-sentence three times at your mother's birthday dinner... and how could you *not* know I was premenstrual when we took that workshop in New York last year. . . . You should never have walked out on me in front of the whole group!" Imagine how you might feel receiving such a barrage of feelings. Would you feel defensive? Probably. Would you remember these incidents exactly as your partner did? Probably not! Would you wish you'd been told about these grievances sooner so you could clear up any misunderstandings? Perhaps. But just as likely, you might wish you could avoid such discussions entirely. You can; but if you do, the quality of your relationship will suffer, and thoughts of ending it will occur more frequently.

So remember, it's not the fact of being disappointed that affects your love and your trust; it's how you communicate (or fail to communicate) about these issues.

Your Feelings Will Change

When you first meet someone attractive, your attention will be mainly on the things you like. Even if you notice their faults or foibles, these will usually take a back seat to the qualities you appreciate.

One thing that often throws people as they are getting to know someone is the "tip of the iceberg" phenomenon mentioned previously in chapter 9. Again, the human personality is a little bit like an iceberg in that only a small part is visible. Most of the person's patterns, features, and foibles are beneath the surface and cannot be seen. As we get to know a new person beyond the first few months, we may be surprised to discover that there is much more to this person, for better or for worse, than we first suspected.

> There is a certain mysterious wonderfulness to how we seem to be attracted to people whose darker, hidden stuff turns out to be exactly what we need for our own spiritual evolution.

Some people get disillusioned with dating when they discover that what they see is rarely what they get. At first we only see part of the person, but later on what we get is all their unfinished business from childhood and former partners, including their unconscious fears, their demands that we modify our behavior so as not to push their buttons, their unresolved dependencies, their sexual hang-ups, their addictions, and all the control patterns they have taken on as a way of managing the fear of being vulnerable.

That's right. When you first feel that surge of attraction, you're responding, at least consciously, to only the tip of the person's whole being. Of course there is a certain mysterious wonderfulness to how we seem to be attracted to people whose darker, hidden stuff turns out to be exactly what we need for our own spiritual evolution.

Some lack of harmony is to be expected. This is all part of a larger movement toward healing for both partners. By consciously applying Truth Skill #1, Experiencing What Is, and Truth Skill #2, Being Transparent, partners can heal the very wounds that threaten to drive them apart.

Molly and James knew it would take some time to get to know each other's darker, hidden parts. But they also thought they might shorten this time by practicing Truth in Dating. They came to one of my seminars after only knowing each other for a month. During the first day of the two-day experience, they appeared to be the perfect couple — common interests, similar personal styles, no conflicts. But then on Sunday afternoon, something unexpected happened. We were doing an exercise designed to shed light on how people communicated about their sexual boundaries. In the middle of what I thought was a fairly nonthreatening activity, Molly broke into tears, pulled away from James, and curled up on the floor shaking and sobbing. The only words she could speak were, "No...no...NO!!!" When her sobs subsided, she told us that she was recalling the first time she and James had sex together. She had not been ready to have him enter her, but she pretended otherwise. She had realized this recently but did not know how to tell James, since he seemed to be really enjoying that part of their relationship. She was ashamed of herself for not being honest from the start.

When it was time for James to respond with his own feelings, he admitted that he felt some anger but mostly relief. He confessed that he had felt something was off between them but had been afraid to bring it up. As Molly and James talked further, she shared that she had a pattern of becoming sexually active with men before she was really ready. Her story was she had been sexually abused by her stepfather, whom she dearly loved. She was afraid he would go away like her father had if she didn't do what he wanted, so she got into the habit of submitting. The boundaries exercise helped her connect with a part of her that she had not been conscious of previously.

Telling the truth can help you see yourself and the other more fully right from the start. The more you communicate your present feelings and self-talk, the sooner you'll both get to know the other person's shadow. The shadow is the part of the personality that we tend to keep hidden, not out of any intent to deceive, but more out of unconsciousness. As Molly and James discovered, communication about delicate or difficult matters helps bring unconscious feelings and beliefs into awareness.

Communicating about Difficult Issues: Two Exercises

There are two exercises that you can practice together to foster this sort of communication, "I'm Afraid It Would Hurt You If You Knew…" and "I'm Afraid You Would Reject Me If You Knew…"

"I'm Afraid It Would Hurt You If You Knew…"

Sit facing each other and take turns completing the sentence, "I'm afraid it would hurt you if you knew_____." Both partners have to agree that this is a good time to do the exercise, since it requires presence and risk-taking. People who have used this exercise report feeling lighter and closer to one another afterward, even if they heard "bad news." New partners often keep secrets from each other, either unconsciously or in an effort to protect their fragile bond. If you take a risk and tell the truth, you may find that the bond actually gets stronger. This frequently happens when we disclose things that we have been withholding. We may feel a sense of relief, or even the sense that "this person can love me warts and all." That's what all of us long for — to be loved just as we are.

"I'm Afraid You Would Reject Me If You Knew..."

After you and your partner complete the above exercise, here's another one that will stretch you even further. Sit facing each other and take turns completing the sentence, "I'm afraid you would reject me if you knew_____." Again, both people have to agree that this is a good time to do the exercise.

You Won't Meet Each Other's Every Need

Even when you're enjoying the first blush of romance, you are probably aware (at least in theory) of the fact that you will not meet each other's every need. No one person can meet all your relational needs, and it probably wouldn't even be good for you if he could. If someone did meet all your needs, that would keep you from growing up emotionally. You wouldn't have to get over the normal (but unhealthy) attachment to getting your own way.

All these notions about being emotionally grown-up are great in theory, but putting this into practice can be challenging. Hearing your partner say she wants to go somewhere with a special friend instead of with you... well, that might be hard to accept. Has this happened to you? Have you ever heard a partner say he or she would rather do something else than be with you? If not, be prepared, for you probably will. And if it never happens, well then your relationship is probably not very mature. You are probably still "babying" each other or the relationship, treating it as too fragile to handle such conflicts. In any relationship, there will be things one partner wants to do that do not include the other person. If you avoid

> You cannot entirely avoid frustration or pain. This being the case, why not use this pain to heal yourself?

mentioning such things so as not to cause discomfort, then your relationship will never evolve to its full potential.

Sure, it can hurt to hear someone say that he or she would rather be
with someone else (or alone) than with you. It hurts, but it's good for
you. It is good for you in the sense that
by facing the truth that you do
not meet each other's every
need, you also grow in your
ability to handle life as it is.
Life is full of things that are not
under your control. Accepting this makes
you stronger. If you insist on getting things your way all the time, you
will stay immature, and so will your relationship.

*That's the healing that needs
to happen — to stop avoiding emotional
pain and start feeling it.*

An Exercise in Embracing Differences

Here is an exercise to try with a partner.

1. On a full-size sheet of paper, each make your own indi-
    vidual list of the things you love to do.
2. In the left-hand column next to each item, write *A* for
    things you prefer to do alone, *P* for things you prefer to
    do with your partner, and *O* for things you like to do
    best with someone other than your partner.
3. Now share your lists and talk about your feelings. As you
    share feelings, be sure and start with the words, "I
    feel...." Using "I feel" statements will prevent you from
    attacking, blaming, or judging your partner.

After doing this exercise, give yourselves credit for taking on the
challenge of being honest about difficult things. Being honest about
your needs for separate space will bring you to a deeper level of intimacy.
It will speed you on your way to a relationship based on trust — one
where trust is no longer seen in terms of "I trust you to never hurt me"

(which is unrealistic), but rather in terms of "I trust myself to be able to handle whatever feelings come up between us. I trust that if you do something that hurts me, I will talk with you about it. And I trust that you and I together can listen to each other's feelings non-defensively so we can get to forgiveness and healing." This is what trust means in a real, grown-up relationship.

You Will Get Your Buttons Pushed

We learned about buttons in chapter 10. The reason most people end a dating relationship is because one (or more) of their buttons was pushed, and they did not know how to take responsibility for their own triggers.

Tara and Randy had a date to go out on the town for New Year's Eve. Randy's nine-year-old daughter was with her babysitter that night. At about 11:00 P.M., he got a call on his cell phone that his daughter was having intense stomach cramps. Without consulting Tara, he made an immediate decision to go home and take his daughter to the emergency room. He apologized to Tara and invited her to go with him, but she declined. The next day Tara broke off the relationship.

Randy's sudden unilateral decision to take care of his daughter pushed Tara's abandonment button. Although she was not able to admit it to Randy, she took the decision personally. Instead of disclosing that she was hurt and angry in a way that might lead to a fuller and deeper sharing of mutual feelings, she chose to end things. Randy tried to get her to talk about her feelings, but she stubbornly refused, claiming that she now knew how little he valued her.

When one of your buttons gets pushed, you are in no frame of mind to make an intelligent decision. It's as if you have a bad drug in your system, so you need to talk it out with someone you trust or wait a day or two until you can be more present. Tara didn't know about buttons. She just thought Randy was insensitive to her needs. Perhaps someday, she'll read this book and understand that she has a self-protective pattern of leaving relationships as soon as she gets a button pushed.

Avoiding Pain Leads to Unnecessary Suffering

The bottom-line conclusion of these six relationship maxims is: You cannot entirely avoid frustration or pain. This being the case, why not use this pain to heal yourself? Just the act of admitting that you have buttons is a healing thing to do for yourself — especially if you allow yourself to feel what you feel (the hurt, the fear, the anger) when you get triggered. If Tara had been able to feel and express her pain about Randy's change of plans, she would have been one step closer to healing her childhood wounding from all the times her parents left her alone to go out by themselves. If you get hurt feelings, that's one of your buttons. When you have disappointed expectations, that's about your buttons. Many people leave a relationship (or fantasize about leaving it) if some piece of old painful unfinished business keeps getting restimulated by the other person. If Tara had stayed with Randy, her abandonment button probably would have gotten pushed again, perhaps many times. If she had talked about her own pain each time, and felt the true origin of her hurt feelings, she might have learned how to be with herself in a nurturing way when she felt those familiar painful feelings. That's the healing that needs to happen, for Tara and most people — to stop avoiding emotional pain and start feeling it. Feeling it can connect you to what's incomplete in your past. You feel whatever you were too scared or weak to feel at the time it originally occurred. You comfort and heal yourself by being fully present to your feelings each time they occur. When you know how to do this, you gain a much deeper sense of self-trust and trust in life.

What If Important Wants and Needs Are Not Being Met?

While it is true that wants may sometimes be indicative of unrealistic expectations, your wants may also reveal authentic core values. By knowing and affirming these wants, you are affirming your authentic self. Sometimes it's hard to know which is which — to know when a want is coming simply from the need to avoid discomfort and when it supports your essential nature. Here is an exercise to help you discover the difference.

Think of something the person you're dating does or does not do that causes you to either fantasize about ending it or to think "this person is not good for me." Here are a few possible responses to get you started: "He doesn't have a job"; "He's too critical"; "She's angry at me too often." Now, let's imagine your answer was, "She's angry at me too often." Is that a button or simply an affirmation that you want to be treated with respect? If it is a button, it will keep on getting triggered either in this relationship or the next one, until you accept it as your button, stop blaming the other for hurting you, and aim to be present to the feelings underneath the reaction. To distinguish a button from a bona fide need for respect, notice when

If your button gets pushed in a way that is so painful as to be paralyzing or damaging to your health, then I'd advise ending it.

she gets angry at you: Are you able to be present to the interaction with your own feelings — to feel and express your own anger or fear? If you are, then it's probably not a button. If you find yourself reacting defensively and automatically, then it's one of your buttons. If it is a button, this fear-of-anger reaction will keep calling for your attention, in this relationship or in future ones, until you have had enough conscious experience with it to heal it.

That still leaves the question "If someone's behavior consistently pushes my button in a way that is extremely painful, might it not be necessary to end the relationship with this person just to preserve my equilibrium?" My advice is to look at whether you are able to learn anything about yourself in this relationship, even though you're very hurt or upset. Usually you won't be in a learning frame of mind right at the instant your button is pushed. But later on, after you come back to present-time awareness, you might discover some useful lessons. If learning is happening, I'd say you should hang in there. If your button gets pushed in a way that is so painful as to be paralyzing or damaging to your health, then I'd advise ending it.

Life doesn't serve us what we want on a silver platter. For most of us, intimate relationships are where we get the most frustrated. This is also where we have the best chance to heal our old wounds. If you find someone who is willing to undertake this growth journey with you, someone who is willing to tell the truth and hear your truth, that's worth a lot. If the other person's presence in your life does not support your personal evolution, then it's probably time to call it quits.

Chapter Summary

- In any relationship, you can expect to get buttons pushed and to experience conflict and painful feelings at times. When these things happen, it does not mean that you or the other did something wrong.
- What you see in the beginning is not what you will get later on. As trust grows, people tend to feel safer about revealing more of themselves.
- If some of your dependency needs are frustrated with this person, this could be good for you if it encourages you to develop your capacity for nurturing and validating yourself.
- It's time to end it if: core bottom-line needs are not being met (such as the need for honesty), if the person does not support your chosen path in life, or if being with this person destabilizes you too much.

PART FOUR

Ending It

CHAPTER SEVENTEEN

How to Say Good-bye Consciously

When you know how to say good-bye truthfully
and with caring for the other person's feelings,
then you can exit with both people's self-respect intact.

et's face it, most dating relationships end at some point, and
most people do not do endings very skillfully. Because endings
tend to be uncomfortable, and most of us prefer to avoid discomfort, our control patterns often take over.

Truth in Dating offers a way to notice your patterns and get free of
them, so you can break things off consciously, truthfully, and respect-
fully. If you end things consciously, you won't be afraid of running into
this person in the supermarket or at the next singles mixer, and you will
be more ready to move on without baggage. When you end things
unconsciously or manipulatively, the other person's ghost may stay
around to haunt you.

Suzanne and Roy's relationship ended when Roy simply stopped
calling her after four months of steady dating. She was confused,
hurt, and angry. She dealt with her feelings by gossiping about Roy to
her circle of friends. Then one day, six months after the breakup,
Suzanne and Roy unexpectedly saw each other at a social event. He was

so uncomfortable seeing her that he left the event soon after he arrived. She stayed, but she couldn't enjoy herself for fear that he might reappear.

When a relationship ends the ways theirs did, you are never really finished with it. Suzanne was still carrying anger about how he handled the breakup and confusion over why. Roy was harboring shame and guilt about his cowardly actions. And they were both carrying a fear of running into one another again. As Suzanne and Roy's story illustrates, if you end things poorly, your future freedom may be limited by the need to avoid contact with the other person.

In my interviews, most of the people I spoke with were burdened by wounds from at least one past relationship that did not end well. As a result, they felt mistrustful and defensive with subsequent partners to some degree.

The ending of a relationship is an important transition and one that requires sensitivity. If you end things in an unconscious way, you will carry the unfinished business from this relationship into your future.

How to Know If It's Over

The decision about whether to end things is often a difficult one. The relationship may have some very good things going for it and still not be viable. My personal rule of thumb is that it's time to end your relationship if any of these conditions are present:

- one or more of your authentic needs are not being met (e.g., the need for touch);
- your partner's behavior violates one or more of your basic requirements, such as honesty or keeping agreements;
- you are having so many unhappy times together that you can't remember the good times;
- you do not feel safe to be yourself;
- when you bring up your feelings to clear the air, your partner is unable to listen or respond appropriately;
- you are doing most of the giving and your partner is doing most of the taking;

- the pain is so intense that you are unable to learn the personal lessons that seem to be "up" for you (such as learning to assert your wants);
- the pain is so intense that it is affecting your health.

If any of these eight points is occurring in your dating relationship, it may be time to call it quits. If you want to be in integrity, I recommend that before you end things, you let the other know that the situation has become intolerable for you. Be specific about what needs to change, and let the other know that you are considering ending the relationship. Some people can only hear your wants when you express yourself very strongly. You may be surprised at how some people will respond to the threat of possible ending with, "I didn't know you felt so strongly about it. I can change this rather than lose you."

If you end things consciously, you won't be afraid of running into this person in the supermarket or at the next singles mixer, and you will be more ready to move on without baggage.

What's Your Style?

We all have different styles of dealing with endings, with some people finding endings very difficult and others appearing to take this transition more lightly. The ending point of a relationship is a good time to do an honest self-assessment, including an examination of your characteristic ending style. Here are some questions to ask yourself.

1. Are you typically the "dumper" or the "dumpee?" Some people rarely or never end a relationship. Samantha was such a person. In over twenty years of dating, she always found herself in the position of the one who got left. It wasn't that she was unattractive. She just could not stand to hurt someone's feelings.

   If you are always the dumpee and never the dumper, what might you be avoiding? Do you, like Samantha, fear hurting others so much that you stick around until things get intolerable, and the other person finally takes action? Or do you have so much fear of being alone that you cannot leave a relationship even if it is not good for you? Or perhaps you aren't very good at picking up a partner's cues that he is not satisfied.

If you tend to be the one who gets dumped, how have you responded when the other told you it was over? Did you try to get away from the situation as quickly as possible? Did you ask questions to help you understand? Did you share your own feelings? Did you get angry or judgmental? Did you act cooler than you really felt? As you read these questions, notice if feelings and memories arise. If there is pain, allow yourself to feel it, and find a reliable way to console or soothe yourself. Use Truth Skill #1, and allow yourself to Experience What Is. When you fully experience your feelings, they change; whereas when you try to suppress or deny what you feel, you stay stuck.

> Blaming supports you in feeling righteously wronged. It prevents you from getting over your angry feelings, so you're likely to be stuck with them.

Some people have rarely or never been left. They are the ones who leave first. If this is your pattern, what might you be avoiding? Are you so afraid of failure or rejection that you take matters into your own hands and end it before things get really bad or before the other person gets tired of you? Or are you so easily bored that you cannot stay with one person?

Any time you notice a pattern in your way of doing things, it's a good bet that this pattern is about avoiding discomfort. If you become aware of your patterns, you can free yourself from them by moving toward situations you once avoided. Thus, if you have always been a dumper, try hanging in there longer than you're comfortable with. If you are usually the dumpee, take a risk and end a relationship as soon as you are sure it isn't working for you.

2. Do you blame yourself? Blaming is a control pattern designed to help you understand why something happened about which you feel powerless, thus helping you feel more in control. Any time you blame anyone for anything, you are not facing reality.

   Maureen had a pattern of blaming herself any time a relationship ended, whether she was the dumper or the dumpee. She told me this helped her cope with feeling powerless to make her relationship the way she wanted it. I encouraged her to allow herself to fully experience her helpless feelings. With my support, she was able to revisit these feelings and to grieve for all the other times in her life she has felt this way. In doing this, she realized that feeling helpless can be a real feeling. It is a valid human experience that occurs when we want something that we cannot have. Everyone alive needs to come to terms with this form of helplessness sooner or later.

3. Do you blame your partner? Blaming others is a form of anger, but it does not allow you to really experience your anger and take full responsibility for it. Blaming supports you in feeling righteously wronged. It prevents you from getting over your angry feelings, so you're likely to be stuck with them. Blaming is a control pattern that keeps you in the victim posture.

   After her breakup with Louie, Raquel felt she had been the victim of betrayal. She had caught him cheating with another woman, so she felt justified in blaming him. As she soon learned, blaming can have a number of secondary gains besides helping you feel in control. If you can convince others that you were victimized, this gives you a way to get sympathy and attention for many weeks to come. It also keeps you safe from being hurt again because it keeps you stuck where you are and thus unable to open up and trust. If you never trust again, you cannot be hurt. At least that's the theory.

Unfortunately, when so much is going on in your subconscious mind, you are not living in the present. When you are not present, this reinforces feelings of powerlessness beyond those that are a normal part of being human. This is an unhealthy type of powerlessness. Eventually, Raquel realized this. But it took her over a year of bad-mouthing Louie and dramatizing her suffering before she woke up to what this pattern was costing her.

4. Do you overlook or deny your real suffering? Troy was having a hard time ending it with Tamara. For over two years he had been telling himself, "Things aren't good, but they aren't that bad.... Sure she speaks rudely to me almost every day... sure she never wants to make love... sure she is critical of my friends and tries to control whom I spend time with... but nobody's perfect.... If things get really bad, I'll leave. Until then, I can hang in here a while longer."

Troy had a little-known addiction — the addiction to stability. He hated change and simply could not bring himself to risk the unknown. As we say in the psychotherapy profession, "Some people would rather endure a known sickness than risk an unknown cure."

Eventually, after much coaching and pressure from his friends, he admitted how much pain he was feeling.

He could only dare to feel this after he made it his conscious intention to deal more skillfully with change. He took action, ended the relationship using some of the tools in this book, and realized that taking a risk and surviving is one of the most self-empowering things a person can do.

How Not to End It

We know endings are often painful, and people don't like pain. Let's look at the nine most common control patterns people use to minimize the discomfort of ending it. While these strategies may appear to ease the pain to some degree, they are all short-term fixes. As you'll discover as you read on, they all backfire. See if you recognize yourself, your current partner, or a former partner in any of the following.

> Some people need to pick a fight or create a crisis in order to feel justified in calling it quits.

1. The disappearing act
2. Let's just be friends
3. Create a crisis
4. Make his or her life a living hell
5. Grow cold and distant
6. On again, off again
7. Plot an escape
8. Immediately find a replacement
9. Have a secret affair

The Disappearing Act

In the hit song "Fifty Ways to Leave Your Lover," this is the style known as "slip out the back, Jack." You just suddenly disappear one day never to be heard from again. The problem with this approach is you lose self-respect each time you do it. And people lose respect for you. Another problem is that you aren't able to get closure or a sense of completion.

If you have been left by someone without explanation, do what you can to get in contact with the person to learn what happened. Even if you do not get an honest answer, you will have the satisfaction of knowing that you did what you could to get closure. And just hearing how this person deals with your question could help you recognize that "it's really over," or even "it's really a good thing that it's over."

Regina and Wilson had been seeing one another about five nights a week for six months. They had professed their love for each other many times. One evening he called her to cancel a date, saying that he was being seriously considered for a new job in another state and had to go there for an interview. He told her he would be gone for a week and that he would call her from there or upon his return. She never heard from him after that.

She waited a month and then realized he was probably never going to call and that if she wanted to know what was going on, she would have to take action. She knew where he had been working before, and while she was reluctant to violate his privacy this way, she decided to visit his workplace or former workplace — she wasn't sure which. She felt she needed to learn the truth so she could get on with her life.

> Some people end a relationship in their mind long before they ever let their partner in on the decision.

When she got to his office and inquired as to whether he still worked there, she was greeted by his secretary, who said in a sober tone, "I'm afraid I have bad news for you." The secretary then told Regina that Wilson was married with three children. She took Regina into his office and showed her the family photos on the wall behind Wilson's desk. Regina was shocked and hurt, but she was glad she had pursued the matter. It was a lot easier to let go now, knowing what she did about Wilson, rather than fantasizing about someone who, in one sense, did not exist. She was able to grieve, comfort herself, and reflect on what she could learn from this painful experience.

Let's Just Be Friends

Sometimes, to protect the other's feelings, you tell her that you want to stay friends — when the truth is you do not. You may even go through the motions of friendship for a while, perhaps talking to her on the phone occasionally, all the while wishing she'd hurry up and end the call. Eventually the friendship fades, and since you've done your penance, you're able to move on without guilt. Or are you?

If you suspect that the person who says, "Let's stay friends" is insincere, mention your suspicion to him, and notice how he responds. If he shows genuine caring or concern for your feelings of doubt, you'll feel one thing. If he gets defensive or angry, you'll feel something else. Notice how your body feels as you listen to his response and share this with him. The goal here is not to find out if he's lying so much as it is to express your own feelings and impressions so you can end things feeling you did so in a way that was true to yourself. You can never know for sure what someone else feels, so don't waste your energy playing supersleuth. Just mention your feelings and self-talk, staying on your own side of the net.

Cynthia felt guilty about breaking up with Layton, so she said almost as an afterthought, "I hope we can still be friends." Layton said he'd like that. About three days later, he called and asked if he could come over for a friendly visit. Being caught off guard, Cynthia said, "Yes, of course," knowing that this was not her true feeling but figuring that she would deal with this when he got to her house. When he arrived, he was so obviously happy to see her that she didn't have the heart to tell him the truth — that she was not interested in him, even as a friend. They talked for an hour, and finally he left. A few days later, he called again, and a similar meeting occurred. This time she decided it was easier to put up with his occasional visits than to hurt his feelings. Their "friendship" went on for a year before Layton fell in love with someone else and began calling Cynthia less and less.

As you can imagine, Cynthia's self-respect took a nosedive during that year of keeping up the pretense of being a friend to Layton. If you were in Cynthia's place, what would you do? Can you imagine telling Layton the truth, perhaps using Truth Skill #7, Revising an Earlier Statement? Remember, it's never too late to go out and come in again.

Create a Crisis

Some people need to pick a fight or create a crisis in order to feel justified in calling it quits. This is a way to put distance between themselves and someone else — presumably so leaving will be less painful. The problem with this strategy is that any decision made in the heat of anger is not trustworthy, and it often does not stick. While partners may end the fight with one yelling, "I'm outta here!" and the other shouting, "Fine!" such decisions do not hold up when tempers cool off. People who use crisis as a way to end things, even if the ending does stick, are likely to be carrying a lot of unfinished business into their future relationships.

If your partner tries to end things during a fight, do not "accept her resignation." Say, "I hear you saying it's over between us. I want to wait and make a final decision about this when we're not so upset. Can we let things cool down and talk in a few days?"

Bernie and Bobbi had been dating only three months when Bernie realized he wasn't getting some important needs met. The only trouble was that he had never actually mentioned his wants to Bobbi. Still he was pretty certain that the relationship was not going to work for him. As his mind churned with all the times he had felt frustrated by Bobbi's "insensitivity," he got more and more angry. Finally, that night, he uncorked his bottled-up rage, telling Bobbi that he had never been happy with her, had never been in love with her, and had been caretaking her instead of expressing himself honestly. He said he was not willing to spend another day in a loveless union, and no matter what she said he was finished with her.

Bobbi was devastated and shaken. She tried to talk to him, but he interrupted her, saying it was of no use. She felt powerless, so in her attempt to regain a sense of control, she screamed at him, "Okay, I hear you. I'm not willing to stay where I'm not wanted. Don't call me again . . . ever!"

A week later, Bobbi realized that if she had been more present, she would have handled the crisis differently. She wished she had asked him to have another conversation with her after he'd had a chance to reflect on the decision. She regretted what she had said, and wished she could do it over. She tried to contact him so that she might have a chance to go out and come in again, but he did not return her calls. In the end, all she could do was write him a letter speaking all the feelings that she had wanted to say on that difficult night. He never responded, but the process of writing and sending the letter allowed her to resolve the matter in her own mind. She said to herself, "It didn't work out the way I wanted, but at least I did what I could and expressed what I wasn't able to say at the time. That makes it easier to let go and move on."

> Some people cannot stand to reject another person. So instead, they hurt and disappoint their partner over an extended period of time hoping their partner will eventually reject them.

Make His or Her Life a Living Hell

Some people just cannot stand to reject another person. So instead, they hurt and disappoint their partner over an extended period of time hoping their partner will eventually reject them. This sounds crazy, but it happens. If your partner is behaving in a way that continually hurts you, and if you have talked about it and nothing changes, and you're pretty sure there is nothing useful to be learned by staying with your painful feelings, then go ahead and end it yourself. Don't stubbornly hang in there just to force him to admit that he's the one who wants to call it quits. Be merciful and put an end to everyone's misery.

Grow Cold and Distant

This pattern is similar to "making life hell." The person who wants to end things is afraid to take action — either because she doesn't like to reject anyone or because she does not trust her instincts that the relationship isn't going to work. So she forces the other to make the decision.

If you suspect your partner is using this strategy, once again go ahead and be the decisive one. If the other is cold and distant, and you have shared your feelings repeatedly using the ten truth skills, then you have done all you can do. This is not a healthy situation for you to stay in, so get out.

Brandon and Verona had been exclusive lovers for two years, and their sex was always satisfying for both of them. But that was the only thing that was working from Verona's point of view. So, as difficult as this was, she decided to wean herself and him from the sex so it would be easier to end it. She took a second job and began to work longer hours. That way she could honestly say to him that she was too tired to make love.

Her plan worked. She never actually had to break things off formally. The two of them simply drifted apart, and pretty soon he told her he was dating someone else. Verona was relieved. This strategy, while effective in one sense, did damage her self-esteem. She says now that she wishes she could have been more honest with Brandon about her feelings.

> The fear of being alone can drive you to tolerate things that are not good for you.

She carries some unfinished business from this relationship in that she still does not trust herself to get sexually bonded again with a man. She holds herself back from the new men in her life because she doesn't want to risk a repeat of what happened with Brandon.

Verona's story reminds us that when you do not end things in a self-respecting way, you tend to feel incomplete about that situation — which makes it hard to move on free of past baggage.

On Again, Off Again

You've undoubtedly heard the phrase "Can't live with him, can't live without him." You break up, but then you realize you miss him. You reconcile, but things still don't work between the two of you. So you break up again. And so on. When this sort of pattern occurs often in a relationship, it usually means that one or both partners are addicted to the relationship, but neither one has the inner strength to make a definitive decision to end it.

Technically, this is not really a strategy for ending it. It's really a way to avoid ending and avoid commitment, because any definitive decision would bring up too much anxiety. Both partners are ambivalent. There's too much bad, so they can't accept "the bad with the good." But there's also a lot of "good," so it's difficult to let this go. If a relationship has so much good that you're hooked but so much bad that you'll never be able to fully commit, it certainly will be hard to take decisive action. But leaving is probably the best course.

Plot an Escape

Some people end a relationship in their mind long before they ever let their partner in on the decision. Instead of putting energy into the relationship, they are fantasizing about how their life will be when they get free of the other person. This is a control pattern for dealing with anger. It is a favorite strategy of those who have learned that it's not safe to express anger. Sometimes, you'll catch them saying things under their breath like, "You're gonna miss me when I'm gone," or something similarly hostile or cryptic.

If you hear such remarks, ask your partner if she is angry or is having thoughts about ending it. Do this in a relational way, a way that communicates that you really are open to hearing the truth. The person may not be ready to be candid, but at least you have begun the conversation — so it should be easier to reopen this discussion if and when these remarks occur again. Any time you hear cryptic or spiteful remarks, use Truth Skill #1 (Experiencing What Is), saying what you heard and what you imagine: "I heard you say 'I'm outta here,' and I imagine you're angry. Are you?" Or "Are you thinking about ending our relationship?"

If you find it impossible to do what you know would be in your best interest, find a professional counselor or coach to assist you in standing up for yourself. You don't want to look back on your life at the end of it and think, "I had a safe and secure life, but I never really lived *my* authentic truth."

Immediately Find a Replacement

Some people, driven by the fear of being alone, cannot leave a relationship until they have a new one in place. If this applies to you, it's very important that you develop your ability to be alone with yourself. The fear of being alone can drive you to tolerate things that are not good for you. If you are able to see and admit that this is your pattern, it's time to address it. You may need a counselor or coach to help you get through the rough spots as you learn to live without a lover or special someone in your life. Once you learn that you're just fine on your own, your relationships will be much healthier.

If you find yourself paired with someone who cannot be alone, notice how his dependent behavior affects you. Do you feel stifled by his jealousy? Do you feel trapped? Do you resent his attempts to control you? If you are afraid to speak about these things, perhaps you, too, are afraid of being alone. Anyone with this fear will have a hard time practicing Truth in Dating.

It is likely that if a person like this does leave you, he or she will already have another person to go to. Or he will find one in very short order. This may cause you to feel that he did not really love you. Just know that anyone who is this dependent could never love you in a mature way. It's not that he did not "love" you in his own way, but what looked like love was actually dependency. There's a big difference.

Practicing Truth in Dating helps you grow up. Not telling the truth keeps you small and weak. It reinforces the belief that you're too fragile to handle the consequences of being honest. As long as you treat yourself as though you are fragile, you will remain fragile.

Have a Secret Affair

Often when a person feels that his needs are not being met, he will find someone who can fill those needs but neglect to tell his partner about it. This type of behavior is usually motivated partly by anger at the first partner for not loving him the way he wants to be loved. The person fails to effectively assert his needs and winds up feeling resentful. While this strategy is similar to the previous method, the motivation behind it is different. It is more about avoiding anger or conflict than avoiding aloneness. For some people, it's just easier to "switch than fight." He may have tried telling his partner about his needs, but he has not done this in a very assertive way, so his partner has no idea of how dissatisfied he really is.

> The experience of ending a relationship is quite different when you have someone else waiting in the wings. You don't have the alone time necessary to confront your own responsibility for why things didn't work.

As the affair proceeds, he becomes more intimate with his new love interest and less intimate with his partner. Since it's hard to feel close to someone you're lying to, eventually he feels closer to the new person. So he changes partners without ever having to go through a real ending process. Sure he has to tell partner number one that it's over, but the experience of ending a relationship is quite different when you have someone else waiting in the wings. You don't completely grieve, and you don't have the alone time necessary to confront your own responsibility for why things didn't work.

What to Do When It's Done to You

Have you ever been on the receiving end of any of these nine common exit strategies? If you have, notice any feelings or judgments that come up as you recall the specifics of the situation. What were your feelings while you were in that relationship? Were there any feelings that you're aware of now that you tried to suppress or ignore at the time? Just notice your feelings and memories, and open up to the pain. It could be pain about your own actions or pain about how you were treated. It's healthy to allow this pain to come up to consciousness so you can comfort yourself. Remember also that when you allow yourself to feel pain in the present that is similar to pain that occurred when you were a child, you are taking a step toward freedom — freedom from the belief that you are not okay if you are in pain, freedom from the control patterns you have used to avoid your feelings, freedom to feel whatever you feel and to be your authentic self.

In my own life, a recent breakup brought up some painful feelings that helped me connect to some very old unconscious fears about my loveability. When the man I had been dating for six months made it clear to me that he was not sexually attracted to me, even though he loved me in every other way, I realized this was the first time I had ever experienced such a "rejection." I decided to mine this rejection experience for all it was worth, so I allowed myself to sit with this pain over a period of months without starting a new relationship. As I let these feelings sink in, I would frequently feel as if I were a tiny infant wanting to be held and touched, but feeling frustrated when I wasn't.

If you have both been telling the truth all along, the conversation about ending it will probably come as no surprise.

When I let myself go into this experience more deeply, a sense of bewilderment would come over me: "Why doesn't she (my mom) love me?... What is wrong with me... am I not lovable?" Even though I did not have access to this vocabulary as an infant, I am certain that I was feeling these things as I waited for my mom to pay attention to my needs. I got in touch with a sort of "background sadness" that I think I have always carried in my demeanor. It is something I was unconscious of but others could see or sense.

It has been painful to let these old feelings into my awareness. But I feel more whole as a result. I am grateful to the man who "rejected" me, since I was able to use the experience to know and accept more of myself.

How to End It Consciously

If two people have been practicing Truth in Dating all along, it is quite likely that the decision to end it will be mutual. When you do not practice complete honesty, you usually have to deal with the more difficult situation where one person is ready to end it and the other is not. This fact is another argument in favor of making honesty your practice. Even if it's only unsatisfactory for one of you, if you have both been telling the truth all along, the conversation about ending it will probably come as no surprise.

If truth-telling has been your ongoing practice, it is also quite possible that a redefinition of your relationship may be more appropriate than a complete ending. There are many gradations of intimacy and friendship between the two extremes of "lovers/mates" and "no relationship at all." Truth in Dating allows room for more of each person's individuality. It encourages people to be themselves rather than fit themselves into a traditional mold.

I believe that our culture's definition of "being in a relationship" is too narrow — you're either part of a couple or you're not in a relationship. In actuality, people's needs are varied and complex and do not always fit into one of these boxes. If more people practiced being "real, unique, and open" instead of generally trying to be "right, safe, and certain," if they really explored the full range of what's possible, our culture would see many more options for relating than we currently do.

So if you really like and trust someone but feel that somehow it's not working as a couple thing or as a sexual thing (or whatever your thing is), you may be wise to explore the question, "What *is* it?" You might get to the point of realizing: "We're not a couple...we're not being sexual...but we do like each other, and we do certain things very well together." If this is true, don't end it. Instead, redefine your expectations to fit reality.

Rules of Disengagement

Now, let's say you have agreed that something is not working for one or both of you, and you want to end it or redefine it. What are the "rules of disengagement?"

From my experience and research, here are some tips for staying conscious and intentional rather than operating from one of your control patterns.

1. Take time to consider the matter. Don't be impulsive.
2. Be clear about your reasons and speak honestly about them.
3. Have a discussion where both people get a chance to express themselves.
4. Do an ending ritual during which you clear resentments and share appreciations and lessons learned.

Take Some Time

If you are pretty sure you want to stop seeing this person, you may be tempted to "just do it" so you can get on with your life. If you have only had a few dates, I think it's fine to just do it. But if you having been seeing each other exclusively for over six weeks, I suggest you consider the decision for at least a week or two — and longer if it has been a significant relationship for you.

Have several face-to-face conversations over a period of time. If this is not possible, the telephone is an acceptable option, but letters and emails are not recommended for this type of conversation.

Know Your Reasons

Identify what you wanted or hoped for in a relationship that you are not getting in this one. It often helps to write this in your journal so you can step back and look at it. Then be willing to share your reasons with the other person and answer any questions the other may have.

If you are on the receiving end of a breakup, then be sure and ask the other about his or her reasons. If you're afraid you may get defensive, practice active listening to assist you in Holding Differences (Truth Skill #8). If you are so upset that you might forget or repress the other's explanation, take notes or even tape-record the conversation. For people who may be in shock when they hear "bad news," a tape recording of the reasons can be very helpful later on when the other person is gone and you're still wondering "why?" Knowing why helps you let go.

> "We're not a couple... we're not being sexual... but we do like each other, and we do certain things very well together." If this is true, don't end it. Instead, redefine your expectations to fit reality.

Give Both People a Turn to Express Themselves

Any conversation about ending or redefining should be two-way. If you have taken the lead in ending or redefining it, be sure and ask the other for her input after you have spoken. Otherwise, she may wind up carrying hard feelings or unfinished business about you. This is not in your best interest because it could result in her gossiping about you to others. If you encourage her to say whatever is on her mind, she'll get over her hard feelings more easily.

If you are receiving a good-bye speech, be sure you get a turn to talk, too. Ask any and all questions that you're curious about, even if you fear this may cause either of you discomfort. If you have questions and don't ask them, you're likely to carry around needless baggage after it's over.

Do an Ending Ritual

If the relationship has been a fairly significant one, set aside a mutually agreeable time to talk about any lingering feelings of resentment or anger, any things you especially appreciated, and any lessons you learned with each other. Additional topics that might be useful to cover during such a closure ritual are:

- What will we miss?
- What are we glad we'll no longer have to deal with?
- What do we want to be forgiven for?
- If we had it to do over, would we do anything differently?

Take turns speaking to each of these questions. Besides talking together, you might also do something to symbolize the change in your relationship. I recall when one two-year dating relationship broke up, the man I was seeing, Richard, took me for a walk in the rose garden he had planted for me on my property. Then, he asked for forgiveness for a number of things he had done. With each item he asked to be forgiven for, he picked a rose and gave it to me. This ritual allowed us both to honor the time we had spent together, thus making it easier to remember each other with fondness. And I wound up with quite a large bouquet of roses!

Chapter Summary

- It's important to notice if you have a characteristic ending style. If you do, this is probably a control pattern.
- You know it's time to end it when you are having so many unhappy times together that these eclipse the happy times.
- If you are on the receiving end of this decision, be sure to ask any and all questions that you have about why it's ending.
- Don't end things in an impulsive manner. Don't pick a fight or create a crisis in order to justify ending it.
- If you end it consciously, you won't have so much unfinished business following you into your future relationships.

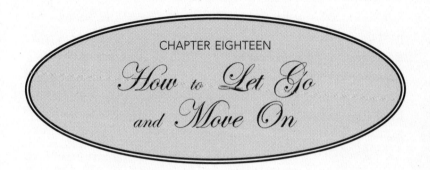

CHAPTER EIGHTEEN

How to Let Go and Move On

*It's easier to let go if you have some lessons
to take with you — lessons that will make you
stronger and more resilient the next time around.*

When a dating relationship ends, it's not always easy to just let it go. Even if it was of relatively short duration, you may feel a sense of failure, rejection, or shame. And if you were together for a longer time, you may need to go through a grieving process.

Ending Is a Time for Connecting with Yourself

The end of a relationship can be an opportunity for connecting more deeply with your feeling nature — for getting in touch with aspects of yourself that you may prefer to avoid. It's a time to notice any feelings of hurt, anger, disappointment, or longing that may have been triggered by the breakup. As I mentioned in the previous chapter, I used my recent breakup to connect with buried self-doubts about my loveability and the background sadness that I carry related to this issue.

It is important not to short-circuit the ending stage of a relationship.

There is much to be felt and much to be learned. It's usually not a good idea to immediately become involved with a new lover, because you need time to assimilate your lessons and process your grief, shame, guilt, resentment, or other painful feelings. Truth in Dating involves feeling what you feel and expressing it where appropriate so you can expand your capacity to experience life as it is (not as you wish it were). Getting involved right away in a new love interest is a control pattern for avoiding being with uncomfortable feelings.

Likewise if you start dating someone who has not given himself time to grieve a broken relationship and complete the past, you are inviting someone else's unfinished business into your life, as well as calling up your own. Be ready to accept the consequences of your behavior.

Getting Closure Can Be Hard to Do

It is generally more painful to end a relationship if it has been going on for a long time because the two of you have probably become more interdependent. But sometimes it can be harder to achieve closure if your relationship was short. When a relationship ends after a short time, you probably haven't had the opportunity to let things play themselves out. It's as if you have interrupted a process before its completion. This creates an unfinished situation in your mind, making it harder for you to let go and move on than would be true if you had taken the time to fully experience your areas of incompatibility. Sometimes it's easier to let go of a long marriage than a brief love affair because in the case of the marriage, you had time to get sick of each other and to see how really hopeless it was.

Many singles in my research for this book reported situations where they repeatedly broke up with someone and then reconciled. They were trying to get to a satisfying place of closure or completion so they could be sure that ending it was the right thing to do. A typical story is that of Jim and Francesca. Jim had an intuition early on that he would never be able to accept how poorly Francesca took care of her health. But he let himself fall in love with her anyway. He tried to interest her in some of his health-oriented practices, and at first she seemed quite willing. She tried a few things he suggested, but he always felt frustrated with her lack of follow-through. The first time he broke off the relationship, she urged him to give her a second chance, saying she needed to feel more secure with him before she could focus her attention on such major life changes. This breakup lasted about two weeks, and then Jim allowed her to convince him that she could change. So they reconciled and tried to start over. But the same problem recurred. He felt frustrated when she promised to practice healthier eating, sleeping, and exercise habits, but did nothing to change her behavior.

> The end of a relationship can be an opportunity for connecting more deeply with your feeling nature — for getting in touch with aspects of yourself that you may prefer to avoid.

When they finally broke up for the last time, Francesca said she was very close to a breakthrough, as she was just beginning to feel secure in his love. She just needed a little more time. Jim refused to reconsider but continued to have nagging doubts about his decision: "Maybe she would change if I could just help her feel more secure...if I just gave her a little more time. Maybe she is the one for me like she says she is. I don't think so, but I can't be sure."

They ended their relationship before Jim got to see how Francesca might be if she really felt secure. This created an "incomplete gestalt" in his mind. As a psychologist, I know how "incompletes" can become mental fixations. In the best of all worlds, we would all get to play out all our fantasies and our curiosities, so that we could put them to rest. But in reality there's just not time for that. Decisions must be made on the basis of insufficient data. Because of this fact, I suggest that you share as much truth-telling as you can while you are with someone so you can at least minimize the number of "incompletes" you'll have if the relationship ends. Incompletes make it harder for you to live fully in present time. They make it harder to let go and move on.

Questions to Consider As You Say Good-bye

Here is a checklist of questions that might be useful to consider in order to end things consciously, forgive, heal, and move on:

1. What did I learn?
2. What did I want that I was not getting in the relationship?
3. What conflicts remain unresolved? What lessons remain unlearned? What feelings remain unexpressed?
4. What will I miss?
5. What am I glad to be rid of?
6. What needs to be forgiven?
7. What amends need to be made?
8. What would I/we do differently if we had it to do over?

Before I elaborate on these topics, I want to emphasize that even a one-date relationship deserves to be dealt with consciously. Some of the above topics will not apply to brief encounters, but it's still important to address the topics that do apply, such as "What did I want that I was not getting?" and "What feelings have I not expressed?" I recommend discussing these questions in person rather than on the phone or in an email. After you have said your piece, always invite the other to share his feelings and thoughts. (I mentioned this in the previous chapter under step 3 of the "Rules of Disengagement.") Even though you are clear that you want to end it, it is still important to invite the other into the conversation. Even a unilateral decision to end it can be done in a relational way.

What Did I Learn?

You will learn something from almost everyone you date. Much of this learning is unconscious. Acknowledging to each other what you have learned can help you be more conscious of your lessons. It can also be very healing. It helps you feel at peace with the time and effort you invested. Sit down alone or together and make a list of lessons learned. Then share your lists. For example:

- I learned not to be so afraid of a man's anger.
- I learned how to negotiate.
- I learned how to play.
- I learned that I am afraid of criticism and that I often do things to attract it.

Do this exercise first, before you deal with the other seven issues in this section. It will set a constructive, positive tone for the conversation.

When Shayna did this exercise after her breakup with Len, she had a hard time letting go until she realized that she had always had a pattern of accepting "crumbs" from her lovers. She had never felt safe enough to ask for what she wanted. As she consid- ered the question, "What have I learned?" she saw that she had had a similar relationship with her alcoholic mother.

You will learn something from almost everyone you date. Acknowledging to each other what you have learned can be very healing.

Her mother was not capable of giving much love or attention, so Shayna had learned not to ask for anything and to try to be satisfied with what- ever crumbs she could get. As she connected with this insight, she saw that she did not have to keep repeating the past in her relationships with men. She was fed up with this pattern. She vowed that from now on she would ask openly for what she really wanted.

What Did I Want That I Was Not Getting?

This is a question that you first need to answer for yourself before communicating your thoughts to the other person. It may help to write down your answers to this question so you can go back over each item and attempt to be specific about what you wanted and didn't get. Many people think in generalities, such as, "I didn't feel heard." Better would be, "When we were driving to your mom's and on numerous other occa- sions, you talked about your feelings, but when I started to talk about mine, you told me you needed space."

Generalities are dangerous. They can lead you to "see" or "hear" something that you fear or expect rather than what is really there. Generalities support keeping your judgments about the other intact, so you never get over them. After writing your list and editing it to be sure you have been specific about what the other actually did or did not do, then share the list. If you share a bunch of generalities, you will not really be clear in your own mind about what happened, so it will be harder to let it go. Being specific in your answers helps you get over these issues so you can heal, forgive, and move on. It also helps the other person do the same.

When Shayna wrote her list for Len, she was careful to include specific incidents that had led her to the general impression that he did not value her very much. One of the specific items on her list was, "When I had you over here for dinner every Friday, you always brought your stock reports to read while we were eating, and when I asked you if we could have a conversation, you told me you needed for me not to be so demanding."

What Remains Unresolved?

If you have been in an intense or deeply bonded relationship, you may have difficulty letting go of your dream of what might have been. Take some time to reflect on the following.

What was the dream I had or we had that we failed to actualize? It's good to admit your failures so you can grieve the loss of your dreams. This will help you heal because you are taking responsibility for your inability to accomplish something you intended to do. For example, perhaps you two wanted to start a business together but learned that your styles were too different. Take a look at what you would have needed to learn or let go of to make the dream happen. Let's say you kept getting into arguments because you wanted to participate in every financial decision and the other wanted to be left alone to make some decisions without your input. Maybe you needed to learn to let go of control a bit; and maybe your partner needed to learn to collaborate better. Usually, partners enter a relationship to learn something from each other. What lesson was your partner trying to "teach" you that you were not able to learn?

Was there something this relationship was asking of me that I could not fulfill? This is another version of the question, "What was I being asked to learn or to let go of that I was unwilling or unable to do?" Often, what's being asked is something in the realm of emotional resilience. In what way were you simply not emotionally strong enough to "take the bad with the good?" When I think of a particular breakup in my own life, I can see that the thing I was not strong enough to learn at the time was how to be fully present when a man is expressing intense anger at me. I got so triggered by his anger that I would become paralyzed. The relationship was calling me to learn to stay present to my own feelings in the face of intense emotions. At some point, I had to admit that I was no match for his anger. (Due to his own fears, his anger was easily triggered.) Eventually, I reluctantly called it quits.

> Generalities are dangerous. They can lead you to "see" or "hear" something that you fear or expect rather than what is really there.

Were there any specific conflicts between us that we could not resolve? Examples of this would be: "We never worked out our differences about how to spend our weekends" or "We never worked out our disagreement about the best time to make love."

Were there any specific complaints or "beefs" that I felt but did not express? This is a big one. Most people do not tell the whole truth — even readers of a book like this. It can be embarrassing to admit at the end of a relationship (even a very short one) that you had feelings or wants that you did not express. You may have hinted, or made sarcastic remarks or helpful suggestions, but you did not express your actual feelings, as in "I feel hurt that you forgot my birthday," or "I want us to make love in the mornings sometimes."

What Will I Miss?

To really get completion with yourself and the other person, it's important to acknowledge the positive things you are letting go of. Make a list (to be shared) of all the good things that you won't have in your life anymore, such as: you'll miss having someone to play tennis with; you'll miss having someone who appreciates your offbeat sense of humor. I suggest acknowledging these things to each other in your good-bye conversation.

When Shayna considered this question, she recognized that in spite of their problems, she would definitely miss having Len as a compatible sex partner and someone to snuggle with several nights a week. But that was about it. That was a pretty short list — which helped her see how out of balance their relationship had been.

What Am I Glad to Be Rid of?

The other half of the "What will I miss?" conversation is "What won't I miss? What will I be relieved to be rid of?" Again, it's a good idea to make a list in solitude and then share these things face-to-face. Face-to-face is best, because the nonverbal energy exchange allows for more real contact; but if that isn't possible, do whatever you can do.

> The other half of the "What will I miss?" conversation is "What won't I miss? What will I be relieved to be rid of?"

By the time Shayna got to this question, she was aware of a number of things she was glad to be rid of. One thing was hearing the words, "You're too demanding." Another was the pain she had gotten used to feeling every time she asked Len to listen to her and he did not respond.

What Needs to Be Forgiven?

When a relationship ends, there is a tendency for partners to blame each other. Whatever you find yourself blaming her for is what you need to forgive her for. Forgiveness is a process of letting go of negative feelings that, if held on to, can affect your physical and emotional health. To get to forgiveness, you need to be able to honestly answer four questions in the section that preceded this one: What was I not getting? What remains unresolved? What will I miss? And what am I glad to be rid of? In dealing with these questions, it is important to use specific language to help you connect to your memory of what actually happened. This will help you experience your experience rather than staying comfortably in the realm of generalizations.

If possible and appropriate, communicate all this to the other person. Speaking about it publicly shines the light of consciousness on it. Consciousness is a healing force.

In Shayna's case, she decided not to communicate her feelings to Len. She was clear within herself that it was over, that it was a good learning experience, and that she was ready for a different type of relationship. Perhaps sometime in the future she would feel differently and want to communicate her feelings to Len, but for now just doing the exercise alone was enough for her.

What Amends Need to Be Made?

A big part of the forgiveness/letting go/moving on process is making amends. One way to make amends is by using Truth Skill #7, Revising an Earlier Statement. So you might say, "Knowing what I know now, if I had it to do over, I would..."

Sometimes just a sincere "I'm sorry" is sufficient. Other times, especially where property loss or other physical damage had been done, more tangible amends may be appropriate. If you have taken money from someone, for example, repay it. If you damaged someone's car, pay the repair bills. If the idea of amends is uncomfortable for you, look fearlessly into the source of your resistance. Often, people do not want to make amends because they are still holding on to the idea that the other person caused them to do what they did. I urge you to search deeply for your own responsibility in everything that seems to "happen" to you. You are not to blame. (Blame is a concept the ego uses to defend itself; it is not real.) But you are responsible.

Making amends is a way of taking responsibility for your actions. And of course it also helps you complete the past so you have more of your attention available for the here and now.

What Would I Do Differently?

Answering this question is a good adjunct to the amends process. Thinking together about your regrets and lessons learned can bring up hidden hurts and resentments, thus allowing these to be seen, felt, and healed. I recall when Donald and I broke up our two-year uncommitted relationship, we each said to the other, "If I had it to do over again, I would have been monogamous with you." Just hearing him say that did a lot to help me heal and let go.

Shayna's list included: "If I had it to do over, I would not fix the whole dinner without asking you for help. And I would tell you what I liked when you were doing things during sex to pleasure me. In other words, I would speak up more in general so you could know what was going on inside me. I feel sorry that I did not express myself more with you. I imagine that allowed you to become more self-centered, which I don't think was good for you or me."

Why Bother with All This?

Taking the time to consciously complete a relationship before too much time has passed is one of the most valuable gifts you can give to yourself and the other. Most people are uncomfortable with endings — so they don't complete things, and they keep accumulating more and more unfinished business. Unfinished business is what interferes with being present. If you find yourself thinking or talking a lot about your past relationships, this may be a sign that you have never gotten complete with those relationships. Practicing Truth in Dating serves your ability to be present to each new moment rather than having a mind that is clogged up with unfinished situations. The work you do at the end of each relationship will help you begin your next one from a place of freedom and openness.

The Five Stages of Grief

Dr. Elisabeth Kübler-Ross, a medical practitioner working with dying patients, has helped thousands of people understand how to grieve the loss of a loved one who has died. These same stages apply to any important loss. Grieving is a process that helps us heal.

Even if yours was a short relationship, pay attention to feelings of sadness and anger, or to the inability to feel anything. These might be signs that you are grieving. According to Kübler-Ross's research, a normal grieving process can take up to two years, although one year is closer to the norm. The intensity and duration of your grieving will depend on many factors. Her five stages of grieving are as follows:

> Pay attention to feelings of sadness and anger, or to the inability to feel anything. These might be signs that you are grieving.

1. *Denial:* Here you may be saying, "This can't be happening. If I just wait, he'll come back. I just have to get him to see how I've changed." Or you may find yourself walking around like an unfeeling robot or becoming depressed.

   This is a time to ease yourself into the reality that it's over and you're powerless to do anything about this. Focus on the things you do have control over. Take especially good care of your physical needs like exercising, eating well, and getting enough sleep. Do things with friends. Do things you used to enjoy doing but perhaps put aside while you were spending time with this person.

During this stage, it may be difficult to remember what your ex said about why he or she wanted to end it (if you are the one who was left). It's a good idea to take some notes or tape-record a conver-

Grieving is a process that helps us heal.

sation on this topic to help you "get it." In order for you to let go, it helps to know in specific terms why it ended.

2. *Anger:* In this stage, instead of turning your anger inward toward yourself, as people do when they're depressed, you're apt to focus more on what you didn't like about your ex. This helps you accept that this person no longer holds such a special place in your life. There may be a tendency to blame the person, so notice this and recognize that no one is to blame for how you feel. You feel the way you do because of who you are (i.e., how you've been conditioned to feel) not because of the other person's actions.

3. *Bargaining:* This may overlap somewhat with the denial stage, or it may come after anger. Bargaining means doing things like telling the person you've "seen the light," promising to change, giving the person a sales pitch about how right you two are for each other, threatening to make her life difficult if she doesn't take you back, and so forth. Watch out for such bargaining strategies. Believing the other's desperate pleas at this stage has caused many partners who should be moving on to reconcile, only to break up again later on.

4. *Letting Go:* This stage is often accompanied by an empty feeling: "Is this all there is to life? Where do I go from here? What do I have to look forward to now?" This can

lead you to sincerely question your values and goals in life — which can be a good thing. Use it as a time to "begin anew," to take stock of what is important to you and what you want to create for yourself. Keeping a journal can be a big help during this stage and throughout the grieving process. Write down your visions and goals in very specific terms. Write down what you learned about yourself while you were going out with this person. Write your feelings so you can see them more objectively and then let them go.

5. *Acceptance:* Now you are ready to put most of your attention on the here and now. Your energy is no longer quite so bound up in dealing with the past. You may think about this person from time to time, but you are not wishing for him or her to come back. You are aware of the benefits of being without this person. There is a sense of freedom and lightness. You are ready to move on.

These five stages occur, with some individual variation, even if you were the one who decided to leave the relationship. They may be less intense in this case, and the subject of your pain may be different, but you will still go through some kind of an adjustment to loss.

If you have children who have bonded with the other person, they will go through these stages too. Knowing what to expect can help you guide them through the process so they can feel their feelings instead of denying or acting out their feelings.

Tools to Help You Grow from the Experience

The ending of a relationship can be stressful. A time of stress or crisis is a good time to expand your resources for self-support.

In this section, let's look at a list of things that others have done to support themselves through this difficult transition.

1. *Talk sweetly to yourself.* Learn how to talk to yourself as if you were a nurturing big brother or big sister. When you are confused, ask your big brother/sister–self for answers, and respond to your own questions from an inner place of wisdom. Often it helps to breathe deeply and center yourself before giving your "wise" reply. Even if you don't have an especially helpful response, at least tell yourself, "I'm here with you, and we'll get through this."

2. *Be compassionately self-critical.* All of us need a sober inner voice that can help us take a realistic inventory of our shortcomings. This is the self-talk where you tell yourself what you would have done differently in the relationship if you knew then what you know now — if you could go out and come in again. After your lover has just told you "It's over," this voice asks: "What signs did you ignore that could have told you this person was dissatisfied?" It is the voice that asks, "What can you learn from this situation, painful as it is?" This self-critique is carried on in a spirit of kindness and compassion toward yourself.

3. *Keep a journal.* I have mentioned the value of journaling elsewhere. A journal can be in any form that works for you. I used to write my dreams, feelings, and reflections daily in a standard size notebook. Now, I occasionally write my thoughts and feelings on any slip of paper that happens to be handy and file it in a folder labeled *Personal.* Many people use their computers for journaling. Find out what works for you, and use it in a way that feels good. If it starts to feel like a chore, try something else.

4. *Write a good-bye letter.* When a relationship ends, it can help to write a good-bye letter, telling the other all the things you'll miss, all the things you won't miss, and what you learned from the relationship. This can help you come to terms with the fact that it's over and that

you did get some useful things from the relationship, even if these things are simply the lessons you are taking away. You do not need to send this letter, but if you feel like doing so after rereading it, go ahead.

5. *Share resentments and appreciations.* I have found it very healing to sit down with the other person after it's over and share all the resentments and all the appreciations I can think of and to invite him to do the same. We each take a turn and say, "I resent you for_____," or "I appreciate you for_____," and then say very specifically what things the other person actually *did* or *said,* not what we imagine he *meant.* Resentments and appreciations can be interspersed — you do not need to do only resentments and then only appreciations. But it does work best if one person takes her full turn (which could last up to thirty minutes) before the other takes his turn.

When I did this with my most recent ex, it was a very positive experience for both of us. We did it face-to-face, not over the phone or by letter. One thing that surprised me was I got more satisfaction from hearing his resentments than I did out of speaking my own. I imagine this is because I intuited that he was harboring these things about me, so I felt relieved to have them out in the open rather than hidden.

6. *Make a list of things you love to do.* Often when we start going out regularly with someone, we give up activities that had been important to us. Make a list of all the things you'd like to do more of — things you used to

love to do but may have stopped doing during your relationship. Celebrate that you now have more time to do what you want.

7. *Pick up the phone.* Since you have more time, pick up the phone and renew your connections with some of the people you didn't see as much while you were seeing your ex. Invite them to do some of the fun things on your list of "things you love to do."

8. *Create a vision for your life.* Take stock of where you have come so far in your life and envision a future for yourself where you are having the life you want. Picture your ideal life, including such things as: an ideal day, what gifts you are contributing to others, how your life looks and feels, where you live, what types of people and community you have around you, how much money you are making, what your lifestyle is like, what your body looks and feels like, and what kind of person or persons you are intimate with.

Do you know what your control patterns are? How about your buttons? Did any of these patterns or buttons contribute to the breakup?

9. *Inventory your relationship strengths and weaknesses.* What do you do well and not so well when it comes to relating? Are there any of the ten truth skills that you need to develop more fully? How real are you when things don't go your way? Do you know what your control patterns are? How about your buttons? Did any of these patterns or buttons contribute to the breakup? Do you know what your partner thinks you did or did not do that contributed to the breakup? This is a good time to take note of areas where you need more skill or more practice. Find mentors, teachers, or practice partners to

help you. Appendix B has a list of resources to help you build your relationship skills, including information on how to locate people who are also looking for Truth in Dating practice partners.

10. *Make a list of the reasons why it ended.* If you are the dumper, make a list of all the needs you felt were not getting met, any things your ex did that violated your boundaries, any broken agreements, and any betrayals you experienced. If you are the dumpee, you should be able to make a similar list, both from your own viewpoint and from your ex's. If you do not know why your ex is ending it, do what you can to find out. And don't argue. If you argue, you will not get the information you need to enable you to face reality and move on.

11. *Create your own ritual.* Some people recognize the end of their relationship by creating a private or communal ritual. I mentioned the idea of a dyad ritual in the last chapter when I talked about my walk with my ex through the rose garden. But you might also do a personal ritual by yourself or a community ritual with friends and/or family. Once when I ended a fairly significant relationship, my partner and I decided to have a communal "disengagement party," to which we invited a number of our closest friends. We recited some words that sounded a bit like marriage vows — except they were actually "un-marriage" declarations — thanking one another for the lessons, taking responsibility for our inability to actualize our dream, and that sort of thing. He even gave me a disengagement ring as part of the ceremony. I think doing this ritual together helped us to let go of the dream we once shared. And I think doing it in the company of our community helped our friends see that they could still relate to both of us in the same room.

Things Most People Need to Learn
Over and Over Again

I have interviewed and counseled hundreds of pairs in the throes of ending it. When people look together at "what we learned from our mistakes" or "what we wish we had done differently," several recurring themes emerge. Here is a list of what people told me they would wish to do differently if they could do it over:

1. Speak about any and all feelings that are triggered by the relationship as soon as we become aware of them.
2. Have a regular time for clearing the air and expressing withheld feelings, resentments, and appreciations.
3. Practice active listening when we seem to be misunderstanding one another or when we are negotiating our differences.
4. Practice truth-telling even at the risk of losing the other's love.
5. Seek third-party help when we're stuck and can't get to a satisfying completion by ourselves.
6. Set aside unstructured time to be alone with one another — for sex and/or for deepening our communion and our communication.
7. Don't do anything out of a sense of obligation. Willing compromise is fine, but obligation poisons a relationship. Always take responsibility for our choices — don't blame our partners because we're giving up something in order to accommodate them.
8. If we're starting to lose interest or get sexually interested in someone else, talk to our partner about it as soon as it occurs. Otherwise we are engaging in deception. This can lead to self-deception, which will erode our trust in our own ability to have a successful relationship.

9. If one of us wants to be monogamous, and the other does not, we will not ignore the importance of this diffrence. (If you two work out a conscious compromise, fine; but don't compromise yourself.)

10. Do not threaten to end it every time things don't go your own way. (If this is your pattern, seek professional help. It means you need help staying with uncomfortable feelings rather than "acting out" your feelings.)

The most important thing you can do when your relationship ends is to look at what you have learned. This will help you find

Look at what you have learned. This will help you find meaning in the process even though things didn't work out.

meaning in the process even though things didn't work out. And it will help you move on with confidence about your ability to be more aware next time.

Chapter Summary

- Ending is a good time for personal reflection and for taking stock of your relationship strengths and weaknesses.
- It is very important to know specifically why the relationship ended. What needs or wants (yours and your ex's) were not being met? What personal boundaries were being violated?
- Grief goes through five stages: denial, anger, bargaining, letting go, and acceptance.
- Most people who look back on their failed relationships wish they had been more transparently honest about their feelings.
- There are a number of questions to be addressed if you

wish to end things in a way that fosters letting go and moving on: What did I learn? What did I want that I was not getting? What remains unresolved? What will I miss? What am I glad to be rid of? What needs to be forgiven? What amends need to be made? What would I do differently?

CHAPTER NINETEEN

Concluding Thoughts

A s I review what I have written in these pages, I feel moved to offer a couple of caveats. The first relates to how difficult it can be to stay on this truth-telling path. The second concern has to do with how communication practices can start to sound like jargon.

The Truth Hurts

I have repeatedly encouraged you in these pages to get in touch with your "bigness," with the fact that you are big now and will not die if someone judges you or rejects you. I have challenged you to stretch the limits of your comfort zone. On the other hand, words can hurt. And when they do, the practices of feeling your feelings and reassuring yourself can be immensely important. Learning to support yourself through pain is an essential life skill, just as important as the ten truth skills. When you trust that you can be kind and loving toward yourself during times of upset, you will have a very important resource to help you get over your phobia about emotional pain. Practicing Truth in Dating often leads people into pain they didn't know was there, which then leads them to discover a self-nurturing capacity that they also didn't know was there.

But what if you cannot do this? What if you get critical or impatient with yourself when you experience pain? This is the type of hurt that really does hurt you, the hurt you inflict needlessly on yourself. The inevitable hurts that come from taking emotional risks do not do nearly the amount of damage as our own self-wounding can. So what to do if you are prone to self-judgment? I say notice this. Experience what is. And then feel what you feel about how you are treating yourself. Feel sadness about the fact that you do not yet know how to be a nurturing parent to yourself. And then aim to connect with the part of you that does know how to be self-supporting. There is a loving, nurturing parent within each of us. Call out to this part of yourself.

When you learn to live in the present, your fear of others' reactions disappears. You discover that fear is usually a head-trip about the future.

Feel what you feel and ask for support from that loving inner parent. If you find this too difficult, hire a professional trained in this work to help you.

Avoiding Jargon

When you first practice the ten truth skills, it's important to follow certain communication guidelines to help you be specific and to help you stay on your own side of the net. For instance, it is important to use "I" statements and to give feedback in a way that specifically describes what happened and what you felt. Following a form like this aids you in becoming more conscious. It helps you unhook from your automatic patterns.

The only problem is that communication that follows a formula is sometimes not very aesthetically pleasing. And it puts some people off.

To deal with this problem, I suggest that you start out, while you are learning to be more self-aware, by following the communication formats suggested here. Then, when you get more fluent and confident, by all means, improvise! For example, instead of saying, "My self-talk is . . ." or "I'm saying to myself . . . ," you could substitute, "Right now I'm thinking . . ." or "I'd like to share what's going on inside me. . . ." Or instead of saying, "Hearing you say that, I feel . . . ," you could substitute, "As I listen to you, my belly is getting tight" (or some other description of your feelings or sensations). The spirit of these communication practices is what's important, not the exact form, but it is necessary to interrupt your automatic patterns in order to become a more aware communicator.

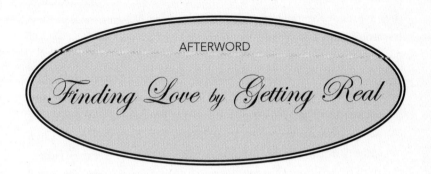

Finding Love by Getting Real

*When you get over being controlled by your fear
of unknown consequences, you become free —
free to live each moment in a state of love.*

Practicing Truth in Dating has made me a more loving person. I think it has made me more loveable as well. Here's my theory about how this works.

Self-expression keeps my energy flowing. When I am fully self-expressive, instead of hiding my true feelings, my life energy is flowing free and without constriction. I have more of the life force (love) coursing through my being, and I experience myself as one with life, not separated or alienated from "others." I have found, for example, that I can express feelings of hurt or anger, and if I do so with the intent of being transparent, I immediately feel more connected with and loving toward the other person.

Transparency helps others relax. As I show myself more transparently to others, without trying to create a particular impression, people trust me more because I am not running a hidden agenda. They feel safe and relaxed around me. Being more trusting and less fearful about my intent, they are more able to feel loving in my presence. When people feel loving around me, I like that. I like to think I had something to do with it.

Being present leads to a sense of basic trust. Practicing the ten truth skills helps me trust myself. The skills keep me living in present-time reality, instead of identifying myself as my story or my beliefs. The experience of being present to what is is extremely empowering. When my identity is based on my capacity to experience what is, instead of my ability to make things turn out the way I want, then my self-esteem and well-being are not dependent on whether the outcome pleases me. I now have a "basic trust" feeling about life that no one can take away from me. I have nothing to fear from others. I am now free to be open and loving as appropriate.

Love is letting go of conditions. I think I am finally learning what love is. Most people have never experienced love, even though this is one of their heart's deepest desires. Most people look for love in all the wrong places. They seek a person who is attractive, who is worthy of their love, and who loves them in return — all positive things. But they do not know how to be in a state of love themselves. So, even if they are lucky enough to find somebody to love, their attention is not really free to love this person — because most of their attention is on avoiding some feared consequence (like being criticized, hurt, abandoned, not seen, et cetera). When your attention is dominated by fear, love gets squeezed out of the picture.

   Being in love depends on being (relatively) free from our limiting beliefs about what we have to do to be worthy of love. It depends on our learning to let go of our ideas about what external conditions need to be met in order for us to be happy, ideas like "I need someone who _____. Then I'll be happy."

Consciousness creates empathy. Another aspect of love is compassion and empathy for others. Truth-telling breaks down the walls between me and my practice partners. I feel more connected, less separate, and so I am naturally more sensitive to what they are feeling. Empathy is not a learned skill. It is the result of a more expanded, awakened level of consciousness.

Honesty gives me practice facing the unknown. Truth in Dating has helped me to let go of my fear about the results of my honesty. Fear of the unknown — of "unknown results" — is probably the most basic fear of all. Honesty has taught me how to face the unknown and step into it, consciously, even joyfully. It has shown me that I can deal with whatever happens, even if the results are unpleasant. As I get over being controlled by my fear of unknown consequences, I become free — free to live in each moment in a state of love.

Learning to take risks and show up open and transparent helps me trust myself more. I am more confident when facing change, chaos, uncertainty, and ambiguity — phenomena that often create fear and discomfort in humans. More self-trust means less fear. Less fear means more love.

It's good to make the first move. I find that by making the first move to practice transparent relating, I am helping to bring more relaxation, trust, and love to the situation. When I take a risk and say what I'm secretly feeling, this seems to give the other permission to do so as well. He will often thank me for helping him feel safe enough to speak about the unspeakable. Usually, after we express something that we have been afraid to say, a whole lot of energy gets released, and we feel more connected, more loving.

Feeling leads to healing. Truth in Dating is also a practice for healing and loving myself. By consciously shining light on my darker, wounded aspects, I am giving myself loving nurturance. By allowing my painful feelings from childhood to now be felt, I am giving attention and acceptance to parts of myself that I used to see as unacceptable or unloveable.

294 TRUTH IN DATING

Sharing my needs is a bonding experience. I have found that I am more loveable when I am being open and transparent about my needs. This occurs because my partner gets a feel for the areas where I need his help. This fosters a stronger, deeper bond between us than would be the case if I presented myself as independent, tough, cool, or together.

To know him is to love him. The more I see how a person feels and thinks, the more connected I feel to him, whether I choose to mate with him or not. Knowing a person well also helps me know what type of relationship is appropriate with this person. He is not hiding certain things in order to seduce me into falling in love with him, for example. So I am free to express whatever feelings I have or don't have. He can take no for an answer because he is committed to experiencing *what is.* There is no sense of obligation on either of our parts. Obligation poisons love. Freedom to feel whatever you feel fosters love.

Keeping up-to-date keeps me open to what is. The ten truth skills have given me a way to keep my relationships continually up-to-date rather than having a mind that is clogged up with incomplete communications. I think this adds to my capacity for love because it helps me be more open and present in each moment.

I am part of something larger than myself. I like feeling a spiritual connection to something larger than myself, in this case to an evolutionary movement that might be called the evolution of human consciousness. I like to feel I am participating in and helping to further the expression of more sensitive and refined levels of being. This is an expression of my love for Life itself. I suppose other words for Life might be: God, the Tao, Being, All That Is, Allah, the Force. You get the idea.

We all want acceptance. It seems to me that everyone just wants to be loved and accepted for who they really are. Truth in Dating has helped me and others accept ourselves as we are. The practice supports us in feeling what we feel, saying what we feel, and then letting go of trying to get approval from others. In the process, we learn to accept ourselves. The very act of being true to our feelings affirms the sense that we are okay just as we are.

Awareness Is Contagious

Taking responsibility for one's own reactions is something that most people are just beginning to learn how to do (most conscious, aware people, that is). This type of awareness is contagious — so let's pass it on! The evolution of human consciousness is everybody's business. As more and more people reach this level of awareness and responsibility, blaming will become obsolete, and so will projecting one's own darkness onto others.

Perhaps one day, when the majority of humans understand what it really means to feel and take responsibility for their own pain, we will find ourselves in a world where love and truth are more prevalent than fear and denial.

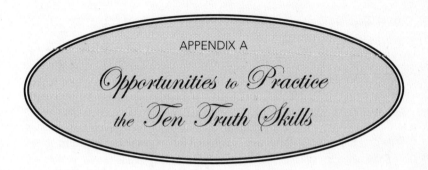

APPENDIX A

Opportunities to Practice the Ten Truth Skills

As I have repeated often, Truth in Dating is a practice that requires willing practice partners. In this appendix, I will direct you to places where you can find like-minded people to practice with via such things as introduction services, teleclasses, and workshops. I will also describe four fun, educational card games that you can use to practice your truth-telling skills.

Truth in Dating Introduction Service

If you want to meet like-minded singles through our internet introduction service, go to www.truthindating.com. Here you will find profiles of potential dates, friends, and practice partners who are also interested in truth-telling as a practice.

Teleclasses

A teleclass is a workshop that takes place over the phone. This is a great way to meet people from all over the world. I offer teleclasses on such topics as Truth in Dating, sexuality, overcoming fears of intimacy, the ten truth skills, and the couple's journey (for couples).

Upcoming teleclasses are listed at www.susancampbell.com.

If you wish to help set up a teleclass for some of your friends or associates (e.g., a work team), call (707) 829-3646 or email drsusan@susancampbell.com.

Workshops

Workshops are another excellent way to meet like-minded people and to locate potential practice partners.

The websites www.susancampbell.com and www.truthindating.com list details about upcoming workshops.

Truth in Dating Online Community

You may join a free online email "discussion list" of people interested in applying the ten truth skills in their relationships. In this online forum, people ask questions about issues in their lives and then give one another feedback and counsel. Sometimes they also play a written version of the Truth in Dating Card Game or the Getting Real Card Game as a way of deepening connections and practicing truth skills.

To join this list, send a blank email with "subscribe" in the subject line to gettingreal-subscribe@yahoogroups.com.

Free Online Newsletter

To subscribe to my free e-zine, *Uncertain Times,* send a blank email with "subscribe" in the subject line to uncertaintimes-subscribe@yahoogroups.com.

Card Games

The Truth in Dating Card Game can be played by two people who are just getting to know each other, or it can be played by couples, groups of singles or couples, or mixed groups. The game brings up topics that dating partners need to address if they are to know themselves and each other well enough to make wise relationship choices. Its questions range from getting-acquainted questions to those that are much more challenging, including many that can be used to uncover unconscious buttons and fears. These and the other games listed here can be ordered from www.susancampbell.com or www.thegettingrealgame.com.

The following are some sample questions from the Truth in Dating cards:

- What is something you imagine you'd have trouble speaking truthfully about to a partner or date?

- What story do you tell yourself about why your last relationship ended?
- What can a lover do or say to help you feel more safe?
- What is something I have done or said that led you to feel closer to me?

Here's what some people have said about the Truth in Dating Card Game:

"I took the cards with me on a date with a man I was just getting to know. We were at a restaurant having dinner, and we each picked our favorite cards and then took turns answering them. I found him very interesting, funny, and refreshingly honest. I had not had this impression of him on previous dates, but after an hour with the game, we felt very relaxed and natural together. Using the cards got our relationship off to a great start."

— Single woman, 37

"We used the 'sex cards' at our men's retreat. These cards definitely had the effect of deepening our communication and our levels of self-awareness. I learned a lot about myself. I want to share this game with my other friends — both singles and couples."

— Married man, 52

The game consists of 150 cards and costs $25.

The Getting Real Card Game (for groups of two to fourteen players) offers the chance to deepen your connections with others, find out how others see you, and practice using the ten truth skills. Players take turns answering self-revealing questions (or dramatizing their answers improvisation-style). These questions are printed on cards, which are placed in four different stacks, representing four levels of challenge.

Here is some sample text from the Getting Real cards:

- Go around the room and say one thing you notice about each person.
- In what ways do you fail to walk your talk?

- What specific feedback do you have for the person whose turn it was just before yours?
- In what areas of your life are you impeccable?
- What is the highest vision you hold for yourself?
- What were you like in high school?

Here's what a few people have said about this game:

"I played the Getting Real Game with my family when I visited my parents for Thanksgiving. My three brothers and their wives and children were all there too. I got to know things about my brothers that I never knew — like how they feel about their lives and their hopes, dreams, and regrets. It was so good for the kids to see their parents being so real. Now we play Getting Real whenever we all get together."

— Psychologist, 59

"I brought the game to my men's group. These are men in all walks of life — the building trades, farming, teaching, the arts. It was an amazing experience. Many of their responses brought tears to my eyes — sometimes because they were so moving, and sometimes because they were so funny! Playing the game together brought us to a new level of sharing with each other."

— Teacher, 40

There is also a **Getting Real Card Game for Young People** aged eight to fourteen. This is similar to the Getting Real Card Game, but the questions have been modified to fit younger audiences. The game can be played by groups of all ages, including parents and children together.

The Truth at Work Card Game is a game of self-expression, skill-building, and fun for work groups. This game offers work groups of any size a fun, structured way to develop better communication and cooperation. It helps bring to the surface issues that may be impeding group performance, and it does so in a way that respects diversity and honors each person's unique style.

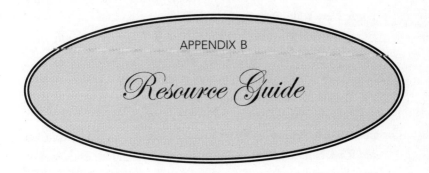

APPENDIX B

Resource Guide

This appendix lists introduction services, books, tapes, and work-shops that relate to Truth in Dating. If you know of a book or other resource that belongs here but is not listed, please send it to me for review at 4373 Hessel Court, Sebastopol, CA 95472.

Introduction Services

These services all appeal to singles whose values include honesty, integrity, spirituality, peace and justice, or ecological sustainability.

www.truthindating.com
www.unitysingles.com
www.greensingles.com
www.concernedsingles.com
www.consciousdating.com
www.natural-friends.com

Books

Blanton, Brad. *Practicing Radical Honesty: How to Complete the Past, Live in the Present, and Build a Future.* Stanley, Va.: Sparrowhawk Publishing, 2000.

_____. *Radical Honesty: How to Transform Your Life by Telling the Truth*. New York: Dell, 1996.

_____. *Radical Parenting: Seven Steps to a Functional Family in a Dysfunctional World*. Stanley, Va.: Sparrowhawk Publishing, 2003.

_____. *The Truth-Tellers: Stories of Success by Honest People*. Stanley, Va.: Sparrowhawk Publishing, 2003.

Britten, Rhonda. *Fearless Living*. New York: Dutton, 2003.

Campbell, Susan. *Beyond the Power Struggle: Dealing with Conflict in Love and Work*. San Luis Obispo, Calif.: Impact, 1980. (This title is out of print but available from the author at www.susancampbell.com.)

_____. *The Couple's Journey: Intimacy as a Path to Wholeness*. San Luis Obispo, Calif.: Impact, 1980. (This title is out of print but available from the author at www.susancampbell.com.)

_____. *From Chaos to Confidence: Survival Strategies for the New Workplace*. New York: Simon & Schuster, 1995.

_____. *Getting Real: The Ten Truth Skills You Need to Live an Authentic Life*. Novato, Calif.: New World Library, 2001.

Covington, Stephanie, and Liana Beckett. *Leaving the Enchanted Forest: The Path from Relationship Addiction to Intimacy*. San Francisco: Harper and Row, 1988.

Deyo, Yaacov, and Sue Deyo. *Speed Dating*. New York: HarperCollins, 2002.

Dhiravamsa. *Turning to the Source: Using Insight Meditation and Psychotherapy for Personal Growth*. Nevada City, Calif.: Blue Dolphin Publishing, 1990.

Fisher, Bruce, and Robert Alberti. *Rebuilding: When Your Relationship Ends*. San Luis Obispo, Calif.: Impact Publishers, 2000.

Hendricks, Gay, and Kathlyn Hendricks. *Conscious Loving*. New York: Bantam, 1990.

_____. *The Conscious Heart*. New York: Bantam, 1997.

Heumann, Suzie, and Susan Campbell. *The Everything Great Sex Book*. Holbrook, Mass.: Adams Media, 2003.

Kasl, Charlotte. *If the Buddha Dated*. New York: Penguin Putnam, 1999.

Lowe, Paul. *In Each Moment.* Vancouver, B.C.: Looking Glass Press, 1998.

Psaris, Jett, and Marlena Lyons. *Undefended Love.* Oakland, Calif.: New Harbinger Publications, 2000.

Tolle, Eckhart. *The Power of Now.* Novato, Calif.: New World Library, 1999.

Videotapes

Campbell, Susan. *The Couple's Journey: Intimacy as a Path to Wholeness.* A thirty-minute interview with Susan Campbell by *Thinking Allowed* host Jeffrey Mishlove. Available at "Products," www.susancampbell.com.

_____. *Getting Real: The Ten Truth Skills You Need to Live an Authentic Life.* Two lively thirty-minute interviews with Susan Campbell by talk show host Asia Powers. Available at "Products," www.susancampbell.com.

_____. *How to Build a Loving Relationship.* Available at "Products," www.susancampbell.com.

CRM Films. *Riding the Wave: Strategies for Change* (based on Susan Campbell's book about "surfing chaos," *From Chaos to Confidence: Survival Strategies for the New Workplace*). 17 minutes, 1999. Available from CRM Films at (800) 421-0833 or from "Products," www.susancampbell.com.

Audiotapes

Campbell, Susan. *Getting Real: Introduction to the Ten Truth Skills.* A recorded interview with New Dimensions Radio host Michael Toms. Available at "Products," www.susancampbell.com.

_____. *Getting Real: Relating More, Controlling Less.* A recorded speech about why we lie, sugarcoat, and pretend, and how to notice when you are controlling vs. relating. Available at "Products," www.susancampbell.com.

_____. *A Guide to Open Communication.* A discussion of the difference between communicating to "know and be known" vs.

communicating to get a certain result. Available at "Products," www.susancampbell.com.

_____. *Overcoming the Fear of Intimacy.* A discussion about why people fear intimacy and how to build your capacity for deeper connection with others. Available at "Products," www.susancampbell.com.

_____. *What Can You Realistically Expect in a Relationship?* A discussion of things you can expect that most relationship counselors don't talk about. Available at "Products," www.susancampbell.com.

_____. *Why Opposites Attract.* A description of why we often attract people who push our buttons. Available at "Products," www.susancampbell.com.

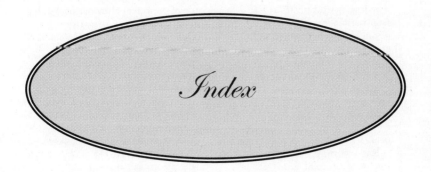

Index

About the Author

Susan Campbell has been a relationship coach, speaker, and workshop leader for thirty-five years and has written seven previous books on interpersonal relationships. She is also the creator and publisher of five entertaining and educational card games for children, teens, adults, couples, work teams, and singles, as well as one for birthday parties. All of her games promote more authentic relating among players.

Susan has appeared on numerous talk shows, including *Good Morning America, The Dr. Dean Edell Show,* and CNN'S *NewsNight,* and she has been published widely in popular magazines.

Her Learning/Discovery approach to communication, conflict, and change are the subject of a twenty-minute professional training video produced and distributed by CRM Films. Based on her book, *From Chaos to Confidence: Survival Strategies for the New Workplace,* the film and accompanying workbook are widely used by Fortune 500 companies and government agencies. As an internationally known professional speaker, Susan speaks on such topics as Surfing Chaos, Honest Feedback in the Workplace, Coping with Constant Change, How to Build a Winning Team, and Successful Win-Win Negotiating. She publishes a newsletter entitled *Uncertain Times,* which she offers free to clients and former clients.

Susan leads public seminars throughout the country and in Europe on Getting Real, Truth in Dating, Truth at Work, and The Couple's Journey: Relationship as a Path to Awakening. For information on her programs, card games, videos, or audio tapes, call (707) 829-3646 or visit www.susancampbell.com.

H J Kramer and New World Library are dedicated to
publishing books and audio projects
that inspire and challenge us to improve the quality
of our lives and our world.

Our books and audios are available
in bookstores everywhere.
For a catalog of our complete library
of fine books and audios, contact:

H J Kramer/New World Library
14 Pamaron Way
Novato, CA 94949

Phone: (415) 884-2100
Or call toll free (800) 972-6657
Catalog requests: Ext. 50
Orders: Ext. 52
Fax: (415) 884-2199

Email: escort@newworldlibrary.com
www.newworldlibrary.com